CROW JESUS

CROW JESUS

Personal Stories of Native Religious Belonging

Edited and with an Introduction by
MARK CLATTERBUCK

Foreword by
JACE WEAVER

UNIVERSITY OF OKLAHOMA PRESS : NORMAN

Library of Congress Cataloging-in-Publication Data

Name: Clatterbuck, Mark, author
Title: Crow Jesus : personal stories of native religious belonging / Mark Clatterbuck.
Description: Norman : University of Oklahoma Press, 2017. | Includes
   bibliographical references and index.
Identifiers: LCCN 2016024725 | ISBN 978-0-8061-5587-6 (pbk. : alk. paper)
Subjects: LCSH: Crow Indians—Religion. | Crow Indians—Rites and ceremonies.
   | Crow Indians—Interviews. | Christianity—Montana. | Syncretism
   (Religion)—United States. | Montana—Religious life and customs.
Classification: LCC E99.C92 C53 2017 | DDC 978.6004/975272—dc23
LC record available at https://lccn.loc.gov/2016024725

1 2 3 4 5 6 7 8 9 10

This book is dedicated to

MALINDA, ALENA, *and* HANNAH HARNISH CLATTERBUCK
and
GLORIA GOES AHEAD CUMMINS *(1931–2011)*

Contents

Illustrations

Foreword

In 1995, I was invited by the World Council of Churches to lead a delegation of American Indians from the United States to the *fiesta de la cosecha,* or harvest festival, in the Guatemalan highlands. The three-day festival was steeped in ritual and ceremony. The first day was traditional Mayan. The second was Roman Catholic. And the third was *evangelico,* or Protestant. What struck me most was that, despite the obvious differences in the celebrations in these diverse traditions, the same Mayan folks attended all three days. I believed then, and I still believe today, more than twenty years later, that more was going on than just people enjoying a great party—or even honoring the harvest. The indigenous cultures of the Americas and the religious systems that undergird them have always been highly adaptive, capable of absorbing into themselves anything that was recognized as having efficacious power. Although I have never conducted any systematic research on any of my several trips to Guatemala, I know that many of those involved in Mayan religious traditions are also practicing Christians.

The indigenes of the Western Hemisphere have been involved with Christianity as the subjects of missionization, as converts, and as practitioners ever since the Columbus event in 1492. In the eighteenth and nineteenth centuries, Indian clergy from the United States and Canada—like Samson Occom, Peter Jones, and William Apess—authored Christian tracts. Children from tribes in California were educated within the walls of the Vatican to aid in the evangelical enterprise. And when the United States purchased Alaska in 1867, they discovered bilingual (or even trilingual) Indians, trained in the Russian Orthodox tradition, acting as missionaries to neighboring tribes. Such examples could be replicated manifold.

Despite this long and intimate history shared by Natives and Christianity, Native American Christianity itself remains woefully understudied. To be sure, there has been fairly extensive study of the coercive and sometimes violent evangelization of Indians. Choctaw historian and clergyman Homer

Noley published an excellent history of Native American Methodists in his 1991 book, *First White Frost*. Five years later, Muscogee scholar of religion James Treat produced an eclectic grab bag of articles by Native Christian thinkers in his edited volume *Native and Christian: Voices on Religious Identity in the United States and Canada*. Most recently, Steven Charleston, the former Episcopal bishop of Alaska and a Choctaw Nation citizen, coedited with Elaine Robinson, a non-Native dean at the Saint Paul School of Theology, an attempt at a kind of Native Christian systematic theology in the 2015 *Coming Full Circle: Constructing Native Theology*. Other than these works and a handful of top-down occasional essays (including a few by me), there is very little on the topic of Native Christianity. Almost nothing has dealt with the voices, beliefs, and practices of Native American Christians on the ground. That is why this book is so important—and so refreshing.

Today in the United States only 10 to 25 percent of American Indians consider themselves Christians (although this figure can be upped considerably if one includes those who adhere to the peyotist Native American Church, a controversial proposition in multiple ways). This estimate has not changed in over a century, and the range is maddening for those of us who study religion through a social scientific lens. The reason that it cannot be narrowed to a more precise number is a phenomenon common to indigenous people through North America and, arguably, the world.

Anthropologist and scholar of religion Joseph Epes Brown labels this phenomenon "nonexclusive cumulative adhesion." Although that label is both accurate and descriptive, I prefer the term "religious dimorphism." From the Greek *di*, meaning "two," and *morph*, meaning "form," it is the practice of two forms of religion. It is distinguished from syncretism, which occurs when two different religions are blended to form a third. Rather, religious dimorphism occurs when a person participates in two different religions. There is no mixing other than within the practitioner. As I have heard Natives say, it is as simple as "This is what I do when I go to church. And this is what I do when I go to ceremony."

I witnessed religious dimorphism in Guatemala, and I observe it regularly throughout the United States and Canada. It pervades the first-person accounts of *Crow Jesus*, as Sun Dance, Native American Church, and Christianity all mingle in southern Montana. Marlon Passes captures its spirit perfectly when he tells Mark Clatterbuck, "A lot of peyote people, members of the Native American Church, a lot of 'em have been baptized Christian. Some Pentecostals, some Catholics, some Baptists. They practice both religions. Just like that tree right there, it's got many branches, but there's one seed that started this tree. That's how I perceive the belief in the Creator, God, Jesus."

In 1869, President Ulysses S. Grant, with his Commissioner of Indian Affairs Ely Parker, instituted a reform that came to be called Grant's Peace Policy, pursuant to which reservations were taken out of the hands of corrupt Indian agents and the military and turned over to Christian denominations. In exchange for assuming this responsibility, the missionaries were given monopolistic control over the reservations they managed. Missionaries from one denomination could not enter a reservation belonging to another without prior approval. When this reservation monopoly system ended in 1934, the denominations involved signed comity agreements with one another, keeping the status quo in place. The only sects that did not abide by the system were those that had either been excluded from it (for example, the Church of Jesus Christ of Latter-day Saints and Seventh-day Adventists) or those that did not exist at the time, like Pentecostals.

Today, virtually all Native American Christians can be accounted for in only four denominations: they are Roman Catholics, Mormons, Episcopalians, and United Methodists. As Clatterbuck demonstrates, however, Pentecostals have established deep roots in the Crow community.

American Indian religious traditions evolved over the course of centuries prior to the arrival of Christianity. They are empirical, based on generations upon generations of observation of the world around them. They are also experiential. There is an immediacy about them, as they speak to the lived lives of the People.

Nineteenth-century Cherokee journalist John Rollin Ridge related the story of one of the first missionaries to come to his people. The man assembled the whole village and began to tell the biblical story from creation through resurrection. One old warrior in the back listened intently. In keeping with the propensity for Natives to adopt anything perceived as having power, he kept loudly interjecting comments, advising his fellow tribesmen to listen to what the missionary was saying. As Jesus got closer to Jerusalem in the visitor's story, the old man fell silent and began to rock back and forth in agitation. When the missionary got to Jesus's crucifix-ion, the Cherokee leapt to his feet and cried out, demanding to know the whereabouts of the evil men who had unjustly put this good man to death, so that he and his warriors could take revenge upon them. The white man was obliged to tell him that the acts he described had happened a very long time ago, in a country very far away. The culprits were not available to have revenge taken upon them. According to Ridge, at that point, the warrior lost all interest in the new religion because it had nothing to do with his life.

The testimonies included herein demonstrate that, despite the historically fraught relationship between American Indians and the colonizer's religion, over the course of centuries the indigenous persons of North America have made Christianity their own. In 1925, E. Stanley Jones published *The Christ of the Indian Road,* discussing how the Gospel of Jesus was being inculturated in south Asia. In the book you hold in your hands, Mark Clatterbuck shows us, more vividly than have any before, the Christ of the Good Red Road.

In 1969, in his classic work *Custer Died for Your Sins,* Vine Deloria Jr., one of the founders of contemporary Native American studies, described an encounter between himself and a clergyman in charge of the Presbyterian Church (U.S.A.) missions to Native Americans. At a public lecture, Deloria lis-tened to the non-Native bureaucrat describe the denomination's efforts among the Shinnecocks on New York's Long Island, one of the oldest, continuous Christian communities of American Indians in the United States. When the speaker entertained questions, Deloria asked him how long the Presbyterians intended to continue mission activities among a people who had been Chris-tian for three and a half centuries. The man replied, "Until the job is done."[1]

In *Crow Jesus,* Clatterbuck demonstrates clearly that, whatever the eth-nocentric disagreements of non-Native church administrators, among the Crows of Montana, the job is done.

JACE WEAVER

NOTE

1. Vine Deloria Jr., *Custer Died for Your Sins: An Indian Manifesto* (New York: Mac-millan, 1969), 112.

Preface

My relationship with a number of Crow families in southeastern Montana began more than twenty years ago. I was serving on the staff of a regional summer youth camp at the time, and dozens of Crow young people were involved in that program. Some of the friendships I developed with their families then have continued over the years; some of those friends are now a part of *Crow Jesus*. More recently, I've spent portions of the past eight summers in the field, exploring the religious history, ritual practices, and religious self-understanding of Crow tribal members. This work has included hundreds of informal, unrecorded conversations, in addition to extensive recorded interview material. It has also involved hundreds of hours of participant observation among a wide variety of Crow church events—Sunday services, camp meetings, baptisms, Bible studies, prayer meetings, processions—and traditional Crow ceremonies.

Three separate studies have come out of these rich oral testimonies and experiences among the Crow Tribe: an oral history of the Catholic Charismatic Renewal among the tribe in the 1970s and 1980s (*U.S. Catholic Historian*, 2010); an oral history and analysis of Crow Pentecostalism (*Spiritus*, 2012); and an exploration of Christianity's influence on current Crow tribal politics (*Journal of Ecumenical Studies*, 2014). I first met some of the participants included in *Crow Jesus* while completing these earlier projects. The majority of the others were introduced to me as respected religious figures, whether lay or clergy, within their church communities.

This volume should not be regarded as a collection of interviews with "religious authorities" whose voices are somehow more important, or carry more weight, than many other voices that could have comprised this book. Rather, my hope for this project has been to gather together, to the best of my ability, a representative sampling of Crow voices speaking personally and poignantly about their Christian faith in relation to tribal identity and traditional religious practices. For this reason, I've included elders and young people, women and men, pastors and laypeople, devout Traditionalists and those for whom Crow Traditionalism is largely forbidden by their Christian convictions.

Most participants selected the location for their interviews. I wanted interviewees to feel comfortable in a setting of their choosing and to allow the context of our discussion to inform the conversation itself. For this reason, the following narratives unfolded at rodeos and powwows, homes and churches, peyote grounds and riverbanks. Regrettably, largely because of length constraints, fewer than half the total interviews that were conducted for this project are included in the present collection. In order to ensure that the stories that don't appear in print here are available to family, friends, and the entire tribe, the video-recorded interviews of all who gave consent are housed in the archives of the Little Big Horn College Library at Crow Agency.

Funding for this project was largely provided through a generous grant from the Louisville Institute, Kentucky. Additional funding for travel and research came from Montclair State University, New Jersey. For nearly all the interviews, I was accompanied by Dave Kapferer, who audio- and video-recorded each session. Most of these recordings are now in the tribe's archives. Most of the photographs in this book are Dave's work as well. I am deeply grateful for his many generous contributions to this project. I also warmly thank the following Montclair State University student research assistants for their important contributions to this project: Kathryn Goldner, Suzannah Leydenfrost, Elena Knoll, and Alaina Thomas. My gratitude also goes to the many students in my religion classes at MSU whose insightful comments have enriched my own understanding of the Native-Christian encounter. I also wish to thank Tim McCleary for offering valuable feedback on this research at various stages; Dave and Bonnie Graber for their tireless hospitality and encouragement; and my wife, Malinda, and daughters, Alena and Hannah, whose spirited support shaped this project more than they know.

Most of all, I thank the members of the Crow Tribe whose stories and words fill the following pages. I consider it an extraordinary honor to have shared in these sacred narratives. In gratitude for your generosity, and toward the continued preservation of the Crow Tribe's oral history, half of all author proceeds generated by this book will be donated to the archives of the Little Big Horn College Library, Crow Agency.

CROW JESUS

Introduction

CROWS, CHRIST, AND THE NEW INDIGENEITY

SIGNPOSTS: JESUS FROM I-90

Visitors to Crow Agency, the tribal capital of Montana's Apsáalooke (Crow) Nation, can learn a lot about the religious landscape of the reservation without ever leaving Interstate 90 as it passes through town. First, there is the towering thirty-three-foot wooden cross that dominates the town's western skyline, each foot representing a year in the life of Jesus. Erected in 2007 on tribal land atop a prominent hill behind St. Dennis Catholic Church, the structure owes its existence to the vision of a devout Crow Catholic who feels a strong devotion to Saint Francis. Flooded by spotlights each night as tractor-trailers rumble up and down the highway from Billings, Montana, to Sheridan, Wyoming, the structure rivals tipis and horses as the town's most iconic visual symbol.

Rising a quarter mile down the highway is the imposing glass facade of the newly dedicated five-hundred-seat auditorium belonging to Spirit

Erected in 2007, the thirty-three-foot wooden cross behind St. Dennis Catholic Church has already established itself as an iconic symbol on the Crow Reservation as it overlooks the tribal capital of Crow Agency. *Photo by Dave Kapferer*

of Life Lighthouse for the Nations Foursquare Pentecostal Church. With state-of-the-art video projection, sound, and lighting systems inside an expansive eleven-thousand-square-foot structure, this is the closest thing to a megachurch on the Crow Reservation. Adjacent to Spirit of Life sits the Community Baptist Church, formerly Burgess Memorial Church, one of the oldest missions on the reservation. Many revered figures from Crow history have called this church their home, including Pretty Shield, the Crow medicine woman made famous by Frank Linderman's 1932 biography of her life.[1]

Another quarter mile down the road, a newly installed billboard in colorful Crow designs declares that "Jesus Christ Is Lord on the Crow Nation." The monument was erected in Warriors Park (also called Veterans Park) with tribal money following passage of a 2013 legislative resolution "to proclaim Jesus Christ as Lord of the Crow Indian Reservation." One may soon spot an Israeli flag waving in that same park alongside the flags of the United States, the state of Montana, and the Crow Tribe. The installation of "an official flag of the State of Israel" was recently pledged to reflect the tribe's support for Israel, an alliance formalized in a 2013 tribal resolution that was later presented to Ron Dermer, Israeli ambassador to the United

The new sanctuary of Spirit of Life Lighthouse for the Nations Foursquare Church at Crow Agency was dedicated in 2010. The congregation traces its lineage back to Nellie Pretty Eagle Stewart, widely regarded as the founder of Crow Pentecostalism in the 1920s. *Photo by Dave Kapferer*

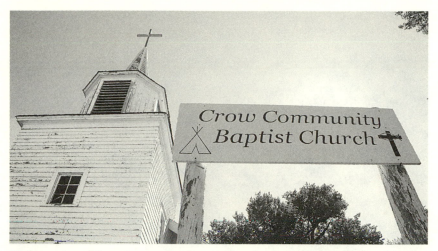

Highway view of Crow Community Baptist Church, which occupies the site of the first Protestant mission on the Crow Reservation, dating to 1891. The church is more commonly known among the tribe as Burgess Memorial. *Photo by Dave Kapferer*

States, during a private ceremony in Washington, D.C. That resolution, which passed with unanimous support from tribal legislators, contains quotations from the King James Version of the Bible promising blessings on all who bless the children of Abraham. A key Senate backer of the alliance calls it a "seed of faith" ushering in spiritual and economic blessings for

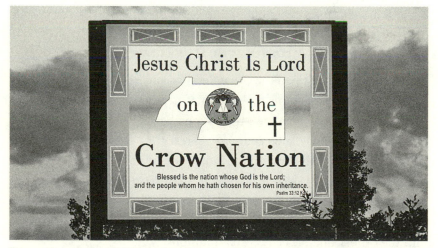

"Jesus Christ Is Lord" billboard in Warriors Park along Interstate 90, Crow Agency. The sign was installed in 2014 with support from the tribal legislature. *Photo by Kenny Pretty On Top Jr.*

A Pentecostal camp meeting canopy awaits service goers in Warriors Park, Crow Agency. Every year since the 1950s, reservation churches have hosted tent revivals here throughout the summer months. Attendees often pitch their own tents or park their campers here for a week at a time, creating mini encampments for these popular events. *Photo by Dave Kapferer*

the tribe. Every year, from June to August, Warriors Park also hosts a continuous series of Pentecostal camp meetings under enormous, circus-style tents. All of these symbols of Crow Christian faith greet the casual driver through Crow Agency—and that's without even exiting the interstate.

MISSIONARIES AMONG THE CROWS: A HISTORICAL OVERVIEW

Signs of Christian faith on the Crow Reservation are ubiquitous. Roughly thirty-five churches dot this reservation of nearly ten thousand residents, the vast majority of whom are enrolled members of the tribe. In the town of Crow Agency alone, nine churches representing five different denominations (the other four churches are independent) stake their claim among the local population. However, of the many Christian denominations active among the Crows today, three may lay legitimate claim to being the oldest, most enduring, and most influential on the reservation. These are the Catholic, the Baptist, and the Pentecostal traditions.

Jesuit missionary Pierre-Jean De Smet was among the first to preach Christianity to the Apsáalooke people in the 1840s.[2] Subsequently, Catholic missionaries were the first to establish a permanent Christian presence on the reservation when Jesuit priests Paul Prando, Peter Barcelo, and Peter Bandini succeeded in founding St. Xavier Mission in the Big Horn Valley by 1887. The mission included a boarding school for Native students that was run by Ursuline Sisters.[3] Today the school continues to operate under the name of Pretty Eagle Academy in honor of the well-known chief Pretty Eagle.

The establishment of St. Xavier was followed in the early 1890s by the founding of St. Charles Mission in the western reservation town of Pryor. This took place largely in response to Chief Plenty Coups's interest in offering educational opportunities for his own people like those being offered at St. Xavier.[4] The fact that Plenty Coups refused baptism until later in life cautions against too readily fingering religious conviction as the primary motivation for the chief's interest in the Catholic mission. Later, St. Dennis at Crow Agency (1905) was founded, and then St. Ann (1909) outside the town of Lodge Grass. St. Ann's Parish relocated to a new building in town in 1932 and was renamed Our Lady of Loretto, the name it retains today.[5] St. Kateri Tekakwitha Parish in Wyola rounds out the Catholic churches currently operating on the reservation.

Catholicism continues to exert enormous influence on the religious and social lives of tribal members. It has also experienced a dramatic shift in attitude toward traditional Crow ceremonies and culture over the years— from open condemnation of virtually all Crow religious ceremonies up until the mid-twentieth century, to active support for many of those same practices today. The five Catholic parishes on the reservation are served by three priests who regularly participate in traditional Crow ceremonies. The seasoned reflections of one of these priests, whose time among the tribe spans more than forty years, are included in the following pages.

A desire among the Crows for educational opportunities for their children was also the catalyst for Baptist missionary efforts among the tribe. The first Baptist mission on the reservation was founded in 1904 in the southeast reservation town of Lodge Grass after local tribal leaders invited the American Baptist Home Missionary Society to open a school in their community. The request was for a day school rather than a boarding school, since Crow families preferred to have their children living at home. The request expressed no interest whatsoever in a mission church. However, the Baptists who met with Crow leaders to negotiate a school insisted they would do so only if they were permitted to build a church as well. Reluctantly, after citing fears regarding church interference with their "games and dances," tribal leaders acquiesced.[6] In the end, the mission was founded, and it established a firm place in Lodge Grass society under the forceful leadership of Dr. William Petzoldt. The day school, as opposed to the Catholic boarding school model, proved so popular among Crow parents that a fierce rivalry soon spread across the reservation between the Catholic and Baptist versions of Christian evangelization.[7]

By 1917, Petzoldt's missionary reach had extended beyond Lodge Grass to include outposts in the districts of Pryor, Wyola, and Big Horn. Over the past century, the Baptist presence has remained a vital one among the Crow Tribe, with Southern and Independent Baptist congregations now established on the reservation in addition to the enduring American Baptist churches. The persistent influence of Crow Baptist missions today surely owes much to the role it played in the lives of venerated tribal leaders in twentieth-century Crow history. These include Goes Ahead and Pretty Shield (Crow Agency, Burgess Memorial Baptist Church), the Sun Dance chief Thomas Yellowtail and his wife, Susie Yellowtail (Lodge Grass, First Crow Indian Baptist), and Joseph Medicine Crow (also from Lodge Grass). Medicine Crow, the oldest member of the tribe until his death in April 2016 at the age of 102, was awarded the Presidential Medal of Freedom by Barack Obama in 2009.

As with the Catholic missions, Baptist activity among the Crows has undergone a significant shift in terms of posture toward traditional Crow religion—although it stops far short of the open embrace demonstrated by the Catholic priests currently serving the tribe. Stories of early Baptist missionaries prodding Crow leaders to throw their medicine bundles into the river in a dramatic renunciation of Indian religion continue to circulate widely among the tribe today.[8] Several of the interviewees included in this collection, including Angela Russell, Marvin Dawes Sr., and Marlon Passes, recount similar stories of their own ancestors.

Pentecostalism arrived among the Crow Tribe when missionary women from Aimee Semple McPherson's newly formed Church of the Foursquare Gospel began holding house meetings, primarily with Crow women, in the

Black Lodge and Reno Districts of the reservation. In 1927, five members of the tribe made their way to McPherson's Angelus Temple in Los Angeles, California, seeking healing for a variety of maladies. After publicly declaring themselves healed, saved, and baptized in the Holy Spirit, they returned as indigenous leaders of the new Pentecostal movement and succeeded in establishing among the tribe the fourfold message of Jesus Christ as savior, healer, baptizer in the Holy Spirit, and soon-coming king. Foremost among these early Crow Pentecostal pioneers were Nellie Pretty Eagle Stewart and Maggie Brass.[9] One of Stewart's great-grandsons, who served in the Crow tribal legislature, is among the Pentecostal voices in the following collection; a granddaughter of Maggie Brass, who pastors an urban Pentecostal congregation just off the reservation, is also included among the voices in the ensuing chapters.

Today, Pentecostalism is arguably the most prevalent Christian movement among the Crows. It accounts for more than half of the tribe's total congregations and exerts considerable influence on tribal politics.[10] While a handful of the reservation's Pentecostal churches are denominationally affiliated (Assemblies of God, Foursquare, Church of God, Pentecostal Church of God, and Open Bible), the majority remain fiercely independent. And every one of them, whether affiliated or independent, is led by a Crow pastor—a remarkable development considering that there is only one Crow pastor among all the other reservation churches combined.

Many factors contribute to Crow Pentecostalism's enormous success. Foremost may be the movement's compatibility with traditional Crow rituals of fasting, healing, vision questing, and sacred dreaming. A second vital attraction is Pentecostalism's pragmatic tendency to predicate spiritual authority on ministerial efficacy rather than on formal training. In this way, a seminary education off the reservation, along with recognition by (largely non-Native) ecclesial structures, are trumped by a perceived "anointing" of the Holy Spirit as manifested in various "spiritual gifts," such as prophecy, healing, and the discerning of spirits. Furthermore, Pentecostalism easily adapts to the historic preference among Crows for holding religious ceremonies outdoors. This is most readily apparent in the wildly popular Crow Pentecostal tradition of holding lively camp meetings under large canopies through the summer months. These festive events are marked by passionate preaching, thunderous praise bands, healing prayer, and altar calls. The tradition of outdoor religious venues is also on display during Crow Fair as Pentecostal groups sponsor floats for the parades, hold services in the pow-wow arbor, and host religious-themed tents among the vendors. Despite such points of continuity with Crow cultural ways, the movement has a reputation for hostility toward traditional Crow ceremonies and, more than any other Christian group on the reservation, preaches that a decision to follow Jesus demands a rejection of so-called Indian religion.

In addition to these three Christian traditions, a number of other denominations operate mission churches on the reservation. These include one church each operated by the Episcopal, Lutheran (Missouri Synod), and Mennonite denominations. There are also a number of churches in nearby towns such as Billings and Hardin that serve a smaller number of Crow tribal members, including at least two Pentecostal churches led by Crow pastors.[11] Substantial missionary activity on the reservation is also conducted by Christian ministries based outside tribal borders. Most notable here is the steady stream of short-term, non-Native youth groups from churches all across the United States that spend the summer operating vacation Bible schools, sports camps, and evangelistic outreach and community service programs among the Crow Tribe. These groups generally operate under the auspices of their own church missions programs, typically in cooperation with one or more reservation-based churches that serve as their hosts.

Nor should the role played by itinerant evangelists be overlooked. In addition to the guest speakers who regularly fill the pulpits at summer Pentecostal camp meetings, an endless train of traveling preachers, prophets, healers, evangelists, and singers—Native and non-Native alike—proclaim the gospel at Sunday morning services and revival meetings year-round on the reservation. Some, like Barry Moen, whose voice is included in the present collection, find a ready-made audience at Crow Fair, where Moen's "prayer and healing tent" among the powwow vendors serves simultaneously as balloon dispensary, water bottle stop, and conversion booth. Moen's evangelistic ministry based in Sheridan, Wyoming, has been following the summertime powwow circuit in Montana since 2010, boasting over sixteen thousand new Native converts to a full-gospel Christian message in the past three years alone. While such strategies and implausible claims raise significant questions about the nature and motivations (on both sides) of such "conversions," the conspicuous role played by itinerant, non-Native ministers among the tribe can hardly be ignored in a study of contemporary Crow Christianity.

Finally, the influence being exerted on the Crow Nation by high-profile international Christian ministries deserves mentioning here. From Aimee Semple McPherson's Miles City crusade of 1934, to Oral Roberts's legendary healing crusade held at Crow Agency in 1955, to recent crusades by Kentucky megachurch pastor Tommy Bates and the Texas-based prophet Chuck Pierce, large-scale and media-savvy Pentecostal ministries have a long history of shaping Crow Christianity. They also figure prominently in the oral testimonies of many Crow Christians today, as some of the narratives in the ensuing chapters will illustrate.

"Native Christians" and "Religious Identity"

Despite missionaries working tirelessly for more than a century to ensure the preeminence of their own sectarian expressions of Christian faith among the Crows, denominational labels are, to put it mildly, held loosely on the reservation today. I spoke with devout Catholics and faithful Baptists alike who love Pentecostal camp meetings, Pentecostals who sing Crow hymns in Catholic Mass, and others whose religious patterns permit as many as four Christian denominations to claim them with roughly equal legitimacy. Denominational affiliations are so tenuous that I have heard even the most generous of missionary pastors vent frustration over how much time their parishioners spend sitting in other pastors' pews. Crow skepticism of Christian denominations also helps to explain why, among Pentecostal churches on the reservation, independent congregations outnumber affiliated congregations by a ratio of two to one.

Crow pastors seem more willing than white clergy to accept, even celebrate, this indigenous fluidity across religious boundaries. A wry smile accompanied the description one Crow Pentecostal pastor offered to me when discussing general habits of reservation parishioners: "When you really come down to it, they go to any church," he said. "As far as denominational lines here on the reservation, I don't think you have them." Sometimes, even the clergy reflect this disregard for sectarian borders. At least two Baptist pastors on the reservation speak in tongues and preach the baptism in the Holy Spirit; I heard one Pentecostal preacher endearingly call these Baptist brethren "the Bapticostals."

Traditional Crow religion is ritual-oriented, community-based, and occasion-driven—traits that account, in large part, for Crow churchgoers' general disinterest in denominational fidelity. They also do much to explain broader habits of Crow church attendance (or nonattendance) that have confounded generations of missionaries on the reservation. As is common among indigenous communities, the well-being of one's clan and one's tribe is widely regarded as the highest good, with religious ceremonies functioning to reinforce those communal ties. Religious behavior is not generally regarded as an end in itself. The failure of many missionaries over the years to respect this understanding of religion in relation to tribal identity remains, too often, a source of frustration. Recently a flummoxed white pastor on the reservation shared with me his irritation over the fact that tribal events so readily trump church obligations among even his most faithful Indian members. "If given the choice between church and a pow-wow," he said with obvious pique, "they'll choose the powwow every time."

Further frustrations and misunderstandings arise when communitarian religious pragmatism collides with Euro-American models, where Christian faith is measured largely by creedal affirmation. Christian missionary endeavors among U.S. tribes have long emphasized correct doctrine and narrowly defined catechetical positions as key indicators of religious devotion, even as Native communities, as noted above, remain far more interested in knowing how participation in one church or another will affect communal cohesion, facilitate meaningful spiritual experiences, and bring healing to body and spirit.[12]

Not surprisingly, this Native tendency to privilege orthopraxis over orthodoxy leads not only to easy passage across different Christian denominations, but also across the steeper institutional walls separating religions. As Father Randolph Graczyk, priest at St. Charles Mission, explains: "I think that's one thing I've learned from the Crows—that we need to be open. They'll tell you there are many ways to God, and all of them are good." He then tells the story about a Crow woman who, as a child, attended St. Charles Catholic School back in the 1940s: "She said that the Sisters there were telling them,

'You shouldn't go to any Protestant services. That's forbidden. Catholics don't do that.' She went home and told her father, and her father told his daughter, 'What the Sisters tell you is good—but in this they are wrong.'" Graczyk adds: "'That attitude of respect is one thing I have learned from the Crows.''

On the other hand, for Osage scholar George Tinker, the admirable indigenous values of generosity and hospitality toward religious outsiders bring with them a grave danger. He writes, "While the virtue of generosity, as it is practiced by different American Indian peoples, can be touted as something superior to the values of civilization that have been imposed on Indian peoples by the europeans [*sic*], it has also become susceptible to abuse in two significant ways: it has been misappropriated by our white relatives and misdirected by Indian people themselves."[13] Among the Crows, it may be precisely because of this spirit of religious "generosity" that widespread participation in both Christian and traditional Crow religions is now standard practice among tribal members. In fact, participation frequently extends to *multiple* Christian traditions alongside *multiple* indigenous traditions for a single practitioner. In such cases, "Crow Catholic Sun Dancer" or "Crow Baptist Peyotist" or "Catholic Charismatic Tobacco Dance Society member" would offer a far more accurate description than "Crow Christian," despite the convenience provided by this familiar shorthand. Indeed, to the extent that the label "Crow Christian" masks the pervasive multireligious habits of the vast majority of tribal members today, that simple phrase functions to extend a colonialist ascription of priority to Christianity over Crow Traditionalism.

For this reason, the unqualified label "Christian," as popularly applied to Crows affiliated in various ways with one or more reservation churches, has increasingly struck me as problematic through the course of this project. The following sampling of four project participants offers a glimpse into the challenges of applying the simple term "Christian" to four Crow voices included in this volume:

- A self-described Crow Baptist has virtually no active relationship with any Baptist church on the reservation today and openly grieves the loss of Crow Traditionalism his family suffered under the heavy-handed tactics of earlier Baptist missionaries on the reservation. He enthusiastically advocates participation in the

Peyote Way, which is the religious community in which he has rooted his own spiritual life for the last thirty years.

- A devout Catholic Crow elder taught for many years at the Catholic mission school in Pryor, the same school she attended as a child through the eighth grade. She holds a master's degree in religious education from a Catholic university in Chicago. She was also steeped in the Peyote Way for much of her life, and still occasionally attends peyote meetings today. She is also a member of the Sacred Tobacco Dance Society and positively reflects on her experience of "speaking in tongues" while being prayed over by a Pentecostal friend.

- A young Pentecostal Crow man grew up in a strong peyote family, his grandfather being a highly revered and widely recognized roadman (leader) in the Native American Church. While he was a student in high school, he and his parents were deeply affected by a Pentecostal revival in a nearby reservation town. For ten years, he abandoned involvement in peyote meetings in deference to the Crow Pentecostal preachers who taught that the two paths are incompatible. Today, as a father of two young children, he wants to teach his children both ways—the Pentecostal way and the Peyote Way. He currently attends church off the reservation to avoid the condemnation of Crow Pentecostal preachers, even as he renews his participation in the Native American Church.

- A lifelong Crow Catholic man decided that one of the best ways he could follow Jesus's example of self-sacrifice, as found in the Bible, was to participate in the traditional Crow practice of fasting and praying in the reservation hills. Through a series of three-day fasts over a five-year period, he experienced a vision that led him to become a dedicated Sun Dancer, sponsoring his own Sun Dance ceremony on the reservation every four years. He now combines an immersion in Crow Traditionalism with a fervent Catholic devotionalism, fasting and experiencing visions in the reservation mission chapels during eucharistic adoration, and declaring that Jesus is drawing the Crow community to himself through the Sun Dance center pole.

This cursory sampling of personal narratives also highlights how the fundamental category of "religious identity" is likewise rendered problematic in indigenous contexts. The term itself implies a more or less exclusive claim made on an individual by a dominant religious tradition. In the context of Native Christianity, "ceremonial belonging" would be a far better designation of religious self-understanding. Where "religious identity" tends to focus on the individual and implies alignment with a single (or primary) tradition, "ceremonial belonging" emphasizes ritual practice, the experience of the community, and the possibility—even likelihood—of multiple traditional alignments.[14] Over and over, the voices of Crow religious leaders emphasize attitude over belief. One Native American Church leader, who also identifies as Catholic, downplayed doctrinal differences across religious borders by insisting that we will all be judged, in the end, by "what's in our heart." During one peyote meeting I attended, the sponsor expressed very similar sentiments when he explained that good religion comes down to one's "attitude." Here he used "attitude" much like Christians speak of the "soul," emphasizing neither doctrines nor denominations, but the interior posture one assumes in the face of life's challenges and joys. Both voices echo the familiar refrain of the late Crow holy man Thomas Yellowtail, who spoke ceaselessly of "proper intention" when performing one's religious duties, whether praying with the pipe, embarking on a vision quest, fasting in the Sun Dance, or praying in a church.[15]

Setting aside familiar conventions of designating Native participation in various forms of Christianity, the religious self-understanding of Christianized Native people as expressed in the narratives to follow, accompanied as these expressions are by complex habits of religious practice, begs the observer of Crow religious life to rethink well-worn models of religious identity by starting, finally, on Native terms. For in practice, despite the imposition of Euro-American assumptions about religion and religious self-understanding from missionaries and scholars alike, Crow religious patterns have, in many ways, succeeded in conquering the religious assumptions of the tribe's colonizers and rewritten the rules of religious identity. Not only will the narratives introduce us to Native people who hold together Christianity and Crow ceremonies with little apparent tension, but we will also find Crows who, despite an explicit renunciation of Crow religion, still manage to be Christian in profoundly Crow ways, defying those who insist that some versions of Christianity are so drenched in colonialist assumptions as to be immune to the indigenizing efforts of Native believers. The phenomenon of Crow Pentecostalism is a perfect case in point, as will be explored later in this introduction.

TRADITIONAL RELIGIOUS PRACTICES
ON THE CROW RESERVATION

In the narratives found in the chapters to come, interviewees reference a wide variety of Crow ceremonies and traditional spiritual concepts that may not be familiar to all readers. Oftentimes, little to no explanation accompanies these references as the speakers themselves are typically so immersed in the culture that they regard the meaning of these terms, and knowledge of these ceremonies, as self-evident. With this in mind, the following brief descriptions of selected concepts and practices is intended as a basic primer of Crow Traditionalism for those who may be unfamiliar with these ways. Since the interaction of Crow Christianity with traditional tribal ways stands at the heart of this study, some familiarity with these terms is necessary for a fruitful reading of these personal religious narratives steeped in traditional Crow culture.

Matrilineal Clan System

Crow tribal society is organized into eight matrilineal clans today. Six of these eight clans are paired into familial groupings, creating a complex network of family relations across the reservation. Members of the same clan share a strong level of solidarity with one another. Even if they don't interact on a daily basis, clan members count on one another in times of financial distress, for political support in tribal politics, and for help with large projects—such as brandings or preparing for a big event. For example, when planning for a graduation celebration, a person would look to clan members to provide the food, money, and gifts required for the feast and "giveaway" to mark the important occasion.

Clan affiliation is determined by the woman's lineage. A father does not belong to the same clan as his children, but is rather a member of his own mother's clan. Even so, a well-defined relationship exists between an individual and the relatives of his or her father's family. The terms "clan aunts" and "clan uncles" *(áassahke)* are used to designate these relationships. *Áassahke*, in turn, refer to their clan "children" as *baakáate*, "my child." According to Rodney Frey, "*áassahke* provide praise, prayer, and protection" to their clan "children" in return for "gifts of respect, feasts, and presents" from their *baakáate*.[16] It can be argued that observing one's clan relations and fulfilling one's clan duties constitute the most basic obligations of being a Crow Indian. Regardless of one's religious practices or church affiliations, clan relations and clan-related duties are universally observed. Even among Pentecostals who refuse to participate in most traditional Crow ceremonies, recognition and respect for one's clan relations are still widely observed, even in cases where Pentecostal Crows may ask church members to fulfill spiritual duties typically reserved for clan relatives in order to avoid violations of religious conscience.

Medicine *(Xapáaliia and Baaxpée)*

Baaxpée is the Crow term for supernatural power. Traditionalists believe that the world is filled with such spirit power, and that it originates with *Akbaatatdía*—the omnipotent, wholly other Maker of all. Many Crows today use the name *Akbaatatdía* interchangeably with "God." However, in its traditional usage, the name denotes a far more impersonal, far less anthropomorphic concept of the divine than that found in most Christian theologies. Crows have long sought *baaxpée* through fasting in the reservation's hills, subjecting themselves to deprivation and suffering in the hope of inciting the pity of some supernatural being ("helper") to give them a spiritual gift.

Crows believe that humans are capable of experiencing *baaxpée*— and, to some extent, harnessing it—through tangible objects known as *xapáaliia*.[17] *Xapáaliia* are essentially material channels for *baaxpée*. The most widely used *xapáaliia* among Crows are medicine bundles.[18] Medicine bundles most often originate when someone, typically while fasting, receives a dream or vision believed to contain *baaxpée*. Often under the direction of a medicine man or medicine woman, the recipient of the dream or vision will construct a bundle of sacred objects that functions to preserve this power, only opening the bundle on specific occasions and according to strictly prescribed ritual guidelines. Medicine bundles have historically been used for a variety of purposes, from bringing success in battle to providing healing power. They may also be transferred to family members or other appropriate seekers, along with the *baaxpée* associated with them.

In addition to medicine bundles, *xapáaliia* come in an almost endless variety of forms. Feather fans used in ceremonies, sacred drums, animal skins, and ritual effigies may all function as conduits of spiritual power. In the narratives of Joe Bear Cloud and Georgine Falls Down that follow, the sacred songs or "hymns" they describe function, in Christian terms, very much like *xapáaliia* function among traditionalists. Like medicine bundles, these songs are "received" through prayer, "carried" (even "owned") by the original recipient, and passed down through generations with their healing power intact, a power that is occasionally unveiled through the performance of ritual singing on behalf of those seeking a healing.

Sweat Lodge

The sweat lodge ceremony is the most common setting for offering traditional, communal prayer among the Crow Tribe. The lodge itself is usually constructed of saplings bent into a half-dome hut that is designed to hold six to eight persons. Blankets or tarps are draped over the wooden frame, completely sealing the lodge from sunlight. A flap covers the east-facing door to the lodge, and inside this door a small pit is dug to hold rocks that have been heated in a fire outside the entrance. After participants have gathered inside the lodge and the pit has been filled with heated rocks, the leader of the ceremony conducts four rounds of prayer while pouring ladles of water over the rocks to create an intense steam bath.

The ceremony is generally understood as a ritual rebirth. In the Crow tradition, men and women sweat separately and are naked during the ceremony, imitating our condition at birth. The sweat generated during the ceremony symbolizes the cleansing of body and mind. At the conclusion, participants exit the warm, dark womb of the earth toward the east, the direction of new beginnings. The sweat lodge is used in many contexts on the Crow Reservation today. While it often functions as a stand-alone ceremony for communal prayer, sweats are also commonly used as both the opening and concluding rite of lengthier ceremonies, including the Sun Dance, peyote meetings, or a multiday fast in the hills.[19]

CROW JESUS

While sweats are common among many churchgoing Crows, there are likewise many who refuse to participate, believing it would compromise their Christian faith. This is particularly common among Pentecostals. But even among fairly conservative Christian congregations on the reservation that are generally opposed to sweats, an increasing number of congregants are discovering freedom to enter the sweat lodge either by (1) transforming the ceremony into an explicitly Christian event or (2) setting aside the spiritual aspects of the ceremony altogether and emphasizing, in their place, the purely physical benefits of the process—such as stress reduction or relief from sore muscles. The interviews with Kenneth Pretty On Top (a Pentecostal pastor) and Jonathan Lawton (a Southern Baptist pastor) demonstrate this development.

Sun Dance

Until its demise in the late 1800s, the Crow Sun Dance was primarily an individual test of spiritual and physical endurance in which a male tribal member fasted alone in the reservation hills, seeking *baaxpée* from the spirit helpers through intensive personal suffering. The primary purpose of the ceremony in those days was to avenge the death of a loved one killed by an enemy tribe. The last known performance of the traditional Crow Sun Dance took place around 1875, after which time the rite was essentially lost.[20] A new version of the ceremony was introduced among the tribe in 1941, when Shoshone medicine man and Sun Dance chief John Trehero accepted the invitation of William Big Day of Pryor to bring the Shoshone Sun Dance tradition to the Crows. To this day, the Shoshone-Crow Sun Dance remains a powerful force in the life of the Crow Tribe, with hundreds of dancers annually taking part in the grueling event.[21]

The Shoshone-Crow Sun Dance is a three- to four-day fast that takes place inside a large, circular, open-roofed lodge. Although the ceremony itself is held during the summer months, dancers make their pledges to participate during the previous winter. At the center of the lodge stands a large cottonwood tree, the sacred center pole, from which are suspended a buffalo head and an eagle upon which dancers focus their prayerful intentions throughout the ceremony. The Sun Dance begins when the dancers, sometimes numbering close to a hundred, enter the lodge and take their places around the periphery of the circle; they'll remain inside this lodge for the full extent of the ceremony—dancing, praying, suffering, and sleeping.

From sunrise to long past sundown, dancers "charge" the center pole to the beating of the drum, offering prayers, blowing eagle-bone whistles, and abstaining from all food and water through the entire ordeal. Each dancer has pledged to pray for a particular intention—whether for a family member, the tribe, or the welfare of all people. The center pole is described by Rodney Frey as "a channel to *Akbaatatdía*, through which *baaxpée* flows."[22] According to Sun Dance chief Thomas Yellowtail, the "dancers are connected to the center pole by an invisible cord coming from the tree and penetrating into their heart." Yellowtail then added, "Everyone present at the Sun Dance knows in his heart that he is at the center of the universe."[23]

The Sun Dance chief is a medicine man who has been given the "right" to lead the Sun Dance in the Shoshone-Crow way. He leads the prayers, conducts the daily sunrise ceremony, encourages the dancers, and oversees the elaborate rituals required of participants. He also conducts the "doctoring" ceremony on the last full day of the Sun Dance, where dancers and spectators alike approach the center pole. There the Sun Dance chief uses his eagle feather fan to bring healing to the people. He puts *baaxpée* into his feathers by touching them against the center pole, and then touches them to each individual who has come for a healing, drawing out the various ailments and casting them away through the Sun Dance door.

A huge number of community members are involved in every Sun Dance. In addition to the dancers and singers, hundreds of family members and friends camp on the Sun Dance grounds and gather each day outside the lodge to "pray on" and offer their support to the dancers. Catholic Crows regularly take part in the Sun Dance religion, and all of the Catholic priests on the reservation give their support to the practice. Father Randolph Graczyk, as mentioned in his interview, has danced in the ceremony seven times. As suggested in the interviews of Newton Old Crow and Angela Russell, many Crow Baptists also follow the Sun Dance religion, though perhaps at a lower rate than Catholic parishioners. Among Pentecostals, however, there is virtually no crossover with the Sun Dance. Of all traditional Crow religious practices condemned by Crow Pentecostal adherents, the Sun Dance regularly tops the list.

Peyote Way (Native American Church)

The ceremonial Peyote Way arrived on the Crow Reservation around the year 1910. Frank Bethune is widely recognized as the first Crow to conduct peyote meetings among the tribe, having learned the religion from the Northern Cheyennes whose reservation is located immediately to the east of Crow Country. A typical peyote meeting takes place in a ceremonial tipi, beginning after sundown and continuing through the night to the following morning. A crescent shaped altar made of sand is constructed on the ground inside the tipi, and an elaborate fire is continuously tended through the night. Participants are seated on the ground in a circle around the perimeter of the tipi as the "roadman" conducts the ceremony. Prayers, short exhortations, and tobacco offerings accompany the central ritual activities of drumming, singing, and ingesting peyote.

Singing takes place all night long, accompanied by the rapid beating of a water drum. The drum is passed around the tipi as participants take turns leading four songs apiece. Each singer, in turn, holds a staff and feather fan in one hand while shaking a gourd rattle with the other. At intervals throughout the ceremony, peyote is circulated around the tipi for participants to ingest, usually in the form of a paste rolled into small balls or a richly brewed peyote tea. Peyote—a small cactus plant possessing psychedelic properties—functions as a sacrament in the Native American Church and is believed to possess supernatural qualities. Most members believe that the Creator gave peyote specifically to the Indians as a pathway to healing and wholeness.

Ceremonial peyote use likely originated in pre-Columbian Mexico before making its way into the southwestern United States. As a structured ceremony, the Peyote Way gained a foothold among the Kiowa, Comanche, and other Oklahoma tribes in the 1880s, before reaching the Northern Cheyennes in the 1890s and the Crows by 1910. In an effort to gain legal protection, leaders incorporated the movement as the Native American Church in 1918. Nonetheless, peyotists continued to suffer widespread persecution as Christian missionaries joined in the efforts of state and federal officials to eradicate the movement. Undeterred, the Native American Church only grew stronger in the face of this opposition, establishing itself as a major indigenous religious movement through the twentieth century. The ceremonial use of peyote by American Indians in the United States finally gained federal protection in 1994 when Congress approved "Amendments" to the American Indian Religious Freedom Act of 1978.

Peyote remains a vital force on the Crow Reservation today. Many Crows who are active in Christian churches are also members of the Peyote Way, often bringing considerable Christian influence with them to the meetings. As Levi Black Eagle details in his interview, his grandfather, who was a prominent leader in the Native American Church, always ended his prayers in the peyote tipi "in the name of Jesus." In fact, evidence of deep Christian influence on Crow peyote practice dates back at least to the 1920s. Timothy McCleary, who teaches at the Crow Tribe's Little Big Horn College, has a peyote banner from this period hanging in his office. It features a large white cross opposite an American flag, a bold white eagle, and the slogans "Jesus Only" and "Love One Another." He explains that a heavily Christianized version of the ceremony known as "the New Way" or the "Jesus Only Way" was widely adopted by the Crows during the 1920s and 1930s in the hope of quieting opposition from outsiders.[24] Today, while Baptist and Catholic Church members are commonly found in the peyote tipi, Pentecostal participation is much more rare. However, Levi Black Eagle, in discussing his own efforts to pair Pentecostalism and peyote later in these pages, suggests that virtually no line of religious separation among the Crows is truly insurmountable.

NATIVE FUNDAMENTALISM RECONSIDERED

While fluid movement across Christian and Traditionalist religious borders is common for many churchgoers on the Crow Reservation, it is by no means universal. As suggested in the previous survey of Crow religious practices, the most glaring exception to this pattern is Crow Pentecostalism, the most populous Christian tradition on the reservation and arguably the most dominant in terms of social and political influence. Adherents frequently speak of their faith as worship of "the true and living God," explaining that Christianity has superseded the "Indian religion" of the old days. While some believe that traditional pre-Christian ways were good for their time but are no longer effectual today, others flatly regard

Crow religious ceremonies as demonic. One Pentecostal pastor included in the following chapters believes the practice of traditional ceremonies is the direct cause for many of the social ills plaguing Native communities today, from rampant alcoholism to a suicide rate several times the national average.

Because of its frequent condemnation of medicine bundles, peyote, the Sun Dance, and many other traditional ceremonies, the Pentecostal movement is regarded by many outsiders as an enemy of Crow culture. Indeed, all across Native America, Native Pentecostalism is frequently maligned by Indian and non-Indian critics alike precisely for its antitraditional rhetoric.[25] On the Crow Reservation, similar criticisms are common not only among non-Christian Traditionalists, but among a wide spectrum of Christian traditions. In fact, even Crow Pentecostals themselves occasionally express dismay over the movement's reputation for its heavy-handed condemnation of the traditional ways.

However, careful attention to the stories of Crow Pentecostals presents a more complicated reality than is suggested by blanket accusations of anti-Traditionalism. As demonstrated in this collection of narratives, Crow Pentecostals represent an enormous range of opinions and attitudes toward what constitutes a proper relationship between Crow culture and Christian identity. Too often in both scholarly and popular treatments of Native Pentecostalism, participants are portrayed as unwitting pawns in the continued devastation of their own cultural heritage by persistent colonial forces.[26] While recent scholarship is increasingly (and rightly) seeing "Native Americans as actors and not merely subjects of the encounter with Christianity,"[27] this trend has been slow to reach studies of Native Pentecostalism.

There should be little doubt that the rise of fundamentalist Christianity among U.S. Native communities does indeed pose certain threats to the persistence of indigenous religions as practiced among affected tribal communities. At the same time, outside observers should bear in mind that Native Pentecostalism is itself an expression of indigenous agency in ways that may not be immediately obvious. Its resistance to white hegemony is evident, for example, in the prevalence of independent Pentecostal churches, as Pentecostal Crows overwhelmingly spurn denominational affiliation to retain oversight of their own congregations and avoid having to answer to white denominational leaders detached from, and often unsympathetic to, Native concerns. Furthermore, we should bear in mind that even to the extent that Crow Pentecostals are complicit in a system that threatens hegemonic oppression over Crow culture and tribal members themselves, Native participation in white structures of dominance inevitably challenges those very structures even while "performing whiteness."[28]

Emerging from these currents of subversive complicity, however, is a far bolder and more sweeping strategy for asserting Native agency while remaining firmly planted in the soil of an adopted fundamentalist faith. Far from rejecting Crow identity in light of their Christian faith, Crow Pentecostals today are creatively attempting to redefine the terms of indigeneity in such a way that they themselves displace their own Traditionalist critics at the center of the tribe's cultural circle, all the while remaining wed to a Pentecostal tradition that has long regarded Christian faith and Native religions as incompatible entities. Here are six ways I see this ambitious strategy unfolding on the Crow Reservation today.

Questioning the Cultural Legitimacy of "Traditional" Crow Ceremonies

In interviews with Pentecostals for this project, I heard many participants express doubts about the authenticity of so-called traditional Crow ceremonies. For example, I was reminded many times that the Peyote Way practiced among the tribe today came from Mexico by way of Oklahoma and the Northern Cheyennes, and that the Sun Dance religion currently surging in popularity among the tribe was imported from the Shoshones back in the 1940s. Such comments were usually offered as a direct challenge to tribal Traditionalists who insist that to be authentically Crow, one must respect, if not practice, the "traditional Crow religions."

Sometimes, Crow Pentecostal attacks on the legitimacy of the traditional ways take a different form. On at least two occasions, I was told that after the Shoshone medicine man John Trehero brought the Sun Dance to the Crows, the tribe allowed the ceremony to change in ways that were prohibited, most notably by allowing women to participate. According to one of my interviewees, these violations in ceremonial protocol led Trehero to later claim, "All my medicine came back by themselves because [the

Crows] did not do what they were supposed to do with it."[29] Others insist that the legitimacy of the Sun Dance, as commonly observed among the Crows today, is disqualified on different grounds. One Pentecostal pastor I spoke with actually expressed respect for the way earlier generations of Crow seekers practiced the Sun Dance in a solitary manner. His dismissal of the ceremony today springs from his estimation that it has become a communal "show-off thing," which runs counter to Jesus's teachings to fast without drawing attention to oneself. Regardless of the argument employed, each accusation alleges that the indigenous ceremonies widely practiced among the tribe are either illegitimate imports or perverted versions of once-true practices, and thus may not be used today as valid indicators of one's authentic "Crowness."

Ancestor Conversion Stories

Another strategy for redefining indigeneity on Pentecostal terms involves the telling of well-worn conversion narratives involving their own once-traditional Crow ancestors. These stories function as a powerful rebuttal to critics who regard Crow Pentecostal faith as a betrayal of the old-time elders. One well-known story describes a visionary encounter that the legendary Old Man Plain Feather had with Jesus. Although Plain Feather was instrumental in reestablishing the Sun Dance among the tribe in the 1940s, and was also involved in the Native American Church, he gradually lost confidence in the traditional ways following a vision that he purportedly had of Jesus. His granddaughter, who is a Pentecostal elder in Pryor, explains that he instructed her, on his deathbed, to abandon the old worn-out Indian religion he once embraced and to follow, instead, "that Holy Ghost"—which, he said, "is way better than what I have." Story after story was told to me of traditional elders whose encounters with "the true and living God" convinced them to forfeit the old ways, embrace Christianity, and instruct their own children and grandchildren—often from their deathbeds—to do the same.

In this way, Crow Pentecostal Christians who renounce medicine bundles, the Sun Dance, the Peyote Way, and other traditional ceremonies are able to counter accusations of anti-Traditionalism by claiming obedience to the instructions of their now-deceased ancestors. In a remarkable twist of irony, this narrative defense of their traditional credentials simultaneously implicates their critics as the *actual* betrayers of the elders' wisdom by virtue of persisting in the so-called traditional ways. Not surprisingly, such stories are, at times, fiercely contested by family members who feel that the Traditionalist legacies of highly revered ancestors are being threatened by revisionist Christian zeal. One Crow Baptist, who wishes to remain anonymous, believes that a serious incident of vandalism at his church was an act of retaliation after his relatives publicized stories of an ancestor destroying the family's medicine bundles in the process of embracing Christianity.

Emphasizing Crow Social Values over Traditional Ceremonies

Another way that some Crow churchgoers attempt to reconcile their rejection of "Indian religion" with their desire to maintain a strong Crow identity is by de-emphasizing the role that ceremonies play in determining who is, and who is not, a "real" Crow. To that end, in response to those who say that participation in traditional ceremonies is a necessary mark of a traditional Crow, many Crow Pentecostals present alternative markers of authentic Crow identity. Kenneth Pretty On Top, pastor of the thriving Foursquare Pentecostal church at Crow Agency, believes that the observance of traditional tribal values like hospitality, love of family, and respect for the land are far more important indicators of Crow identity than participation in Crow religious ceremonies. Even more important, from his perspective, is whether one has Crow blood. During one of our interviews, he bluntly raised the following question: "What makes someone a Crow?" He then offered a litany of traditional activities and Crow ceremonies as possible answers, before offering his own reply: "That doesn't make you Crow. Anybody can dance. Anybody can wear feathers. Anybody can do those things. But being a Crow is when you got that Crow blood. The blood." He then added, "And what makes you a Christian? The blood of Jesus."[30]

Nor are Crow Pentecostals alone in giving priority to tribal values over traditional religious ceremonies when deciding who is truly Crow. Angela Russell, a Crow Baptist who works as an attorney, is a good example. Although she is comfortable with Crows simultaneously observing Christian and Indian ceremonies, she echoes Pretty On Top's comments by downplaying the necessity of ceremonial participation when determining a tribal member's traditional credentials. Instead, she emphasizes attachment to Crow tribal land, strong family relationships, and using the Crow language—especially in preserving the tradition of Crow sacred songs.[31]

Downplaying the Religious Dimension of Crow Ceremonies

While the majority of Crow Pentecostals categorically regard participation in traditional Crow ceremonies as incompatible with Christian faith, the one practice that appears to be gaining acceptance in the Crow Pentecostal community is the sweat lodge ceremony. During a group interview at one Pentecostal church on the reservation, I asked how many of the participants felt comfortable praying in the sweat lodge. Of the ten church members gathered in the circle, two acknowledged attending sweats on a regular basis. Both described a lengthy process of wrestling with guilt over the practice, and both talked about how they had to prayerfully work through opposition raised by fellow Christians.[32]

In both cases, however, a key factor in their eventual decision to enter the sweat lodge was the conviction that the ceremony is not, at its core, a religious event. Rather, they came to see it primarily as a means of purification and an antidote to stress and anxiety. In turn, both emphasized that their chief motivation for sweating was *not* spiritual. They explained that the sweat lodge was originally a means of physically cleansing the body in the days before running water, and also functioned to relieve stress and muscle soreness in a prereservation era marked by intense physical exertion. Desacralizing the ceremony in this way triggered a sense of permission for them to enjoy the benefits of the sweat without violating their own religious convictions. One of the two explicitly said that she does not pray inside the sweat lodge so as to avoid violating her Christian conscience. The other church member conceded that, in addition to seeking relief from stress and muscle tension, he does sometimes join in the prayers. "But me," he was sure to clarify, "I call upon the name of Jesus." He added, "The bottom line is, don't make it an idol." The pastor at another Pentecostal church was less cautious in defending his decision to enter the sweat lodge, rhetorically asking with pointed good humor, "What's wrong with a bunch of men getting together to pray?" He punctuated his defense of Christians attending sweats by saying he knows of several conversions that have taken place in the sweat lodge.

An Alternate, Spiritualized Clan System

While some Crow Pentecostals have discovered a degree of freedom to practice selected Crow ceremonies by means of downplaying the religious significance of the rites, others have done so by carefully realigning the community within which traditional Crow ceremonies are observed. For example, it is common for Crow Pentecostals to harbor grave concerns regarding the spiritual implications of traditional naming ceremonies, as well as the traditional blessings offered by clan aunts and clan uncles. Many feel that the spiritual power—called "medicine"—involved in such practices is antithetical to Christian faith. Some regard it as tantamount to witchcraft or idolatry. However, some have found a way to bridge the divide between Christian faith and Crow culture in ceremonies involving traditional clan relations. In cases where Pentecostal Crows wish to participate in such ceremonies, but are wary of relatives who are deeply traditional, some will simply ask a highly respected Pentecostal believer—if not from their own family, then from another within their congregation—to fulfill the role traditionally reserved for clan aunts and clan uncles.

One Pentecostal lay leader humorously referred to this phenomenon as the NBA of the Crow Reservation: the Native Believers Association. Many Crow Pentecostals are willing, and even eager, to observe the roles traditionally reserved for clan relatives, but will do so only for those belonging to this newly defined spiritual clan—a clan determined not by Crow blood, but by the blood of Jesus. In this way, in the absence of a clan relative who is a devout Pentecostal, a functionally parallel clan structure is spontaneously springing up across the reservation that is based on Christian belief and one's standing in the church rather than on one's place within the matrilineal clan structure of the tribe. This surely stands as one of the most remarkable expressions of a newly emergent, faith-based indigeneity developing among fundamentalist Christian circles on the Crow Reservation today. Again, the desire is not to abandon the traditional ways, but rather to reinvent and redefine them in terms compatible with Pentecostal convictions.

Doubly Empowered Native Identity

As suggested in some of the stories above, the relationship between Crow blood and Christian identity is playing an increasingly important role in the religious vision of many Crow Pentecostals. This development is perhaps seen most clearly in the influential work of Jim and Faith Chosa, whose nationally recognized Day Chief Ministries is based near Fort Smith in the reservation's Big Horn District. According to the Chosas, indigenous peoples of the United States possess a kind of geospiritual authority over their ancestral homelands, and to them alone belongs "the true ownership of the spiritual landscape of the continent." This spiritual framing of indigenous authority naturally affords considerable significance to all Native bloodlines in the United States.

To born-again Native believers, however, the Chosas impute even greater authority. They represent a kind of pan-Indian supertribe that bears unique spiritual responsibilities, including serving as gatekeepers for the collective blessings and curses that fall on their land. "Native Americans," they claim, "are still the earthly host authority for the land of America, and the Native believers as new creatures of Christ restored to heavenly authority in the Name of Jesus are the only ones who can righteously and permanently deal with any and all ancient issues of iniquity affecting the spiritual and natural landscapes."[33] It is no surprise that such a spiritual vision is gaining more and more traction among Crow Pentecostals today as it blends aspects of classic Pentecostal theology, tribal pride, and an empowering sense of indigenous privilege in God's universal salvific plans.

STORYTELLING: NOTES ON METHODOLOGY

The chapters in this volume are devoted to Crow people sharing stories and personal perspectives related to their own practice of Christianity. Despite persistent scholarly interest in the contemporary religious beliefs and practices of American Indians across a widening range of academic disciplines, surprisingly few studies are devoted primarily to the voices of Native people themselves. It is my hope to offer here some small corrective to the glaring lack of material devoted to the religious perspectives of Native women and men expressed in their own words.

With the exception of one that was recorded in 2009 (with Gloria Goes Ahead Cummins), all of the interviews in this collection occurred between 2012 and 2015. Furthermore, each is focused primarily on the relationship between Crow identity and Christian faith in the participant's own experience. While I often opened these conversations with questions about historical context (for example, "To your knowledge, when and how did your congregation begin?" and "In what ways have you been involved in the work of this church through the years?"), the bulk of each interview was dedicated to exploring personal religious practices with an eye to how Christian faith interacts with Crow culture and contemporary Crow Reservation realities.

Toward that end, interviews typically revolved around questions such as the following: "What role do you believe the traditional tribal clan system should play in the lives of Christian Crows?" "Do you believe it's okay for Crow churchgoers to participate in traditional Native ceremonies involving medicine bundles, the sweat lodge, vision quests, or the Sun Dance?" "Some critics of Christianity on the Crow Reservation contend that Christianity is a threat to traditional tribal culture. How do you respond to them?"

Despite entering each interview with a set of prepared questions, I was far more interested in hearing stories of spiritual significance, rooted in the experiences of daily life, than I was in gathering statements of faith or successive replies to a series of questions. I pursued this approach not only because it is better aligned with indigenous patterns of religious self-understanding,[34] but also for the way that narratives—more than philosophical discourse—seem capable of communicating religious experiences arising from within *any* religious tradition. As Nancy Tatom Ammerman explains in *Sacred Stories, Spiritual Tribes*, "For the experts, cognitive coherence is critical, but for the non-experts, ideas about the nature of God and of the world are most often carried in stories. We don't tell stories about God intervening in the world if we do not believe that God exists, but what we know about divine character and divine interaction with humanity is carried by the stories that play out across the domains of our lives."[35] The narrative turn that has marked so many disciplines in the social sciences in recent years is being felt in religious studies as well. In undertaking this project, I self-consciously place myself within that trajectory.

Drawing from years of experience working on oral history projects with indigenous communities, one enrolled tribal historian with whom I met explained his own approach to interviews like this: "One of the things we found out about interviewing Indian people, especially the elderly, is that it's best just to let the person talk. A regular white man talking—their mind is set. They say, 'You stop me, ask me questions, and I'll answer.' Then more questions. But Indian people—the best thing is to let them go."[36] And so, after discussing my project with each participant and briefly reviewing the key questions I hoped to explore during our interview, I tried, as much as possible, "to let them go." At points where I did seek clarification or further elaboration during interviews, or where interviewees requested prompting, I've edited my own brief comments out of the following transcripts. This decision was motivated by my desire to keep readers focused on the interviewees by minimizing potentially distracting conversation that took place with me as the interviewer. In place of my questions and comments, I've inserted topical headings throughout each of the transcripts to provide helpful context originally contained in questions now redacted from the transcript. For those participants who gave written consent to do so, video recordings of the interviews, containing my comments as well, are housed in the Little Big Horn College archives at Crow Agency, where tribal members and nonenrolled researchers alike have full access.

Indeed, many times, after politely reviewing my sheet of questions, an interviewee would deliberately lay aside the sheet and embark on a continuous narrative arc that sometimes lasted well over an hour. In addition to answering the majority of my questions (though never in the scripted order), such interviews invariably revealed crucial questions I had failed to ask. This revelatory function of narrative freedom was especially effective in correcting some of my assumptions about the nature of discontinuity between Crow identity and Christian faith. While my own understanding of this tension tended to focus either on apparent theological incompatibilities between Crow religions and Christian doctrine, or the pains of colonial missionary history, listening more and talking less during my interviews revealed that, among Crows who identify closely with Christianity, these are seldom their primary concerns. Rather, participants were much more concerned with how Christianity (1) addresses a pervasive desire for tribal belonging, (2) facilitates encounters with the spirit world, and (3) promotes healing in the community—physical and spiritual, individual and communal.

In preparing the following interviews for publication, I have attempted to retain the style, tone, and rhythm of the speakers' original oral narratives.

For this reason, colloquial expressions, syntactical errors, and many other nonstandard English conventions appear frequently throughout this volume. For purposes of clarity and readability, only minor changes have been imposed on the interview transcripts as they appear here, such as omitting distracting verbal clutter or excessive repetition. Footnotes have been kept to a minimum to help keep the focus on the narratives, serving only to provide necessary context for readers who may be unfamiliar with aspects of Crow culture or history referenced in the narrative. In some cases, where the meaning and continuity of a narrative is evidently improved, I've relocated segments of an interview either earlier or later in the narrative than they originally appeared. For example, there were times at the end of an interview when a participant remembered—and proceeded to tell—a story relevant to a much earlier portion of the interview. In such cases, I've attempted to place those interjected segments where they most naturally belong in the narrative.

My relationship to families and individuals on the Crow Reservation dates back more than twenty years, with more extensive contact taking place over the last six summers. In choosing participants for this project, my priority was on selecting voices that would, taken together, offer a representative sampling of contemporary Christian beliefs and practices on the Crow Reservation. While each of the voices included in this project is individually introduced in the course of the book, a few comments should be made regarding my selection of participants. First, I wanted to include voices from each of the most prevalent Christian missionary traditions on the reservation: Roman Catholic, Baptist (American and Southern), and Pentecostal (denominational and independent). Second, I wanted to include adherents from each of these Christian traditions who simultaneously participate in traditional Crow religious ceremonies in order to reflect the prevalence of multireligious participation that currently exists among tribal members. Third, I felt it was important to include a wide demographic of Crow tribal members, so that women, men, elders, young adults, clergy, lay members, and married and single churchgoers are each represented in this project. Fourth, I chose participants who are generally well regarded within their respective communities. Every religious community has its outliers, and there is much to be gained through careful attention to those who inhabit the edges of any religious tradition. However, my intention is to offer representative portraits of Christian faith as widely practiced among the Crows, rather than a survey of extremes. Fifth, I was committed to representing diverse geographical regions of the reservation—from Pryor in the west, to Crow Agency in the east, to Lodge Grass in the south.

Finally, I chose to include one non-Native clergy member from each of the three most dominant missionary traditions on the reservation. This decision was not based simply on the historical significance of outside missionaries among the tribe, but on the influence they continue to exert today. While non-Native clergy persist in dominating the ordained leadership of Catholic, Baptist, and other mainline Protestant churches among the Crow Tribe, even among Pentecostal congregations (all of which are currently led by Crow pastors) non-Native-led ministries exert considerable influence. Indeed, Pentecostal evangelists, healers, teachers, and preachers from off the reservation fill the pulpits of Crow Pentecostal churches and camp meetings all year long. Therefore, I felt it was imperative to include at least one non-Native Crow Pentecostal voice in the final part of this narrative collection.

One group that was intentionally omitted from this project deserves mentioning. While there certainly exists an outspoken, though relatively small, number of people among the tribe who are publicly opposed to Christianity's presence on the reservation and who regard its influence as a grave threat to tribal well-being, I chose not to include these voices for two reasons. First, the further I got into this project, the more it felt like voices of opposition to Christianity belonged to quite a different—if equally important—project than the one I have undertaken here. Given the range of participants I wished to include, as well as the breadth of issues I have attempted to explore with respect to Crows who, to some extent, embrace the Christian faith, it became increasingly clear to me that the project could not achieve these goals if it also attempted to fairly represent significant voices antagonistic to Christianity. The second reason is more personal. Almost without exception, when I discussed with Christian participants the possibility of including voices openly hostile to Christianity, many expressed deep misgivings about appearing in a collection alongside them. Respect for their wishes, coupled with my own sense that adequately representing anti-Christian sentiment would stretch the project too thin, has led me to keep the focus of this collection on Crows affiliated with one or more Christian traditions. Even so, readers of this volume will have no trouble finding criticisms of Christianity among the participants included here, reminding us that some of the most penetrating critiques of any religious movement often come from within.

THE VOICES

The following first-person narratives are organized into six topical parts. Since a detailed introduction precedes each of the interviews as well as each of the parts, I'll offer at this point only a brief overview of the voices included in this project. The first part, "Crow Catholic Visions," contains the stories of four tribal members who all identify strongly with the Catholic Church, though in quite different ways. Geneva Whiteman is a lifelong participant in the Catholic Church with a strong devotion to Saint Mary, while also being an active member of both the Tobacco Dance Society and the Native American Church. Larry Hogan was raised in a strictly Catholic home before entering the Sun Dance religion as an adult in an effort to imitate the sufferings of Jesus. Bobby Lee Stops At Pretty Places is a Third Order Franciscan who spearheaded the project to erect a thirty-three-foot wooden cross towering over Crow Agency. Gloria Goes Ahead Cummins, who rounds out the part, was profoundly influenced by the Catholic Charismatic Renewal that swept Montana's reservations in the 1970s and 1980s.

The part titled "Pentecostalism, Culture, and Politics" contains the stories of four Pentecostals. Two are independent Pentecostals, and two are denominationally affiliated. Each one struggles with the effort of reconciling a love of Crow culture with the movement's condemnation of many traditional Crow ceremonies. Rhea Goes Ahead, who pastors the Full Gospel Revival Tabernacle in Billings just north of the reservation, discusses how the early trademarks of the Crow Pentecostal movement continue to exert influence today—including a strong tradition of fasting, the prominent role women play in the movement, and the conviction that dark spiritual forces animate Crow religion. Fannie Plain Feather Ward served for more than two decades as youth minister of a denominational Pentecostal church in Pryor. Her narrative describes some spine-tingling experiences with "Indian religion" that led her to abandon it altogether in favor of exclusive loyalty to Christianity. Pastor Kenneth Pretty On Top Sr. likewise speaks against "compromise" and "syncretism," but also offers a blunt critique of the anti-Traditionalist judgmentalism he sees among some of his Pentecostal peers. The final voice here is that of Conrad "CJ" Stewart, a former Crow tribal legislator and a fourth-generation Pentecostal who was instrumental in passing two recent resolutions advancing an overtly Christian agenda among the tribe.

Two interviews comprise the third part, titled "The Baptist Middle Way." Although early Baptist missionaries on the Crow Reservation condemned Crow religion just as thoroughly as other Christian denominations did at the turn of the twentieth century, the Baptist tradition now represents a wide range of attitudes toward Crow Traditionalism—from persistent rejection to eager embrace. Both voices found in this part express a deep commitment to holding diverse traditions together, the posture most commonly found among Baptist Crows today. Newton Old Crow Sr. has been an American Baptist pastor on the reservation for many years. A well-known rodeo cowboy who was steeped in Crow Traditionalism as a child, Old Crow actively brings indigenous practices into Christian worship while chiding Pentecostals for refusing to do the same. Angela Russell grew up in a family with a long relationship to the historic First Crow Indian Baptist Church in Lodge Grass. She balances praise for the Baptist legacy of education among the tribe with open criticism for some of its past mistakes, all while insisting that the core Crow values of land, family, and language are entirely consistent with Christian faith.

"Peyote and Christ" is the next part, featuring three tribal members with close ties to the Peyote Way, also known as the Native American Church. Each one identifies with a different Christian denomination. Marvin Dawes is a committed Catholic, a devotee of Saint Mary, and a peyote roadman. He distinguishes between "religion" and "ceremonials," contending that Christianity belongs to the former and Native traditions belong to the latter. Even so, he feels no contradiction in practicing both, and actively challenges Crow church members who fail to respect the traditional tribal ways. Marlon Passes tells of his grandfather's decision to participate in the efforts of Baptist missionaries at the turn of the twentieth century. He recounts the destruction of his family's medicine bundles at the urging of these early missionaries, while expressing his own conviction that the Bible and peyote are fully compatible paths. Levi Black Eagle, grandson of the renowned peyote leader Sonny Black Eagle and son of recent tribal chairman Cedric Black Eagle, was steeped in the Peyote Way until a Pentecostal revival abruptly changed his spiritual path. Now as a young adult, he discusses his decision to reenter the peyote tipi in a rare effort to reconcile the Pentecostal and peyote traditions in his own religious practice.

The venerated Crow tradition of receiving, carrying, and sharing sacred healing songs is explored in the part "Healing Hymns." While fasting in the mountains, Crows have long sought and received holy songs for ceremonial purposes. When Pentecostalism gained a foothold among the tribe in the 1920s, that tradition was easily translated into Christian terms as Pentecostal hill-fasters continued receiving spirit songs of healing power in the Crow language. They were analogous to traditional Crow songs in nearly every way, except that the lyrics were filled with biblical imagery and an urgent expectation of Jesus's second coming. Joe Bear Cloud, the first inteviewee in this part, was an itinerant Pentecostal preacher before his recent appointment as pastor of an American Baptist congregation at Crow Agency. He is also a founding member of Crow Hymns Ministry, an interdenominational organization that gathers, records, and performs these Christocentric sacred songs across the reservation. Georgine Falls Down, a decorated powwow dancer and devout Christian, describes receiving her own sacred songs, which she freely shares with those who request their healing power.

The last part, "Missionary Voices," contains the only non-Native contributions to this project. Randolph Graczyk is a Capuchin Franciscan priest serving St. Charles Parish and School in the reservation town of Pryor. Graczyk is a University of Chicago–trained linguist who has dedicated the past forty years of his life to authoring a comprehensive volume on Crow grammar.[37] He believes that the Catholic faith and Crow Traditionalism are thoroughly compatible with one another, a conviction reflected in his own immersion in Crow ceremonies, including the sweat lodge and Sun Dance. Jonathan Lawton has served for twenty years as pastor of Apsáalooke Southern Baptist Church. Before that, he spent several years pastoring a church on the Navajo Reservation, just as his father before him had done.

He discusses his struggle to understand the extent to which Christian faith and indigenous ceremonies may properly be practiced by Crow parishioners of his own church, as well as by himself. The third and final voice in this part is that of Barry Moen, a Pentecostal evangelist from Wyoming who travels the Montana powwow circuit each year, seeking Native converts to Christianity in his mobile Prayer Tent. His account draws attention to the scores of ministry teams from all over the country that visit the tribe every year to evangelize in the name of Christ.

A POSTMISSIONARY ERA?

"There have been those who have considered the conversion of the Crows a dream that would never be realized." So conceded the Bureau of Catholic Indian Missions in its 1921 appraisal of missionary activity among the Crow Tribe, even while hoping against hope that from its own missionary failures would "burst forth the brilliant blooms of abundant success."

Assessing "the conversion of the Crows" has always been a contested business, beginning with an utter lack of agreement over what the term "conversion" among the Crows even implies. While attempts at gauging missionary success according to the heroic sacrifices or sterling intentions of missionaries have been resoundingly rebuffed in recent decades, appeals to baptismal records, church attendance, and other "hard evidence" are equally suspect.[38] As the following narratives make abundantly clear, measuring Christian devotion by church membership and denominational loyalty is a doomed enterprise, failing to account for the enormous range of Native intentions leading to participation in Christian activities. Such efforts make no attempt to assess Christian faith and practice among the tribe according to Crow terms. After all, the desire for educational benefits bestowed by missionaries, a felt need to follow the spiritual lead of one's elders, the pursuit of spiritual power and healing "medicine," the hope for economic blessings, and a host of other intentions have all been expressed by Christian Crows when explaining their identification with Christianity.

For these and many other reasons, the category of religious conversion, so central to the Christian missionary enterprise across denominations, continues to be a profoundly problematic concept in the context of American Indian communities. As Michelene Pesantubbee reminds us, religious conversion, when considered in tribal contexts, can only be adequately explored in relation to a complex web of related issues, including "gender, preservation, . . . revitalization, poly-religious experiences, intertribalism, and pan-Indianism."[39] The Crow Tribe is no exception. Nor can we ignore the inescapable fact of Christianity's colonial complicity that persists in marking, however faintly, every indigenous decision to identify with Jesus Christ, whatever the circumstances and motivations may be. In the words of Joel Martin, reflecting on the work of George Tinker: "Christian conversion was the interior analogue and affective accomplice of more visible forms of dominion and displacement of indigeneity, and in some ways, the more destructive form of assault against Native peoples, which continues today."[40]

It is telling that, in the majority of narratives that follow, so little attention is paid to classic Christian conversion, particularly to the familiar notion that one must become something new—something one was previously *not*—in order to be a Christian. Even among Crow Pentecostals, for whom dramatic conversion narratives (referred to as being "born-again," "saved," or "delivered") frequently play a key role in religious self-understanding, we find fundamental challenges to classic Pentecostal models of soteriology. For one thing, many Crow Pentecostals discuss their Christian conversion in experiential terms that betray deep roots in Crow religious practice—namely, visions, fasts, healings, dreams, spirit visitations, and the reception of sacred Crow-language songs. Furthermore, many Crow Pentecostal "converts" are—creatively, painstakingly—blazing new paths of integrated Crow-Christian religious practice that meaningfully wed their dual identities in new ways of synthesized religious praxis. Some of these paths have already been outlined above, and still others will become apparent in the narratives that follow. Even among devout Pentecostal lay leaders and clergy, we find some who are experimenting with meaningful participation in the sweat lodge or peyote tipi, despite maintaining a measured rhetoric of condemnation against traditional Crow ceremonies.

As highlighted in the opening paragraphs of this introduction, Christianity's influence on the Crow Tribe is ubiquitous. Yet, even in the face of all the apparent success this missionary religion has enjoyed among the tribe in the 175 years since Father De Smet's first sermon among them, one may yet agree with those who labeled "the conversion of the Crows" a "dream that would never be realized." Even while tribal members fill Pentecostal camp meetings and Catholic Corpus Christi processions, there is enormous room for debate concerning both the nature and extent of conversion among churchgoers of every Christian tradition across the reservation. As the following accounts make clear, Crow Christian identity is now set firmly on Native terms, challenging which tradition—Christianity or Crow Traditionalism—has achieved the greater conversion. Crow congregations are today so deeply informed by indigenous ritual practices and indigenous ways of conceiving the sacred that one is justified in wondering which religion is acting as missionary, and which is the missionized.

Even among Pentecostal churches where traditional missionary notions of exclusive religious belonging and radical religious conversion are still commonly found, the leadership structure is now so thoroughly indigenous and the ceremonies (fasting, sacred songs, vision seeking) are so thoroughly informed by Crow tradition that to call Crow Pentecostalism a "missionary movement" utterly fails to capture how Crows experience the tradition themselves.

In fact, beyond noting that Crow Pentecostalism is the most thoroughly Crow-led Christian movement on the reservation today (which it certainly is), one might even be tempted to argue that it has, in important ways, become even *more* indigenous than some of the so-called Indian religions. The movement's influence among Crow tribal leaders certainly adds to this argument. So, too, does the fact that one may find more white participants in the reservation's Sun Dances than one typically finds in an independent Crow Pentecostal church on any given Sunday. Perhaps more than any other Christian movement on the Crow Reservation, an indigenous-led Pentecostalism is forcing a hotly contested reappraisal of what "authentic" indigeneity looks like in relation to Christian faith and tribal identity.

Put another way, a willingness to publicly declare Jesus as Lord and abstain from most Crow religious ceremonies may no longer prevent a Crow Pentecostal from making a convincing argument that he or she is a truly traditional Crow. We might join several of the voices contained in this collection who raise, in so many words, the following question: Is a fourth-generation Crow Pentecostal living on ancestral tribal lands, speaking the Crow language, elected to office in the tribal legislature, fasting and seeking visions in the Crow Reservation hills, singing Crow-language healing songs, and faithfully attending an all-Crow religious community led by a Crow pastor somehow less authentically Crow than an outspoken Crow Traditionalist or a Crow critic of Christianity?

The following narratives present an unapologetically complicated and intimate portrait of contemporary Native Christian faith. Taken together, these stories rebuff attempts at blithe caricatures and trouble popular assumptions about Native religious identity and the persistence of Christian missions in a postcolonial era. After listening closely to the voices of those who have managed to transform Christianity, along with its messengers, as much as they themselves have been transformed by the encounter, we may soon agree that the time has come to start talking about a postmissionary era among the Apsáalooke Nation.

NOTES

1. See Frank B. Linderman, *Pretty-shield: Medicine Woman of the Crows*, 2nd ed. (Lincoln: University of Nebraska Press, 2003). For the role that the Baptist mission played in Pretty Shield's life, see the biography of her granddaughter: Alma Hogan Snell, *Grandmother's Grandchild: My Crow Indian Life*, ed. Becky Matthews (Lincoln: University of Nebraska Press, 2000), 50–54 and 76–88.

2. There is some disagreement about the timing and frequency of De Smet's visits among the tribe. Frederick E. Hoxie mentions a single visit that De Smet made to the Crows in 1842; see *Parading through History: The Making of the Crow Nation in America, 1805–1935* (Cambridge: Cambridge University Press, 1995), 198. However, the 1921 "Crow Number" of *The Indian Sentinel*, a publication of the Bureau of Catholic Indian Missions, claims that De Smet made two missionary visits to the tribe during the 1840s, one in 1840 and another in 1844. The author writes, "No doubt, it was on these two occasions that the Crows obtained their first knowledge of Christianity." See L. Taelman, S.J., "St. Xavier Mission among the Absaroke or Crow Indians," *The Indian Sentinel* 2, no. 6 (April 1921): 254, Department of Special Collections and University Archives, Raynor Memorial Libraries, Marquette University.

3. Hoxie, *Parading through History*, 198–203. For a more detailed description and analysis of St. Xavier Mission's early years (1887–1921), see Karen Watembach, "The History of the Catechesis of the Catholic Church on the Crow Reservation" (M.A. thesis, Montana State University, 1983).

4. Hoxie, *Parading through History*, 203.

5. History of St. Ann and Our Lady of Loretto Churches, courtesy Father Jim Antoine, O.F.M.Cap., interview by author, Our Lady of Loretto Church, Lodge Grass, Montana, June 13, 2012.

6. Becky Matthews, "Changing Lives: Baptist Women, Benevolence, and Community on the Crow Reservation, 1904–60," *Montana: The Magazine of Western History* (Summer 2011): 3–29.

7. Hoxie, *Parading through History,* 207–8. Hoxie notes that the earliest Protestant missionary enterprise established among the Crows was the Montana Industrial School, which was overseen by a group of New England Unitarians (204). The project lasted only nine years.

8. For an account of Goes Ahead throwing his family's medicine bundles into the Little Bighorn River near Crow Agency to declare his faith in Jesus as preached by Baptist missionaries, see Snell, *Grandmother's Grandchild,* 50–51. Snell claims that Goes Ahead thereafter served as the first Baptist deacon in the reservation's Reno District.

9. For more on the early history and steady rise of Crow Pentecostalism, see Mark Clatterbuck, "Healing Hills and Sacred Songs: Crow Pentecostalism, Anti-Traditionalism, and Native Religious Identity," *Spiritus: A Journal of Christian Spirituality* 12, no. 2 (2012): 248–77.

10. For a discussion of Pentecostalism's influence on Crow tribal politics in the late twentieth century, see Timothy P. McCleary, "An Ethnohistory of Pentecostalism among the Crow Indians of Montana," *Wicaso Sa Review* 15, no. 1 (Spring 2000): 117–35.

11. These churches are the Full Gospel Revival Tabernacle, led by Pastor Rhea Goes Ahead, Billings, Montana, and the House of Hope Mission, led by Pastor Buddy Rogers, Hardin, Montana.

12. The priority of concrete, communal well-being over attachment to abstract theological affirmations among indigenous tribes has obvious consequences in the Christian theology being done by, and for, American Indians today. One of the most serious Native Christian theological projects undertaken in recent years is the groundbreaking work of Clara Sue Kidwell, Homer Noley, and George Tinker, titled *A Native American Theology.* The authors contend that a Native theology must begin by challenging the very structure and process of Christian theology itself, including a linear notion of history and a hierarchical approach to doctrinal affirmations. As they explain in their preface: "Our intent is to challenge the traditional categories of Christian theology with a new understanding of Native views and to bring new insights to an understanding of Native theology, in its broadest sense." This new understanding, they contend, "must be built on Indian cultures, values and religious traditions, even as it responds to the devastating history of colonialism." See Kidwell, Noley, Tinker, *A Native American Theology* (Maryknoll, N.Y.: Orbis Books, 2001), ix–x, 1.

13. George E. "Tink" Tinker, *Spirit and Resistance: Political Theology and American Indian Liberation* (Minneapolis: Fortress Press, 2004), 68. While Tinker is

specifically addressing problems associated with Native religious leaders having a difficult time refusing requests from non-Natives to participate in traditional Indian ceremonies, his cautions are every bit as applicable to the enduring tendency of many Native communities to permit missionary activity in keeping with tribal habits of hospitality, often despite deep concerns about the consequences that such activity will have on the tribe.

14. For an insightful study of recent Christian responses to multireligious belonging in an increasingly pluralistic global context, see Catherine Cornille, ed., *Many Mansions? Multiple Religious Belonging and Christian Identity* (2002; reprint, Eugene, Ore.: Wipf and Stock, 2010). Unfortunately, the study gives no attention to the Native North American context.

15. Tom Yellowtail was a well-known and widely respected Sun Dance chief among the Crow Tribe, as well as a practicing Baptist for many years. On the foundational emphasis he placed on right intention, see Thomas Yellowtail and Michel Oren Fitzgerald, *Yellowtail: Crow Medicine Man and Sun Dance Chief* (Norman: University of Oklahoma Press, 1991), throughout. One long-serving Catholic priest among the Crows recently described Yellowtail to me as "the holiest man I have ever met."

16. Rodney Frey, *The World of the Crow Indians: As Driftwood Lodges* (Norman: University of Oklahoma Press, 1987), 46. For more on the organization, functions, and duties associated with the Crow clan structure, see Frey, *World of the Crow Indians*, 40–57. Frey acknowledges the important earlier work of Robert H. Lowie, *The Crow Indians* (New York: Farrar and Rinehart, 1935; repr.: Lincoln: University of Nebraska Press, 1983).

17. For one of the finest treatments of *xapáaliia* and *baaxpée* in traditional Crow culture, see Frey, *World of the Crow Indians*, 59–76 (ch. 4).

18. The classic ethnographic treatment of Crow medicine bundles is William Wildschut, *Crow Indian Medicine Bundles*, 2nd ed., *Contributions from the Museum of the American Indian Heye Foundation* 17 (New York: Museum of the American Indian, 1975).

19. The most accessible description of the Crow sweat lodge is likely the one offered by Thomas Yellowtail in his autobiography. See Yellowtail and Fitzgerald, *Yellowtail*, 106–14.

20. For detailed studies of the traditional (pre-1900) Crow Sun Dance, see Lowie, *Crow Indians*, 297–326, and Fred W. Voget, *The Shoshoni-Crow Sun Dance* (Norman: University of Oklahoma Press, 1984), 77–128.

21. For the most comprehensive study of the Shoshone-Crow Sun Dance tradition, see Voget, *Shoshoni-Crow Sun Dance*.

22. Frey, *World of the Crow Indians*, 109.

23. Yellowtail and Fitzgerald, *Yellowtail*, 165–66.

24. Timothy McCleary, conversation with author, July 11, 2015. McCleary cites evidence that, by the early 1940s, the New Way had almost completely died out among the Crows.

25. For one of the most illuminating recent analyses of Native Pentecostalism's anti-Traditionalism tendencies, see Kirk Dombrowski, *Against Culture: Development, Politics, and Religion in Indian Alaska* (Lincoln: University of Nebraska Press, 2001).

26. Andrea Smith's groundbreaking work has consistently challenged scholars and other outside observers of conservative (including Pentecostal and Charismatic) Native Christian movements to avoid caricaturing these movements as simple extensions of the hegemonic, colonialist impulses at work within the Christian tradition. See Smith, *Native Americans and the Christian Right: The Gendered Politics of Unlikely Alliances* (Durham, N.C.: Duke University Press, 2008), especially the units "Native People within the New Charismatic Movements: Performing Whiteness" and "Native People within the New Charismatic Movement: Contesting Whiteness," 81–114. Among the most recent contributions to the study of Native Pentecostalism that offer a highly nuanced analysis of the complex relationship between Native Pentecostal convictions and tribal identity, see Angela Tarango, *Choosing the Jesus Way: American Indian Pentecostals and the Fight for the Indigenous Principle* (Chapel Hill: University of North Carolina Press, 2014).

27. Mark A. Nicholas, "Conclusion: Turns and Common Grounds," in Joel W. Martin and Mark A. Nicholas, eds., *Native Americans, Christianity, and the Reshaping of the American Landscape* (Chapel Hill: University of North Carolina Press, 2010), 276.

28. Smith, *Native Americans and the Christian Right,* 81.

29. Anonymous, interview by author, Crow Reservation, Montana, July 10, 2011.

30. Kenneth Pretty On Top Sr., interview by author, Spirit of Life Lighthouse for the Nations Four Square Church, Crow Agency, Mont., June 23, 2013.

31. Angela Russell, interview by author, Custer Battlefield Trading Post Cafe, Crow Agency, Mont., June 22, 2013.

32. For the majority of Crow Pentecostals, the general prohibition against participation in non-Christian ceremonies clearly extends to the sweat lodge. The prohibition is based on a host of reasons. Even among those who may feel personally free to sweat, many still choose against the practice by citing I Corinthians 8, where Paul warns mature Christians to avoid exercising their liberty of conscience in a way that scandalizes weaker Christians: "Take heed lest by any means this liberty of yours become a stumbling block to them that are weak" (I Cor. 8:9). Others believe it is too closely tied to false religion, since it involves, as one pastor described it, "burning sage and gettin' your rattles out and feathers." Some refrain for fear of the "medicine" that may have been used in the construction of the lodge. Many cite the danger of the practice becoming "an idol." Finally, for some, the Crow practice of sweating in the nude is the biggest hurdle to overcome, referencing passages in the book of Leviticus censuring public nudity. One Crow Pentecostal pastor told me he has seen churches split over the issue of whether or not it is permissible for church members to enter the sweat lodge.

33. Jim and Faith Chosa, *Thy Kingdom Come: A First Nations Perspective on Strategic Keys for Territorial Deliverance and Transformation* (Yellowtail, Mont.: Day Chief Ministries, 2004), 137.

34. See, for example, chapter 5, "Story as Indigenous Methodology," in Margaret Kovach, *Indigenous Methodologies: Characteristics, Conversations, and Contexts* (Toronto: University of Toronto Press, 2009).

35. Nancy Tatom Ammerman, *Spiritual Stories, Spiritual Tribes: Finding Religion in Everyday Life* (Oxford: Oxford University Press, 2014), 7.

36. Marvin Dawes, interview by author, Hardin, Mont., June 11, 2012.

37. See Randolph Graczyk, *A Grammar of Crow: Studies in the Native Languages of America* (Lincoln: University of Nebraska Press, 2007).

38. Among the most incisive and scathing critiques of attempts at using "good intentions" as a criterion for measuring missionary success is George E. Tinker, *Missionary Conquest: The Gospel and Native American Cultural Genocide* (Minneapolis: Fortress Press, 1993).

39. Michelene Pesantubbee, "Foreword," in Martin and Nicholas, eds., *Native Americans,* xii–xiii.

40. Joel Martin, "Introduction," in Martin and Nicholas, eds., *Native Americans,* 2.

Part I

❀

CROW CATHOLIC VISIONS

The chapters in this part explore the religious beliefs and practices of four self-identified Crow Catholics. Each has a lifelong association with the Catholic Church, and each describes ongoing involvement in one or more of the Catholic parishes on the reservation. All speak of visions or dreams, all demonstrate a considerable degree of multireligious participation, and all declare at some point in their interviews that there are many sacred paths to follow in this life. At the same time, their narratives represent very distinct spiritual pathways, as each blends Catholicism, Crow Traditionalism, and other religious influences into richly creative patterns of religious belonging. In each case, deep communal commitments are balanced by highly individualized habits of ritual expression.

Geneva Whiteman grew up in both the Catholic Church and the Native American Church. She's also a member of the tribe's Tobacco Dance Society and speaks very positively of her encounters with Pentecostal religious practices. In addition to earning a master's degree in Catholic religious education and serving for many years as an educator at St. Charles Catholic School on the Crow Reservation, Geneva has always maintained her involvement in traditional Crow ceremonies. Larry Hogan, who's featured in chapter 2, likewise pairs a lifelong commitment to Catholicism with traditional Native ceremonies. In Larry's case, it is the Sun Dance that both satisfies his longing for Traditionalism and serves to deepen his Christian faith. The Catholicism of Bobby Lee Stops At Pretty Places blends an evangelical Christian zeal with familiar Crow practices such as hill fasting, vision seeking, smudging, and pipe ceremonies. His story also draws attention to the tribe's continuing proclivity for large-scale public demonstrations of Christian faith, as he describes his successful campaign to plant a thirty-three-foot cross behind St. Dennis Catholic Church.

In the fourth and final interview of this part, Gloria Goes Ahead Cummins gives voice to the highly influential Catholic Charismatic Renewal that dominated Crow Catholicism in the 1970s and 1980s. As her story makes clear, elements of that movement continue to inform the religious lives of many Crow parishioners to this day. While her story illustrates well the Crows' pervasive pattern of religious boundary-crossing, the backlash she encountered from Pentecostals and Catholics alike reminds us that indigenous challenges to tidy denominationalism still pose a threat to Christian institutions operating among the tribe today.

1

Frank Sinatra Sings in a Peyote Meeting

AN INTERVIEW WITH GENEVA WHITEMAN

Geneva Whiteman taught for many years at the St. Charles Catholic School in the Crow Reservation town of Pryor before her retirement. In addition to being a graduate of the University of Montana (Missoula), she also holds two master's degrees: one in special education from Eastern Montana College (now Montana State University, Billings), and one in religious education from Loyola University in Chicago. Her career in education included several positions she held at Eastern Montana College over the years, including counselor, instructor of Native American studies, and

Geneva Whiteman at St. Charles Catholic Church in Pryor, Crow Reservation, Montana. *Photo by Dave Kapferer*

coordinator of Native culture. She explains that her grandfather was given the name "White Man" after teaching himself to speak English, a highly unusual accomplishment for Crows at that time.

One of the central themes of Geneva's story is the rich cross-fertilization of diverse religious traditions that marks her own spiritual beliefs and ritual practices. In addition to her long-standing participation in the Native American Church (the Peyote Way) and her adoption into the Tobacco Dance Society, she is also a lifelong Catholic with a strong devotion to Mary. Additionally, she studied for a short time in a predominantly Mormon school in Wyoming and has also experienced "speaking in tongues" when prayed over by a Pentecostal friend.

Beyond highlighting the legacy of competing Christian missionary efforts among the Crow Tribe, Geneva's story also sheds light on the delicate balancing act performed by missionaries who have long felt the strain of denominational expectations that are sorely out of step with realities on the ground among Native Christian communities. Her fond recollections of the mid-twentieth century Jesuit priest who "looked the other way" when it came to peyote meetings in Pryor District, and how his tolerance brought her own father back into the Catholic Church, reminds us that the appearance of a name on a baptismal record or list of converts among a tribe does not necessarily mean that traditional ceremonies, even those publicly condemned by the church's hierarchy, were abandoned by those church members.

Geneva concludes her narrative by describing a recent dream in which the Catholic crooner Frank Sinatra is singing sacred songs in the Crow language inside a peyote tipi. In Crow tradition, the reception of a sacred song through a dream or vision is a powerful spiritual gift. The earnestness with which she expresses her hope to receive the dream again in order to remember the song's words is humorously juxtaposed with the incongruity of Sinatra serving as carrier of the Crow language spirit song. It's a lighthearted story that captures the rich blend of indigenous and Euro-American traditions that inform Geneva's religious experience—not only in her waking hours, but even while she sleeps. Indeed, the pervasive good humor with which she recounts the contradictions attending her own brilliantly varied religious identity is no mere window dressing in this story. To the contrary, humor functions as a constitutive part of this and so many other narratives of contemporary Crow religious life.

The following interview with Geneva took place at St. Charles Catholic School in Pryor, where Geneva is both an alumna and former teacher. She continues to be an active member of St. Charles Catholic Church.

❁

GENEVA'S EARLY EDUCATION

My name is Geneva Whiteman. My Crow Indian name is *Aannée Baax-páa*. I have lived here in Pryor practically all my life. I am a graduate of St. Charles Catholic Mission School, where we are today.

My parents were both Catholic, and on my father's side my grandmother was half Irish. Her father was from Vermont. They were all Catholics. All I knew was Catholicism. When I graduated from the eighth grade here at St. Charles, my father had friends in Cowley, Wyoming, and they offered to take me in because we didn't have a high school here in Pryor, and we didn't yet have a bus taking high school students to other area schools. Most of the graduates back then went to Indian schools. I went to Cowley, Wyoming, which was strictly Mormon territory. They were all out to convert me and it about gave me a nervous breakdown. So I ran away! Got on the bus and went to Billings. My aunt was a waitress at one of the restaurants, so I went there and she found a ride for me to come home. I told my parents what I was going through. My father didn't understand. All he wanted was for me to get a good education and he wanted to take me back [to Cowley], but my mother cried with me so I didn't have to go back. They arranged to have different families take turns taking us to Edgar public school, just off the reservation, so we could go to high school. We eventually moved into an apartment there and my aunt sent us to school, and then we finally got a bus the following year.

PEYOTE, TOBACCO DANCE SOCIETY, AND GLOSSOLALIA

My father was a believer of the Native American Church (the Peyote Way). When I was about two years old, I nearly died from food poisoning. I ate some old corn. At that time no one had refrigeration, and I guess I reached up to the table and got some corn and ate it and it nearly killed me. There's an old Crow tradition that when you think a baby is going to die, you throw the baby away and whoever comes and picks up the baby then has the say-so over the child.[1] The only one at our house back then was my father's uncle, my great uncle. He picked me up and he gave me my English name, Geneva. He was a blind man and he had gone to school in Great Falls [Montana], a school for the deaf and blind. He had heard of Geneva, Switzerland, and was told that it was the most beautiful city in the world. So he named me after the city. And then he also gave me my Indian name. *Aannée* is "a path" and then *Baaxpáa* is "holy." Sacred Path is my Indian name. And he had the say-so of my big decisions in life. When I wanted to do something like getting adopted in the Tobacco Dance Society and all that, my father referred me back to this uncle who decided if I should do it or not. There was a man, who was also blind, from Lodge Grass who wanted to adopt me in the Tobacco Dance Society. But my uncle said, "No." And my father said, "Well, what shall I tell him is your reason for refusing to have him adopt her?" He said, "I want her to have a mother." So this man's sister and husband then adopted me in the Society.

Entering the Society was a formal adoption ceremony with the Crows back then. And it also involves a lot of prayer. Even today, in the adoption ceremonies, they pitch up two tipis and they dance, sing some songs inside the tipi, and then they come out, like in a procession, and they sing several songs as they continue to the second tipi. The person that's being adopted— like the last one I went to, my son was being adopted—they had him ride on horseback. Whatever was on the horse—and the horse, too—was given to him. Besides, he was completely outfitted in buckskin. He was adopted by the Big Days. His daughter was just little at that time, about four years old or so. The first form of worship for the Crows was the tobacco, praying with tobacco. And then at one time I think the whole reservation was Catholic. And then the Baptists came in, and later the other religions.

Back when I was in high school, I didn't think I was going to live. I have a medical condition that gave me a lot of kidney infections. So my aunt, Ruby Goes Ahead, invited me and prayed for me and I was blessed with the Holy Spirit and started speaking in tongues. My father was really afraid I was going to roam away from the Catholic Church! But I found, like with the Native American Church, that I am able to combine all the beliefs. At one time the Catholic Church was against the Native American Church. They actually, according to my parents, were ready to oust people who had gone into peyote meetings as outcasts of the church. But then we got Father Brown. He was a Jesuit priest educated from back East. I think he was an orphan and was adopted and then became a Jesuit priest. When we had him here, he just looked the other way, you know, and I thought that was good. Because a lot of people came back to church, including my father. He died an untimely death of a heart attack when he was only forty-eight years old. At that time he was making it to daily Mass because Father Brown was here, and I was thankful for that.

Nowadays, I only go to peyote meetings that I put on, or if it's a close family member. Later this month my son is having a meeting for his daughter who graduated out of high school in Hardin.[2] It's going to be here in Pryor. I'm kind of thinking of going. I have a bad back and it's really hard for me to sit on the ground all night for the meeting, but I'm praying about it, whether I'll go or not. It would be nice. It's a good experience. My father used to say that the springtime is the best time to go into a peyote meeting because you come out and the grass is green and the birds are singing. There's new life, you know. It is a good time.

Visions of Mary and Dreams of Sinatra

I would say those who believe you need to choose between Christianity and Indian religion are narrow-minded. Usually it's a result of, well, tunnel vision. Their perspectives are limited to the reservation. They haven't been out and about to see that you can find life more fulfilling by combining the religions and spiritual beliefs. Personally, I just combine everything. I believe in saying my Hail Marys, the Lord's Prayer, the Glory Be, and the rosary. I am very close to Saint Mary. I had a religious experience when I was going through surgery. I was at St. Vincent's Hospital in Billings. It affected my kidneys and I was in the hospital for twenty-nine days. My children thought that I was going to die. They were little then, and it was really hard on them and hard on me.

Early one morning, I walked down the hall of the hospital and I got to the end, and I looked outside and here I saw a statue of Saint Mary. So I stood there and, you know, they say the most sacred time of the day is when the sun is rising. So it was that time, and I was looking down. And I saw the statue of Saint Mary. So I prayed for healing and I stood there for quite a while and then I returned to my room. The wind was blowing outside and a lot of papers and trash were blowing around the statue, so I promised I would go down and pick the trash up after I got out. When I finally got out, I was working at Eastern Montana College then. I was a counselor in Student Special Services, then eventually I became Native American studies instructor, and then I became a coordinator of Indian culture. When I returned, when I finally got well and I went to pick up the trash, there was no statue. I went back in to the hospital and I asked the Sisters what happened to the statue. And they said there was never a statue. So I think that Mary appeared to me.

Another time, when I was going through my divorce, it was a very painful experience and I went into the sweat bath with my sister. It was down by the creek, by their trailer. We were watching there as the lodge was being prepared, and we were thinking of reconciling so my husband was there as they were taking rocks into the sweat. My sister and I were standing there watching. And right over the fire, in the smoke, I saw Saint Mary—Our Lady of Guadalupe. She was small, just like a statue. I can't remember if I knelt down right away, but I started praying. And my sister was just standing there, and I said, "Do you see her?" And she said, "Who?" She didn't see anything. But I did. That, I think, was given to me because after that, life was very, very difficult because I did go through with the divorce. I needed that experience.

Because of those experiences and the pain that was in my life, I prayed for God to use me in whatever way so that I could give back and help people. I thought I left teaching for good, but eventually I returned and taught here at St. Charles Catholic School and I think I was able to reach a lot of students. I am just thankful. I feel that we, as a people, are blessed in having Father Randolph here at St. Charles Church. While attending Loyola University in Chicago, I went in the summers because I worked during the school year teaching. I went for nine weeks every summer to Loyola, the Lake Shore campus. I still have dreams about it. I really loved that place. Especially going to the lakeshore and watching the sun come up and praying. In fact, I just named my cousin's wife. I was asked to give her an Indian name, and I gave her the name that means "One Who Prays by the Lakeside."

And I'm praying now. I've been asked to name my niece's little boy. They say that if you are really fortunate, you will hear the name in a dream and that often happens. So, I love Frank Sinatra songs and I've been reading a book about his life. Last week I had a dream of him and he was in a peyote meeting and he was singing! In the dream I was so astonished that he was able to sing Indian that I didn't pay attention to the song he was singing. I wish I had. Because the song is given to the person if you hear it in a dream. I'm praying it'll come to me again.

NOTES

1. As explained by Timothy McCleary, chair of the general studies department at Little Big Horn College, Crow Agency, the Crow custom of "throwing away" a very sick child is linked to Crow beliefs about the soul. According to Crow tradition, a soul (*iilaxe* in Crow, more like "willpower" than the classic Christian notion of soul) is capricious, and when a child is born, it is not fully attached to the physical body. The ritual of naming the child is thought to attach the soul to the body. When a child is sickly, it is believed that the soul does not like its name, and so the name is changed. If the child continues to be ill, it is believed that the soul may not like the family it was born into. At that point, the child is "thrown away" to another family. The child is literally left outside of her home, and the new parents come and pick her up. She can have nothing from her former life—no clothes, toys, etc. If the new parents decide to do so, they may keep the child permanently. Sometimes, when a child has fully recovered, she will be returned to her original family, while still maintaining close ties to her second parents. Strict Nativists will generally not return the child under any circumstances. McCleary, personal correspondence with author, July 4, 2014.
2. It is common for Crow families in the Native American Church to hold a peyote meeting to honor and pray for a child or grandchild following graduation from high school. Chief Plenty Coups was a strong proponent of education for the tribe in the early twentieth century, and many Crows seek to maintain that tradition today.

2

Sun Dance Spirits and Visions in the Monstrance

AN INTERVIEW WITH LARRY HOGAN

Larry Hogan was raised in a family that emphasized commitment to the Catholic faith; he was taught by his father that there is "nothing else!" Not until he was a young adult did he begin seeking a stronger tie to traditional Crow religion. He says he was particularly drawn to the rigors of Crow hill fasting, as well as to the physical, mental, and spiritual exertions involved in the Sun Dance. Compelled by a desire to imitate the sufferings of Jesus in his own ritual practices, Larry undertook a series of austere four-day fasts, intermittently spanning several years, up in the Crow Reservation mountains. In his fifth year of seeking a vision, he was finally rewarded by an encounter with a powerful Sun Dance spirit man during a solitary fast up in the reservation's Big Horn Mountains. Since receiving the vision more

Larry Hogan explaining the directional orientation of the Sun Dance lodge near Fort Smith, Crow Reservation. *Photo by Dave Kapferer*

than ten years ago, Larry has sponsored a Sun Dance in the Shoshone-Crow tradition every fourth year.

In the narrative that follows, Larry describes the vision he received as well as various elements of the Sun Dance that have become an integral part of his own religious identity and practice. Along the way, Larry offers many personal reflections on his dual religious identity, both as a devout Catholic and a dedicated Sun Dancer. He explains how his beliefs about the Sun Dance differ from those of non-Christian participants in the ceremony, and how his Catholic faith is strengthened through this grueling four-day fast under the summer's hottest sun.

His testimony is particularly poignant for the ways that traditional Crow religious practices (vision questing, fasting in the hills, Sun Dancing) so thoroughly permeate the religious life of a self-described Catholic, even as his Catholic devotion shapes his experiences in the Sun Dance lodge. This dialectic of integrated, polyreligious identity is highlighted, for example, when he describes the life-changing visions he received while combining a Crow-style fast with eucharistic adoration in the chapel of a Catholic mission. At another point, he notes his growing conviction that the Catholic Church is the only true path to salvation "because we're the only ones that have the body of Jesus Christ." At the same time, he believes that it is through the center pole of the Sun Dance lodge that God is drawing the Crow people "to the Catholic way."

The degree to which Catholic and Sun Dance traditions inform one another for Larry is further illustrated by his story of how the spirits in his Sun Dance vision instructed him to seek spiritual advice from one of the reservation's Catholic priests. The following interview took place on Larry's Sun Dance grounds near Fort Smith on the Crow Reservation.

❁

JESUS INSPIRES LARRY'S SUN DANCE FASTS

The reason I got interested in fasting out in the hills, in the mountains, is that you read so much about Jesus going through penance, and I wanted to do that—to fast, make my body hurt. That's why I still do it. I think of the scourging at the pillar, his way to Calvary, all that torture. And so I wanted to sacrifice all this worldly stuff. When I go out there and fast in the hills, there in the mountains, that's tougher than going to a Sun Dance because you're doing it by yourself. Again, the reason I fast is because the Bible says to imitate Jesus Christ, and for me that's one of the best ways to imitate Jesus Christ—it's to try to imitate his suffering. When you're out there fasting, you're by yourself. It's just you and God. If your faith is powerful, or you feel you've got faith, that's what's going to carry you through your solitary fast out in the hills. Some guys even do it at home—fast at home, or in the mountains. It gets pretty tough out there.

A Sun Dance Spirit Man Comes to Larry

My brother goes to a certain spot up there in the Big Horn Mountains, so I went over there toward where he fasts. That's where that effigy came to me in a vision about ten years ago. Before that, I'd been fasting and praying that that effigy would come, a Sun Dance doll, so I could have a Sun Dance doll. Here that spirit came to me and said I could use him for a Sun Dance doll.

That Sun Dance doll has a spirit helper, and that helper told me that there's some real Sun Dance dolls, and there are some that people haven't earned. You have to earn them. Or, like a lot of times, these Crows will pass it on to another, usually the oldest boy, or it'd be like the grandfather giving a Sun Dance bundle to the oldest son. But you really want to go up there and fast and get it yourself. It took me a while to receive it. Five years since I first started asking.

When you fast, a spirit might come to you, and whatever vision you have of that doll is what you make in an effigy. Mine—people are afraid of mine because when that spirit stood there in front of me, he must have been seven or eight feet tall. And his body was close to four feet wide. And his hands were huge, 'cause he grabbed me on the arms and his palms went from the tips of my fingers all the way to my shoulders. And he said, "My hands, that's where I let my power come out—from my hands. That's why they're so big."

He looked liked a kachina doll. He had a small head and he had a black canvas hood over it and little slits like a kachina doll does.[1] He had little slits for his eyes and a little slit for his mouth. And he had one of those dresses on. It was a long-sleeve pullover made of canvas material. His leggings and his moccasins were canvas, too. But that black covering he has over his head—Crows are afraid of it because they were told that when you make a Sun Dance doll, don't use black. 'Cause it's kinda like a bad omen to the Crows. Me, I can't help it. That Sun Dance doll came, and he had a black canvas hood over him.

I showed the pictures that I made of that doll in my vision to a longtime, respected Sun Dance chief here and he said, "I'll make that effigy for you." You put that doll on the tree during the Sun Dance. That effigy has a spirit that we believe goes out and talks to the sun, talks to everything, lets them know that there's a Sun Dance going on, that the Crows are having a Sun Dance, and invites all of them: the earth, the trees, the air, the clouds, the sky—invites all, everything you see, from Mother Nature.

Anyway, that Sun Dance man that came to me in the vision, he said, "Go ahead and use me. I know you've been asking about me." I said, "I don't even know you!" He said, "That don't matter. On this side we already know everything, and you were praying and asking for me. I'm the one. Go ahead and use me."

A Dream, A Fast, and Another Spirit Encounter

No one ever told me about what comes with a Sun Dance effigy. We came off the mountain after that fast, and I told my brother what happened to me. But something told me I wasn't done with my fast, so I came back and took a sweat bath and prayed about it. I don't know—it was just too much. That Sun Dance spirit man, he came to me in a dream and said, "You have to go up there again, and they're going to tell you something." So I took that sweat and rested that day, and the next evening I went and made a fasting bed up on our dad's rimrocks there between Lodge Grass and Crow Agency. And I fasted.

That night, this old man came from the East. He was close to seven feet tall, except he had long silver hair down to the middle of his ribs, and he was light-skinned, and blue-eyed, and kinda narrow built. He wasn't a bulky man. He came and he sat down and said, "You've been fasting all this time asking for that Sun Dance man to come to you. Well, we finally let him go to you. You can use it, but I want you to know that that Sun Dance doll is real medicine."

I said, "You look like a white man!" He said, "That don't matter. On this side, that don't matter. I just made myself look like this when I talk to you."

He said, "I could make myself look like you if I wanted to. On this side, you can do anything. This is the spirit world. But I have to tell you, that effigy we sent you—I'm the one that talks for him. I'm the one that watches over him. And I'll watch over you, as long as you listen to me. There are some things that come with this Sun Dance man we sent you. There's some rules that you gotta go by. As we go along, I'll tell you. I'll tell you what you can do and what you can't do. And if anybody does something wrong to that effigy, or mistreats that effigy, that's when I come after them. And when I come after somebody, I take 'em back with me."

I looked at him and I said, "Geez, I don't want that!" He said, "You can't say that, because we already gave him to you and you've got to accept whatever comes with him. I come with him. I'm the one who takes care of him, talks to him, talks for him. You have to know that if he's mistreated, if they're not being good to him, I'll come after whoever's doing that. You people that ask for these effigies, you don't know about that. But you have to know that. Now you know."

I went and told one of the Sun Dance chiefs here on the Crow Reservation—he's been a Sun Dance chief nearly his whole life—and he asked me, "Did that doll, that effigy, tell you that you could use him? That's what you need to hear. That's what you have to experience. You better make sure." He said, "I've met a few guys that their Sun Dance doll wasn't real. They just made it up." Then he told me that when you put that doll out on that center tree, there are some other people out there who have medicine and they'll find out with their medicine if that doll is real or not. If it's not real, some of them will put bad medicine in there and use it for themselves. In other words, they'll send a bad spirit into that doll. And that medicine will hurt the owner because he shouldn't have done that in the first place because he doesn't have medicine. He said that's what's dangerous about that medicine. There are people out there who know how to go about finding out if there's medicine in there. And if not, like that doll, they'll send that bad medicine in there and they'll use that doll to do their dirty stuff, their dirty work, and it'll hurt that person who says he owns that doll.

I just fall back on what Father Charles [of St. Dennis Catholic Church] told me about my vision. He said that if it's of God, then it'll stay with you and help you in this life. And if it's not, ask God to take it away and then he will. 'Cause every time I pray about the Sun Dance doll coming to me, I'd say, "If it's your will God, then your will be done. If it's not, then just forget about it." That was gonna be my last year praying and asking for a Sun Dance doll while I fast. 'Cause I figured, geez, about five years now and, well, this'll be the last pass I'm going to ask for it. Maybe it's not meant to be. If it's his will, it's his will. If not, then let it go. That was one of the most terrifying fasts I ever had when that guy showed up. I almost took off! I was sitting there and he said, "You've been praying about me and I came." And I looked at him and I said, "Are you a Sun Dance doll?" He said, "I'm a Sun Dance man. And I'm gonna show you some of my power." And that's when he grabbed me on the arms and lifted me up and—holy mackerel!

LARRY'S DESCRIPTION OF THE SHOSHONE-CROW SUN DANCE

When Crows put up a Sun Dance lodge, we put it up the same day we go in. The buffalo head goes right here on the center tree facing the Sun Dance chief. They call this the Chief Pole—this rafter running from the center pole to the western post of the lodge. They all have to have it. The Chief Pole always has a fork on it. That fork, it's a reflection of the Sun Dance chief—good and bad. Most of the times it's a reflection of ourselves. We're good and bad. I mean, it's just human nature. You're good and you're bad, even though you try to find a way of always being good. That's this tree.

This Sun Dance we do here in this lodge is actually the Shoshone way, brought to the Crows in the 1940s. Before that, the Crows' old Sun Dance was a dance of death and revenge.[2] They say, even today, if someone had that ritual—the old Crow Sun Dance—even if they were just imitating it, someone in their family would die because it's the dance of death and revenge. That's what the old Crow Sun Dance was all about: revenge. Go out there and kill that enemy that killed their father, or son, or daughter, or attacked the tribe and killed a bunch of Crows. It's all about death. But we can't have that. That won't get you anywhere!

Nowadays, the Crows and Shoshones put up their Sun Dance lodge and then go in the same day. The Crows and Shoshones go in when a star comes up in the east there. I don't know if you ever noticed it, but there's a first star that comes out in the evening, the Evening Star some call it, comes up right over there in the east.

On a four-day Sun Dance, you have two Medicine Days that are between the first and last days. It's tough. Lots of people come in who want to be prayed for during those days, and, boy, that sucks your energy. Friday and Saturday are called the Medicine Days on a four-day Sun Dance. It's just Saturday on a three-dayer. On those Medicine Days in the morning, between seven and nine o'clock, they put up what they call "gates"—a stall for each dancer. They say that the trees used to make these gates protect the dancer from the spirit of that buffalo that comes in here. Protects them from the spirit of the buffalo and other spirits that come in here that want to do battle with the dancers. That's why the dancers paint themselves during the Sun Dance, too. The paint protects them. I don't know if you ever seen it, but some dancers literally fly through the air.[3]

That happened to a couple guys my brother used to dance with. They went flying through the air. Afterwards, they said, "What happened?" And my brother told them, "We were all dancing, and you guys flew through the air!" They said, "That buffalo hit us!" After it hit them, they were out—they were out for the rest of the Sun Dance. That happened there at Gas Cap Hill, right there at Crow Agency. And then another time down there in Cedar City, Nevada. You just tell them, "Don't be afraid—that's part of the Crow-Shoshone Sun Dance." Their prayers are answered, I guess, when that happens.

"DOCTORING," PRAYER, AND EUCHARISTIC ADORATION

During the ceremony, the Sun Dance chief will ask a dancer, "Where are you hurting?" They'll fan off that spot, and work on that spot, and then a lot of them you'll see shaking the feather fan toward the eastern opening of the lodge, letting that sickness, bad medicine, spirit, or whatever it is go present itself to God. And he'll do with it whatever he wants to. The Sun Dance chief Tom Yellowtail said, "Once this center tree is put in the ground, God's power is there." And the prayers of the people are just added to it. Especially when dancers come up and they touch the pole, it's just adding to the power that's already in there. Yellowtail and John Trehero said that once that pole's in the ground, all Sun Dances are like the center of the universe.

There's still some of those traditional guys around who pray to the sun when they Sun Dance. Some of them will go over there and say, "We pray to that Old Man," and they'll point at the sun. But I just try to keep the peace, you know. Otherwise you get into a big old argument that'll amount to nothing. But they're praying to that sun. They say the sun gives us life. If the sun wasn't there, there'd be no life, no trees, no nothin' here on Earth. It would be like the moon. And that's what they say about the Old Man Sun. Or some of them, like the Sioux, they call him Grandfather. And the moon they call Grandmother. The Old Man, he's the one they pray to. He sends that energy in there, if that's your philosophy.

But me—I take it just like Tom Yellowtail and John Trehero said. God made that power that runs through the earth and goes out to the whole universe. Right there and up through a tree, that center pole, and around the earth, and into the heavens. Not heaven itself—but the sky, the stars, the moon, the sun. In Crow, I call him *Akbaatatdía*, the One Above Who Makes Everything.

Our dad brought us up strictly Catholic, and that's what he just drilled in our heads. "Nothing else!" he said. Which is true, I guess. Because we're the only ones that have the body of Jesus Christ. I thought all the other churches had him, too. But there's no body of Christ there, and I really missed that 'cause, man, our dad really drilled it into our heads that you gotta have that—or you're gonna go to hell! And I'm starting to believe that.

I did a fast in the Catholic church there at Crow Agency, a forty-hour fast where you start on Friday and end with Mass on Sunday. That's where my most powerful fasts were. Father Charles would say, "Go ahead. You can take that monstrance out with the luna, and put it in there with that host. And you can do benediction," he said. "I'm a priest and I'll give you that. Go ahead." And there's a lot of things I've seen in that host. I've seen Jesus. I've seen angels. I've seen demons. I've seen everything in that host.

One woman, she asked me, "Did you see anything?" I said, "Do you really want to know?" She said, "Yeah." I said, "I've seen from demons to angels in that host." And she said, "Oh, God!" She never asked me after that. But it's—I don't know. After seeing all of that—I mean, I've seen Jesus Christ walking, when I was looking at that host in the monstrance. I've seen him walking, turning. I've never seen that anywhere else. Boggles my mind when I talk about it sometimes.

Father Randolph [of St. Charles Mission in Pryor] was in my Sun Dance dreams. Those spirits, they told me to go to him. They said, "That man right there is a good man. Go to him. He'll help you." I said, "That's Father Randolph!" I told him about it, and he said, "Yeah, come over. Come over, and we'll talk." So I went over there a couple times and fasted—did that forty-hour adoration. And that's when I talked to him, and a few other times. I was surprised when those spirits all told me, "Go to that man. He's a good man. He'll help you." I was like, "Holy mackerel! The spirits know him." That guy, he's pretty good.

In the Sun Dance, I feel like that Christian spirit is going out there and drawing the people. Not to the Sun Dance itself, but God—sending his power through that tree—is drawing those people to the Catholic way. Ever since I seen all that stuff happening in that Eucharist, in that host, it gives me goose bumps sometimes to talk about what I've seen in that host. That was the most powerful fast I ever had. God is the one that's sending that power through that tree. It's not that Old Man Sun or Grandfather. If it wasn't for God, there wouldn't be no Old Man or Grandfather. There wouldn't be nothing. He's the only one that can create something from the uncreated. He's the only one. Not even the devil can do that. The devil's powerful here on earth, can show you visions and show you your dead relatives. But only God is the Creator.

NOTES

1. Kachinas (or *Katsinim*) are spirit beings central to the spiritual lifeways of many Puebloan people, including the Hopis. Kachina dolls are small, carved, sacred effigies of these spirit beings. While some modern kachina artists have begun depicting more realistic features on these effigies, traditional kachinas have highly stylized features, where eyes, mouths, and other features are often represented by single bold lines, like those described here by Larry.
2. The old-time, traditional Crow Sun Dance, which Larry references here, is believed to have last taken place around 1875. As Larry says, the central purpose of the ceremony was to secure revenge against an enemy for the death of a family member. For more on the prereservation era Crow Sun Dance, see chapter 3, "The Traditional Crow Sun Dance," in Voget, *Shoshoni-Crow Sun Dance,* 77–128.
3. For a description of dancers being "hit" and "knocked down" by buffalo visions during Shoshone and Ute Sun Dances, see Joseph G. Jorgensen, *The Sun Dance Religion: Power for the Powerless* (Chicago: University of Chicago Press, 1972), 212–16.

3

Raising the Cross over Crow Agency

AN INTERVIEW WITH
BOBBY LEE STOPS AT PRETTY PLACES

On a prominent hill behind St. Dennis Catholic Church, a thirty-three-foot wooden cross dominates the skyline of Crow Agency. The enormous fir-tree structure is easily visible from Interstate 90 and is illuminated by spotlights each night, making it one of the most recognizable symbols on the reservation. Erected in 2007, the impressive structure owes its existence to Bobby Stops, a devoted member of St. Dennis Catholic Church. Bobby recalls having a vision of a cross as a child and regards the construction of this monument over Crow Agency as the fulfillment of that vision. Bobby explains his hope for everyone who sees the cross in one simple phrase: "I want them to recognize Jesus Christ."

It took Bobby five years to gather the necessary support and resources for the project, including a land grant from the tribe. Financial assistance was provided by West Hills Presbyterian Church in Omaha, Nebraska. That same

Bobby Lee Stops At Pretty Places in the sanctuary of St. Dennis Catholic Church, Crow Agency. *Photo by Dave Kapferer*

church also sent a team of volunteers to help erect the monument. The completed project was dedicated during an outdoor Mass presided over by Father Charles Robinson of St. Dennis Catholic Church. The late Carl Venne, who was tribal chairman at the time, was among those who attended the dedication service. The *Billings Gazette* ran a front-page story covering the event.[1]

While the size and impact of this project made it somewhat unique, the appearance of highly public, tribally supported monuments to Christian faith has become a familiar pattern on the Crow Reservation. More recently, the Crow Tribe funded construction of a billboard along Interstate 90 declaring, "Jesus Christ Is Lord on the Crow Nation." The illuminated sign, located less than a mile from Bobby's iconic cross, is the product of a 2013 tribal resolution "to honor God for his great blessings upon the Crow Tribe and to proclaim Jesus Christ as Lord of the Crow Indian Reservation."[2] Senator Conrad J. Stewart, who sponsored that bill, is among the voices included in this volume.

Bobby is a lay affiliate of the Order of Saint Francis and a deeply committed Catholic parishioner. However, as his narrative repeatedly demonstrates, he is emphatically nonsectarian in his approach to religious belief and spiritual practice. As he says below, "I'm a Catholic, and I also believe in Crow tradition. Because in every religion, we all have a way to get to heaven and meet the Creator." Woven into his own story are strands of Catholicism, Crow Traditionalism, mainline Protestantism, and Pentecostalism. Significantly, while self-identifying as a Traditional Crow Catholic, Bobby is married to the daughter of Harold Carpenter. As the most influential preacher in Crow Pentecostal history, Carpenter's fiery condemnation of Traditionalism continues to exert a powerful influence on the reservation today.

St. Dennis Parish itself offers a striking example of the rich confluence of traditions commonly found among the Crow Tribe. In addition to the congregation's long-standing partnership with West Hills Presbyterian Church, their services regularly include traditional Crow rituals such as cedar smudging—where cedar is burned in a small tray as people use their hands to draw the smoke over their bodies for a cleansing or a blessing—and, occasionally, pipe ceremonies. Bobby's description of the Sunday Mass when his mother received special prayer also highlights the impact that the Catholic Charismatic Renewal continues to have on the congregation, marked by anointing with oil, laying on of hands, and healing prayer. The

Catholic Charismatic Renewal among the Crows is explored more fully in the narrative shared by Gloria Goes Ahead Cummins in chapter 4.

Like so many other personal stories contained in this collection, Bobby's story of religious practice is punctuated by visions he has received at various stages in his life, visions that have guided his decisions and sustained his religious faith. The first half of this interview took place on the hilltop where the cross now stands at Crow Agency; the second half was conducted inside the sanctuary of St. Dennis Catholic Church, where Bobby describes several visions he has experienced in that space during eucharistic adoration.

❀

PLANTING THE CROSS AT CROW

My name's Robert Stops. I'm a member of the Crow Tribe, and I'd like to tell you a little bit of history on the cross that stands over Crow Agency here on the Crow Indian Reservation. I'd like to tell you how it came about through a vision that I had as a young child when I saw this cross come up and I drew a picture of it. When I got older, in reality, it happened.

I had several sponsorships for the project, including the good people from Omaha, Nebraska, that come to our church. They're Presbyterians. Several members of their congregation helped out a lot. I'm really thankful for that. And the Crow Tribe helped a lot. This is Crow land that I put the cross on, which I got permission to use.

Also, I'd like to tell you a little bit about *where* I put the cross. So it was a Saturday night. Father Charlie Robinson was in the church here at St. Dennis, and I went to confession to cleanse myself so I'd be prepared. Then I came up here on the hill and spent the night. The cross wasn't even up yet. I took my Bible, blanket, and chair—sat up all night, prayed, read the Bible. And as I was reading the Bible, I felt something move on this side here to my right, and a person approached.

It wasn't a scary feeling. It was a good feeling. As I looked at it, an orange light came out from the face, right into the ground. And it lit up the whole top of this hill. When it did that, I knew that was the place where I was supposed to put that cross in. Then he dissolved away. And as he dissolved away, I looked up into the sky and the stars parted. It was the most exciting thing. I spent the rest of the night right here on this hilltop, and I marked that spot where I was going to put the cross. When the sun came up, that's when I came down the hill and told Father Charlie, "I found the place where to put the cross. Someone came to me and showed me."

That was early Sunday morning. On Monday and Tuesday, we came up here and dug the hole. When I tried to dig the hole in a different place—a place where I wanted to put it instead of where that orange light went in—the ground kept caving in. My good friend Gene had a little loader we were using to dig the hole, so I finally said, "Let's put it here. It's supposed to be here anyway." And when we did that, it went right down. We dug down five feet, got it level, and then the metal sleeve came. After the metal sleeve came, the concrete came next. And after the concrete, the cross came. All in one week. That Friday is when we dedicated the cross. Father Charlie and about fifty people came up here and we had services that dedicated the cross. The tribal chairman came, too, and different people from the community. It was really exciting.

When the cross went up, semitrucks along Interstate 90 were pulling over, and people were coming out of their offices down from the hill and clapping. It was the most exciting thing you could see when that cross went up. It was really a good thing.

The Community's Response to the Cross

This cross was meant to be here for a reason: so people will recognize Jesus Christ, whether they're traveling through, or if they live here. I think it is very important that Jesus came and died for us, for our sins. This cross is thirty-three-foot high. That's how many years Christ was on this earth. Putting up this cross meant a lot to me. I see it every day. It even lights up at night. People say they drive by, they see the cross, and they just think it's the neatest thing that's ever happened at Crow Agency. It's truly a good thing.

Before all this happened, a few of us were talking one day after Mass about putting the cross up here on this hill. They said, "Where are you going to get the money for this? It takes a lot of money to put up a cross like that." But someone said, "Well, we have these icons here in the church, and it was a miracle that we got 'em. It can be the same way with the cross. If it's meant to happen, if it's truly meant to happen, it will go up." And it did. Everything fell into place. It was a pretty neat thing. It was in July of 2007 when we put this cross up. It took five years to put it up, but it all fell into place.

People in the community all like it, too. People that pass through here that live in Hardin just north of here, they say, "Oh, I've seen the cross lit up at night. It was really neat!" They all say, "I'm glad you put that up." It really is a good thing for the community.

When we came up here to dedicate the cross, the *Billings Gazette* even came, and the story made it on the front page of the paper. Man, I'll tell you what, you see this cross up here, you see it from the highway—even my kids, when they were going to school, the kids were saying, "Hey, that cross at Crow really looks neat!" Even the young kids notice the cross. That's what I want them to do. I want them to recognize Jesus Christ.

This is Crow tribal land, and they allowed me to put the cross on it. The chairman at the time was Carl Venne. He's also the one who sponsored the electricity to come up here, from that pole down there to this meter, so the lights stay lit all night long. When we first got the cross up, me, my dad, and my brothers used to come up here and turn the lights off and on by ourselves every night because we didn't have the sensor. Then we got a sensor put on, so now it shuts off and on by itself. It lights up on both sides. That way, the people that live here behind us can see it, the people that live down in the valley can see it, and also the people coming along the highway. They can see it from all angles.

Bobby's Altar Visions and "Conversion"

It was a little over ten years ago, probably a little longer, that my conversion started. I came into church to pray with some people. We had the monstrance up here on the altar, and we were prayin' and sayin' the rosary when they started seeing things. They were always seeing things in the monstrance. But I never saw it. I never saw things in there. They'd all say, "C'mon, you can see it. It's there, look!" But I couldn't see nothing. Then all of a sudden, I saw something. My faith started growin' through somebody else's faith, and then that's how it all got started. My conversion was when I started seein' things. It helped my faith grow.

I saw Jesus as a man and as a baby. I saw it in the monstrance, right in the host. And it kept changing back and forth—man, baby, man, baby—goin' faster and faster, and then it got to be a blur. But it was lettin' me know I had to grow in faith. From that point on, everything started changing. I started seein' many things in the monstrance. I saw the Last Supper. I saw John the Baptist, the wild man, with his hair all messed up and crazy-lookin'. Then I saw Saint Francis of Assisi. And the reason why I say it was Saint Francis is 'cause a dog was sittin' right next to him. And I saw the Holy Family—Jesus sittin' on Mary's lap and Saint Joseph right next to him. Now all these things that I was seein' was helpin' my faith grow. And I saw it in shades of brown, kinda rust color. And I saw many things in there. I saw infant Jesus laid in a blanket. It was quite a sight, the corner of the blankets folded and stuff like that.

This went on for like a year, or a year and a half. I'd come in here to the sanctuary to pray every night. Sometimes I'd spend the night in church and pray all night, just by myself. One-on-one with Jesus is real good. We got a relationship. We talk. When he talks to you, it's not like words that come out of your mouth. It's here, in your mind, when it comes in. You know what I mean? What he says to you is spiritual. It's thought. I've experienced a lot of things in church that have helped my faith grow.

Jail Ministry: Catholicism Meets Pentecostalism

Then I started goin' with Father Charlie to the jail and having Mass. We'd have healin' services and different things like that. But I want to tell you a little story about a lady I met there. She's a eucharistic minister and she's Pentecostal. She was in jail havin' services with the prisoners, and she had a vision. She saw me and my wife, and, based on that vision, she found us. Apparently the Lord talks to her and she listens. She found where I was at. She talked to my wife and this lady described me. She didn't even know me, but she saw me in a vision. And that's how I got to know her. She'd come one Saturday of every month. She would come and we'd pray together and we'd visit. Every day was something different. Some days she would read the Bible. Other days she would bring an instrument over and sing.

But I want to tell you the story of how my leg got healed. One weekend she was prayin' over me, and when she got done I said, "Well, what did the Lord have to say?" But in my own mind, I was thinkin' I wanted her to pray over my leg to have Jesus heal it. And before I could tell her that, she already knew because the Lord had told her. She said, "He wants to pray over your feet, your legs." So we got a bowl, and she cleansed my feet with water and dried 'em. And after she dried 'em, she anointed them with oil. And it was like night and day.

I got healed. My legs got healed. I no longer limped—and before that, I was limpin' pretty good. But it went away. The pain went away. Jesus healed me.

HEALING PRAYER FOR BOBBY'S MOTHER

Let me tell you the story about the time I asked for help in church when my mother was sick. I was in tears, and I needed someone in my parish to help me with my mother. And the Lord actually told me which chair the person would be sitting in who was going to help me. It was actually that one right there, the third from the left. This was a Saturday night late when I was here in the church. Then on Sunday morning, I got to church and I was sittin' over there when I thought, "Maybe I better check who's sittin' in that chair." And, sure enough, there was someone sittin' in that chair. So I decided to wait and see if that person's gonna come to me. My mother was there, and I didn't know they were gonna have her come up and pray over her and anoint her. 'Cause my niece went and told Father Charlie she wanted them to pray over her.

So I helped my mother up to the front of the church where she sat down while Father Charlie anointed her with oil and prayed over her. The whole parish gathered around and laid hands on her. After we were done praying and my mother sat back down, that person right there in that chair touched me on this side and says, "When they were praying for your mother we saw Jesus—right in front, like this, with his arms stretched out. I'm supposed to tell you everything's gonna be alright. You got nothin' to worry about. Your mother'll be fine. And I'm supposed to tell you that." See, the Lord told me someone was gonna help me and it would be that person sittin' right there. And that's what happened. That lady still comes to our church. The Lord used the person. And that person didn't have a clue that I knew already that it was gonna happen. And it did.

MORE VISIONS OF JESUS

There's quite a few experiences here that I could tell you. I could go on all night! When the monstrance is out and people are up here prayin', it's like continuous Mass goin' on when they're prayin' in front of the monstrance. One time when people were in here prayin', I did have an experience while drivin' by outside the church—because I saw someone behind the altar with their arms stretched out. So when I saw our priest on Sunday, I said, "Father, what were you doin' in church so late? Why were you havin' Mass?" And he said, "That wasn't me. I wasn't in church." What I saw was Jesus in back of that altar, with a sincere face and his head was turned sideways, arms stretched out. But it seemed like he was taller—he was up higher because I saw the whole upper figure above the monstrance. And Father Charlie told me, "You know, Bobby, when someone's prayin' with the monstrance out, it's like continuous Mass goin' on."

And that's what I saw. Jesus was there havin' Mass—he was prayin' when it was goin' on. And it happened several times. A lot of times people would come in and gather around in church and you would see 'em prayin'. It's such a good feeling to have our congregation prayin' together. When we say the "Our Father" during Sunday Mass, we get in a big circle and hold hands. I think that's the neatest thing—saying the "Our Father" with everybody holding hands together.

TRADITIONAL CROW ELEMENTS DURING MASS

I'm a Catholic, and I also believe in Crow tradition. Because in every religion, we all have a way to get to heaven and meet the Creator. That's the stairway of getting to heaven. And everyone has their own beliefs. But I believe that in every church, even in the traditional Crow way, they're praying to the same Creator in their own way. We do a lot of traditional Crow things in our church, and it's really nice. We use cedar in our church. We go around and have people cedared during the Mass.

During special events, like at the Corpus Christi procession, we have the pipe ceremony. They come down and they have a pipe, and they smoke it and they pass it around. It's kinda interesting to see that. It's really neat that certain people can do that. There's a lot of tradition that goes on in our church. You see, there's a lot of Native Americans in church and they all pray to the Lord—ask Jesus to help them with their problems and everything that they need. And also it helps their faith. Their faith grows and that's one thing we all need is our faith to grow.

NOTES

1. Becky Shay, "Vision Fulfilled: Presbyterians Help Catholics Erect Highly Visible Symbol," *Billings (Mont.) Gazette*, July 28, 2007: 1A, 10A.
2. LR 13-02 (March 6, 2013).

4

Catholic, Crow, and Charismatic

AN INTERVIEW WITH
GLORIA GOES AHEAD CUMMINS

The late Gloria Goes Ahead Cummins, though originally from Pryor, lived much of her life near Lodge Grass in a part of the reservation known as *Bínneete* ("No Water District"). She was baptized as a child at St. Charles Catholic Parish in Pryor, and attended Catholic school through the eighth grade. In 1947, as a high school freshman, she moved away to attend the Flandreau Federal Indian School in South Dakota. She enjoyed a great deal of academic success that year, explaining: "I had it easy 'cause all the lessons they taught us, I already had 'em at the mission. It was just like review. So I made the honor roll and I got the highest grades."

Through her adult life, Gloria was a faithful, longtime member of Our Lady of Loretto Catholic Church, located in the town of Lodge Grass. The

Gloria Goes Ahead Cummins in her home near Lodge Grass, Crow Reservation. *Author's photo*

Catholic Charismatic Renewal that swept across the United States in the 1970s had a powerful impact on Montana's tribes well into the 1980s, and the Crow Catholic community at Lodge Grass was among those deeply affected.[1] It was there, during a Holy Spirit seminar in 1977, that Gloria received "the baptism in the Holy Spirit," followed a few months later by the experience of "speaking in tongues." For many in that parish, the next few years were marked by a steady stream of charismatic house meetings, prayer and healing services, and charismatic conferences. In the summer of 1979 there was a three-day ecumenical healing event held at the Crow fairgrounds that attracted national leaders of the Catholic Charismatic Renewal, drew an estimated 2,500 attendees, and claimed a prominent story in the *Billings Gazette*.[2]

Although this represented a relatively brief period in Gloria's long life, it shaped her religious beliefs and practices in profound ways for the next thirty-five years. In many ways, the movement is still alive among members of the parish today. This is also the case for Father Jim Antoine, Loretto's current priest, who arrived at the parish midmovement. He still prays for healing and uses tongues with parishioners when requested, as Gloria would sometimes do. However, compared with its heyday in the late 1970s, the movement had fallen into sharp decline by the mid-1980s, leaving Gloria to relish memories of days filled with so many "powerful" experiences, experiences that restored the happiness she had lost following her husband's death in 1974.

Throughout the interview, Gloria insists that full participation in Crow cultural practices is compatible with Christian faith. She openly expresses frustration with Crow Pentecostals who say that Indian ways are "of the devil." In contrast, she argues that the Bible calls Christians to enjoy life and to celebrate family and culture. For Gloria, this translates into a deep love for Crow Fair, powwow dancing, and annual tribal parades.

Despite similarities in religious experiences that might have served as a bridge between the two groups, Crow Pentecostals often accused Catholic charismatics as operating under "a different kind of bad spirit," distinct from the Holy Spirit. Gloria describes how, because of her Catholic loyalties, Pentecostals regularly snubbed her when she attended their camp meetings. At the same time, opposition to the movement also came from within the Catholic Church itself. Gloria recalls Crow Catholics who accused charismatics in the Church of "turning into Pentecostals." Non-Indians in the parish were particularly severe critics of the charismatic renewal taking place among many Crow parishioners at the time. They even insisted on holding their own separate Mass each week. According to Gloria, their complaints to the bishop were ultimately responsible for driving away the deacon and the Sisters most supportive of the movement, effectively bringing the charismatic renewal to an end in Lodge Grass.

Gloria's narrative reflects a strong biblical devotionalism blended with indigenous ways of accessing the spirit world. For example, her discussion of Bible stories is punctuated with descriptions of dreams and visions that are, in turn, filled with Christian images—from encounters with the Virgin Mary, to a run-in with a white preacher in a Bible distribution warehouse. Her belief in the complementarity of Catholicism and Crow Traditionalism is reflected in the large mural adorning the altar wall of the sanctuary at Our Lady of Loretto Church, which she attended for so many years. Gloria told me with pride that she served on the parish council that oversaw the installation of that mural. At the center stands a crucifix planted atop a sharply rising hill. A flying eagle approaches the suffering Jesus from the upper right-hand corner of the mural; in the opposite corner stand three large tipis at the foot of the hill. According to Gloria, the mural "says the power to the cross, to get to Jesus, is through that power of the eagle. Through there, to get there to the cross, that's what it means. The three tipis resemble the Trinity—the three persons of the Trinity."

The following interview took place in Gloria's living room, just days before Crow Fair.

❁

How the Catholic Charismatic Renewal Came to Lodge Grass

There was a priest that used to be at Crow Agency whose name was Father Noel. I guess he was praying, and then he got the Holy Spirit and started praying in tongues. And that's where it started. He left St. Dennis Catholic Church at Crow Agency and came and stayed here at Lodge Grass after our one priest left. There were three Capuchin [Franciscan] priests that had come to Lodge Grass. Then they all kind of transferred away. After those three young guys left, that's when Noel came here.

Father Noel started having what he called "area Masses." We had them on Saturdays. He invited people from Billings and Sheridan that were Spirit-filled. They were non-Indians, most of 'em. But they always came, and we had Mass at our church here at Lodge Grass, at Our Lady of Loretto Catholic Church. We had prayer meetings, too. And that's how it all started. All those people were Spirit-filled and they all had testimonies. Then they started praying, and it was really powerful.

That was around '76 or '75. I was born-again in October '77. And that was powerful. It's something that you can't explain. It's so powerful. That happened down at the Catholic Church here in Lodge Grass. We had a prayer meeting there. All the priests were Spirit-filled, the ones that were at St. Labre at the time, and even the nuns were, too.[3] They came from Labre for that area Mass. There were about three priests and two nuns. They were Franciscan Capuchin priests.

Before that happened, I lost my husband in January '74. I have seven children. Four of them were still underage when he passed away. I really went through a lot. When Father Noel was here, that's when he had those area Masses. And I kind of got familiar with the Holy Spirit. There was also this Catholic deacon, Brother Joe Kristufek. He's the one that came with Father Noel. I guess they used to have conferences at Steubenville Franciscan University in Ohio. Anyway, I guess those conferences there, with the priests and the nuns, were all about the charismatic renewal. I think Noel and Joe met at a conference there, and then Noel invited him over to stay here in Lodge Grass with him. And Joe sings, too. He plays guitar and sings. When he sings he really stirs up the Holy Spirit. We also had three nuns here, at the time, who were Spirit-filled. One of them played guitar and sings pretty good, too. So we had real good music when we had prayer meetings. They were the ones that kind of brought that in and taught us about the Holy Spirit.

Gloria Is Baptized in the Holy Spirit
and Speaks in Tongues

In the Catholic faith, we know the Holy Spirit; but they never taught us how to accept it. We read the Bible, but we just know some of the important stories that they teach us. I think that's all we know. In the Catholic Church, we never hardly read the Bible. Anyway, one Saturday Joe wanted to have a Holy Spirit seminar. He said, "I want you to come to that meeting. Any plans you have, just let 'em go. I want you to be there." So me and my sister-in-law went, and it was just powerful. That's when we accepted the Holy Spirit—both of us at the same time. That's how we kind of started.

Sometimes you can receive tongues right at the time when you first get baptized in the Holy Spirit. But I didn't use it 'til like three months later. That's when it came to me. I still pray in tongues now. When I'm alone and I pray, I just pray in tongues. When I can't think of anything else to say, I start praying in tongues. And it's really a powerful thing. They say that it's just prayer to God—that the devil don't even understand it when you pray in tongues. So he doesn't know what to do. So it's important that you pray in tongues.

Anyway, that's how we started. They prayed for us. My sister-in-law was with me, and one of my daughters was there, too. During the meeting, they asked whoever wants to be prayed over to come up to the front. And those priests and those nuns were there. I felt like going up. It felt like someone was pushing me to go. I was sitting by my sister-in-law and daughter, and I said, "Shall we go?" And they kind of just looked at me, and I don't think they wanted to go. The second time they announced it, I said, "Let's go! Let's go up there!" They kind of looked at each other and smiled, and I said, "I'm going up." So I just walked right by 'em. But then they followed me up there.

When they prayed for us, all them priests and some others, there were about six of us ladies in the middle. They told us to hold hands, and we did, and they started praying for us. We were holding hands, and pretty soon I felt something hit me right here in the head. I didn't know what it was, and I was really fighting it. But it just kind of filled me up. Then I started shaking, and my hands went up. And I started to cry. I was really holding it back, but when I heard this other woman crying I just really started crying, too. Then my hands went up, and I felt the lady next to me hold my hand up here. When they all left, just me and my sister-in-law were there. Our hands were up and we were singing and crying. You know, I never did believe in holding your hands up like that when you pray. I never even believed that. But they just went up by themselves, you know? And I thought someone was holding my hand up all the time—but it was just me. It was just powerful. And I can't explain it. You have to experience it yourself to know. It's just so powerful.

We went back to our seats and sat down. And this Brother Joe came to us and said, "Hey, you two ladies got zapped, didn't you?" And here we looked at each other and we started laughing. After all the crying, and now we couldn't stop laughing. We just laughed and laughed. I felt so happy. You know, I never felt that happy after I lost my husband. And all that grieving, I didn't realize that I was never happy after that. He died in January of 1974. This was three years later in 1977. But, finally, I was happy again.

During that time, we had prayer meetings like every Saturday evening. Sometimes it was at somebody's house, but most of the time we met at the church. And different ones would come. That's how it really started, like we prayed for people that were already born-again—we would pray for people, and they'd get slain [in the Spirit] and it's just powerful. We also had prayer meetings every Wednesday night at the church. And house meetings, too. People invited us to have prayer meetings at their house. So we would go, and we traveled all over. Even in the winter. Nothing stopped us at the time! All over the reservation we traveled, and sometimes to Billings and to Sheridan. Different preachers would come, and we'd all go over to their prayer meetings.

An Experience of Healing Prayer

Before all this happened is when I got sick, when I'd get those attacks in my tummy. I'd been to different doctors, and they didn't know what was wrong with me. They took all kinds of tests. They thought it was my gall bladder, but when they tested it and X-rayed it they said there was nothing wrong with it. They didn't know what was wrong. I'd get those attacks, and it was just really so painful. I didn't know what to do sometimes. It didn't help if I walked around, or if I sat down, or if I lay down. No matter what I did, the pain just wouldn't go away. This was before I was born-again, you know—received the Holy Spirit. Anyway, my daughters were outside, and they came in. I was lying in bed and I called them over and said, "You should take me to the hospital. I don't know what to do anymore. This is so painful. I don't care what the doctors say—even if they have surgery on me." I said, "I don't care anymore."

Before they took me to the hospital, the pain was so bad I could hardly walk. I was lying there in bed, and I started reading my Bible. I opened it to Luke 4 where Jesus has his first miracle. It was that scripture about the wedding in Cana when they ran out of wine and the servants brought the jugs and told 'em, "We ran out of wine. What shall we do?" His mother was there, so she said, "Take them to Jesus. He's in the other room. Take them to him." So they took the jugs to him. And he said, "I wasn't ready for a miracle, but fill those jugs with water." So they brought them, and he blessed them, and he said, "Go ahead and take 'em [to the guests]." When they tasted them, they said that was the best wine they ever tasted. And the people said, "We usually serve the best wine first. You are different. You served it last."

That's the scripture I opened to, but I couldn't get nothing out of it. So I closed my Bible and I opened it again. The same scripture! When I opened it the third time to the same place, I prayed, "Lord, I don't know what you are trying to tell me. Let me know. Let me understand it." Then I closed my eyes, and I don't know if I fell asleep or what. But I closed my eyes and heard the Blessed Virgin Mary talk to me. She said, "I want you to trust my son as I have trusted him." And I thought, "Oh, my gosh!" I just sat up. It scared me—it really scared me! It was the first time something like that happened. It was just like a voice. I didn't see it—I just heard this voice, and I knew it was her. That's when my daughters came and took me to the hospital. But on the way, when we were in town, I told my girls, "Stop by Brother Joe's house." And they said, "Why? Why do you want to go up there?"

So we stopped at the Sisters' house and went in. I could barely make it up the steps. When we knocked on the door, that one nun was there. Her name is Sister Diane. She was there alone. And I said, "Is Joe around?" She said, "No, he went somewhere. He's not here." I said, "I came to see him—I want him to pray with me." I told her I was in pain, that I was on my way to see the doctor, but thought I'd stop by and have him pray with me before I went. So I asked, "Since he's not here, could you pray for me?" She just kind of looked at me and said, "Let me finish what I'm doing in the kitchen first." So I went and lay down on the couch by the door. I couldn't even sit. A few minutes later, she came back in, knelt by me, and started praying.

She had her hand on my arm and started praying for me. I took her hand and placed it down where the pain was. And pretty soon, here, I felt this movement making like a bubbling noise. It just went down. The pain, it just kind of left. I stayed there really still, and I didn't feel it after that. It just left like that. I lay there after it stopped, and I said, "Did you feel that?" And she said, "Uh-huh!" I guess she was really surprised, you know? Here I found out later that she had never prayed over anyone before. I think that's why she kind of hesitated, when she went back in the kitchen at first. I said, "That pain left!" And we just started laughing. We talked for a while, and I said, "Shall we go now? That pain is gone. It left! Let's just go back home." So I got up, and here I walked and didn't feel the pain. It was still kind of sore, but that pain wasn't there anymore. I walked out, and it didn't even hurt when I walked down the steps. I didn't even go to the doctor. So we just came back home, and I was all right. Anyway, that's what happened.

ATTACKED FROM WITHIN AND WITHOUT: NON-INDIAN CATHOLICS AND CROW PENTECOSTALS

When we got the Holy Spirit, the non-Indian Catholics didn't like it. They didn't take part in it. They didn't believe it. They thought that it's—well, I don't know what they thought. They didn't even believe in it. And they started having their Mass on Saturday instead of Sunday. One time we were having a prayer meeting with Brother Joe at the church on a Saturday, and he had forgotten to announce the Sunday before that there wouldn't be any Mass that next Saturday. So here we were, praying for people in each corner of the church, and people were slain in the Spirit, laying on the floor—and these two white ladies came in, and Joe looked at 'em and said, "Oh, my gosh! I forgot to tell them that there's no Mass!" And here those ladies looked around and said, "This is disgusting!" And they walked right back out.

Some Crow Pentecostals didn't like us at that time, either. "Those charismatic Catholics, they're having a different kind of bad spirit," they'd always say. They'd say it was a different spirit we were using. You know, the Pentecostals quit everything—they don't even go to dances or basketball games. They think that Indian ways are an evil thing to do. They think that beliefs in our culture and all that stuff is of the devil, they say. And they just quit everything! I said to them, "We don't do that! In the Bible it says that Jesus wants us to enjoy our lives. He wants us to be happy. That's what we're doing."

We were just praying, you know? We didn't care who came into our church. If they wanted prayers, we prayed for 'em. We never said nothing to them. We just welcomed them. But you know how Pentecostals are. Like, if you're Catholic and you go into their meetings, they'll preach about the Catholics. If you go to Sun Dances, they'll preach about that. Peyote meetings—same thing. They think that it's evil. They think it's not of God. But they don't even know. All these different ways—we all pray to God. There's only one God. That's what we're all praying to. It's to God. But the Pentecostals are kind of changing now. They're beginning to realize what they're doing is not the way to do it. Even some of the preachers, I see 'em at basketball games now.

Catholic, Charismatic, and Traditional

At first, Brother Joe was kind of making us think that way about our culture, too. But I talked to my boys about it, my oldest boy especially. I said, "There's nothing wrong with our culture. We pray to God, and we believe in God." A long time ago, my [paternal] grandpa was a real strong Catholic. He was one of the first students that went to that St. Xavier Mission when it was first opened.[4] So they're real strong Catholics. But they still used their culture and they still kept their medicine bundles in a safe place where nobody got into it. That's how he believed in his Indian ways, too. He was always there to teach us, to tell us stuff all the time.

When we were small, there were five of us. My mom had six children from her first marriage before her husband died. Then she married my dad, and there's five more of us. It's nice to have a big family. I don't know how she did it. We're all close family. We help each other and that's how she taught us. She said, "When someone needs help, you help 'em. And don't ask for anything back. Someday when you're in need, it's your turn to get help." We're really close family. Maybe we argue and all that, but we never really fight or things like that. That's how she raised us. And I think she did a good job. She's a real strong Catholic, has a strong Catholic faith. And she taught us that, too.

When the charismatic movement started here, at first the older Catholic members didn't believe in it. They said, "You're turning to be Pentecostals now!" They didn't like that. But some found out that we're just using the Holy Spirit and some believed in it. But some didn't. They thought that we were turning into Pentecostals. But, unlike the Pentecostals, we still believed in our culture. We still would go watch dances, and we still set up camp at Crow Fair. This one lady told me, she said, "How come you're moving to Crow Fair? Me," she said, "I'm not moving—I'm not camping there anymore."[5] At the time, there were some people planning a pilgrimage to Our Lady of Fátima.[6] And I wanted to go. I really wanted to go. That lady wanted to go, too. But when I looked at the date for the trip, here it was the same time as Crow Fair. She asked me again if I would go, but finally one Sunday at church I told her, "You know," I said, "I'm not going to go, because it's the same time as Crow Fair. I don't think I want to go."

And she was kind of upset with me. She said, "Why do you want to go to Crow Fair? There's nothing there that's fun to watch." And I said, "That's part of our culture and it wouldn't be right if I don't set up camp there. I move there so my children can enjoy it, and I like to watch and take part in the parade and dances." At Crow Fair there are parades every morning on Friday, Saturday, and Sunday. On Monday they have a parade dance where they dance through the camp. They stop four times, and that's like looking to the future. That's what that's about. Even our friends from different tribes, they come over. They visit us, they eat with us, and we camp together. My youngest sister and my youngest brother, we camp together, we visit each other, and we eat with each other. We share meals and we visit.

So I told her, "I really enjoy all that. And there's nothing wrong with that." In the Bible it says, "Faith, hope, and love—and love is the greatest." And that's what I'm there for. Because I love my family, and I like other tribes to come and visit us. I love that, and that's why I like to camp there.

"Mom's Gone Nuts!"

Our prayer meetings back then were really something. It was something so strong, and something you feel. It's a good feeling, and you don't want to leave it. I was like really high for a week or so after I was baptized in the Holy Spirit. It was really something when that happened to me. I came back home and my son was there sitting in the living room. I asked him, "Did you eat?" He said, "I tried to, but there's no bread in the house." And I said, "Wait, I'll cook something and I'll make some biscuits." So I went into the kitchen, and my dishes were piled up high. And I started making biscuits and cooking, and I started washing dishes, and I was just really singing and humming this one tune that they sang when they were praying for us. When that happened to me, and I got filled with the Holy Spirit, that song was still in my ear. I had to sing it, and I was humming it, and working at the same time.

Just then, my oldest daughter and her family came into the house. They live in Wyola. I guess she heard me singing, and that was the first time I had done that after their dad passed away. I guess I never really was happy after that. Here I started singing, and she came in and said, "Hey, what's going on? What happened to Mom?" Barney said, "You better go check—I think Mom's gone nuts!" She came in and said, "What are you doing?" I said, "I'm cooking and washing dishes." When I got done, I set the table and we all sat down to eat. And I said, "You should have come to that prayer meeting. It was really something. Something happened to me so powerful—I couldn't stop singing and I just want to jump around!" I said, "You should have been there. It was really something. Me and Regina, we got slain and we got baptized in the Holy Spirit."

I think Regina spoke in tongues right away, but I didn't. It was a couple months later, I think. Here my daughters, they received the Holy Spirit right after that. All were filled with the Spirit. Later on, my sons, too. I feel kind of proud because I was the first Catholic from Our Lady of Loretto Church that received the Holy Spirit in our new building. At least I can say that much! My sister-in-law was with me the same time I got filled, but she's from St. Dennis Catholic Church at Crow Agency. And there was another lady that received the Holy Spirit before I did, but she was in a different church. It was in a Pentecostal church, because her sister is real strong Pentecostal and I think she received it there. So Our Lady of Loretto is a special church for me.

BIBLES AND DREAMS

I used to get dreams all the time about the Bible. I don't get that way anymore. Like when the Pentecostals were saying stuff about us, and that kind of hurt me. They at least should be glad that there's only one Spirit that's from Jesus. And that's what we have, too. "Why can't they believe it that way," I thought to myself, "instead of saying stuff?" Some even said that we're not reading the right Bible. I thought, "Which one is the right Bible?" I thought they're all the same. Maybe the wording is a little different, but it's all the same.

One night I had this dream. I was with my youngest girl, the one I lost. That's her daughter who was just here. I've raised her. She was with me in this dream, along with the second-oldest daughter. We were walking on this gravel road, like in the country. We were coming towards a big building, and there was this little stream we crossed. I saw people going in the building, and then coming out from a different door. And they were carrying something. I told my daughter, "We should go in. Look, people are coming out of there carrying something. Let's go in there and see what's going on."

So we went in there, and here this one white guy, he looked like a preacher, was standing there. He was standing there, giving out Bibles. So we went and he gave us a Bible. Then we came out the other door. I looked at it, and here the cover of the Bible said "The Living Bible." It was kind of like a maroon cover, with gold engraved letters. So we took it and went back towards where we were coming from. We crossed back over this little stream, and there was a big old tree, kind of alone, all shady underneath. I said, "Let's go sit there and look at the Bible." So we went over this fence and walked towards that tree. I sat down in the shade on the grass and started opening it—and here I woke up before I read it!

Ever since then, I kept looking for one of those Living Bibles. And I couldn't find one anywhere. I'd go to those Bible bookstores, and they'd say, "We had one, but we sold the last one!" But, finally, I did get one. I told my cousin my dream, and here that Christmas she found one for me. It's a different color, but she had my name engraved on it and gave it to me for Christmas. I was so happy to get one. It's an easier one for me to read and understand it. It just kind of came apart, so I found another one, and that's what I use now. It's wearing out too, but I always get my answers in the Bible. If I have a worry, I open it, and I get my answers right there. That's why it's called the living Bible—because it's alive. It tells you stuff you want to know. It's right in there.

Changes after Vatican II

I guess the Catholic Charismatic Renewal really began when Pope John [XXIII], the one that passed away, had those changes at Vatican II. When he did that, he changed everything. And I think that had something to do with why this happened. I felt the changes, too. Like when our new church was built, when they had the first Mass, I walked in and all the statues were gone. Just the crucifix was there. I thought it looked so bare. "Gosh, it doesn't even feel right," I thought to myself.

After we came out of Mass, the priest came over to me and said, "What do you think about our new church?" I said, "You know, I felt like I went into the wrong church." And he just laughed! I said, "What happened to all the statues? I just don't feel right about it." "Well, let me tell you," he said. "You can't have those statues—they took it out because a lot of people prayed to these statues when they should be praying to God and Jesus. That's why they took them out. But the Blessed Mother's statue is there, and Jesus," he said. Then I knew what he meant, so it didn't bother me anymore after he told me that. But that's how I felt. Different ones felt that way, too. They even took all the pews out and put chairs in there, so we don't have the kneelers anymore.

Aftermath of the Movement

Little by little, the charismatic renewal kind of moved out of the church. The non-Indians in our church wanted to have their own Mass. And they did—they had their own Mass. Anyway, I think they complained a lot to the diocese about how they didn't like what we're doing. Finally, Sister Diane left on account of that. All the nuns left. That was not long after Father Jim came, maybe around the early '80s.

Some individuals could understand it when someone prayed in tongues, like at the area Masses. Someone would stand up and they would pray in tongues, and then they'd sit down. And then some people had the gift to interpret what they were saying in tongues. That was really something. Sometimes meetings still go on, but not as much anymore. We're not as active as we used to be.

Those who were involved in the movement back then, they still go to

Catholic church here at Lodge Grass. But they also go to Pentecostal meetings, too, like camp meetings. We go to those meetings, too. We go and just listen. I was at a Pentecostal camp meeting a couple nights ago—one of my granddaughters took me there. We didn't get out, we just sat in the car and listened to the preaching. It was a meeting held up in Crow Agency. Sometimes you don't feel welcome. They know what church we belong to, and they don't accept us, like they don't welcome us. They'll just look at you and turn away, like, "She shouldn't be here." At first, I kind of felt hurt. But then I thought, "Gosh, I'm here for God—not for them." I just want to listen to the preaching. So, it doesn't bother me anymore.

Father Jim Antoine still uses tongues in the church. He has the gift of healing, and he really prays for people that ask for prayers. I go to him, too. When he came here to Our Lady of Loretto, he was already Spirit-filled. So that was really good.

Gloria's Family: An Enduring Charismatic Legacy

When my daughter received the Holy Spirit, Brother Joe Kristufek was praying for her in the church. That's when she got slain and was really speaking in tongues, too. At that time, I didn't even have tongues yet. I had a dream about my daughter getting tongues before me. In that dream, I was in the church and was going up to receive the holy communion. And this priest was there—it looked like a bishop because he had that bishop hat on his head—and we were standing there to receive the holy communion. And my daughter was with me. We were standing there at the altar, and he asked me, "Do you use tongues now?" I said, "No. I want to, I'm really trying hard, but I can't." And he said, "Well, just listen to me and follow me when I pray in tongues," he said. He started praying in tongues before he gave me the host. So I was standing there, and I was really repeating him in my mind when he prayed in tongues. Then I heard my daughter speaking in tongues before I did. You see, so I dreamed this before it even happened!

And how I wished, at the time, that I could use tongues, too. When we were traveling to prayer meetings with Sister Diane and Brother Joe, sometimes they'd pray and they would really speak in tongues. And I'd sit back there, and how I wish I could speak it, too! I was really trying hard, and I couldn't. But later on, we had just a few of us there praying where Joe lived right across from the church, and I started praying in tongues. And I really started crying—I was so happy! They thought something was wrong, you know, and they said, "What happened?" And I said, "Didn't you hear me? I was praying in tongues for the first time!"

But all of my children have the Holy Spirit, and my grandkids, too. I have twenty-three grandkids, and I have thirty great-grandchildren. I think it's gonna be thirty-one now—one is on its way. They say you're speaking in a different language when you pray in tongues, and somebody might understand it. We don't even know what we're saying, but God does. That happened to me one time at one of those area Masses. I heard this one man in front of me—we were kind of sitting in the back—and I heard somebody up front speaking in Crow. And I said, "Who could that be?" All of 'em were non-Indians sitting in front. We were standing up praying, and I was really looking. And here it was this older guy with gray hair. And I saw him really talking, speaking in Crow. And he didn't even know! I forget what he said. That's when we were first going to those prayer meetings, and that was the first time I heard it like that. And I was so amazed.

At this one area Mass, there were a lot of people in there. And this one lady got up and started speaking in tongues. When she sat down, I started inter-preting it in my mind. Just before that, something kind of slapped me right here in my forehead. I was sitting there, closing my eyes, really listening, and something just kind of hit me like that. I looked around, because I thought someone threw something at me. But I didn't see anybody there—they all had their eyes closed and their heads down. And I thought, "Gosh, that's funny." So I closed my eyes again, and that's when I got that interpretation. I wanted to say it out loud, but I was so shy. I didn't want to say anything. And this one priest spoke out, Father Ron they called him. He spoke out, and that was the same interpretation that I was supposed to say—and I didn't do it. So he used that priest, instead. I lost it after that—the gift of interpretation. I think that's why the Lord hit me right on the head, because I didn't speak up! I was always so shy to speak up when there's a lot of people.

All my children speak in tongues, and we all have different gifts, too. When you start using the Holy Spirit, the Lord will use you in all those gifts. And where you fit in, that's where he'll keep you. That's what hap-pened to me.

NOTES

1. For more on the Catholic Charismatic movement's influence among the Crow Tribe and surrounding Native communities, see Mark Clatterbuck, "In Native Tongues: Catholic Charismatic Renewal and Montana's Eastern Tribes (1975– Today)," *U.S. Catholic Historian* 28, no. 2 (Spring 2010): 153–80.
2. Lorna Thackeray and Dory Owens, "Rain Mixes with Tears as 'Spirit' Heals," *Billings (Mont.) Gazette,* July 29, 1979, sec. A.
3. Gloria is referring to the St. Labre Indian School located in Ashland, Montana, on the Northern Cheyenne Reservation. St. Labre operates several Catholic Indian schools in Montana, two of which are located on the Crow Reservation: St. Charles School in Pryor, and Pretty Eagle Academy at St. Xavier.
4. St. Xavier Catholic Mission on the Crow Reservation recently celebrated its 125th anniversary. It was founded in 1887. The school located at the site is now called Pretty Eagle Academy, named after a well-known Crow chief.
5. Each year in mid-August, families from all across the reservation set up tipis, tents, and campers for the Crow Fair, located at the Crow Agency fairgrounds. The Crow Fair draws participants and spectators from across the country in a massive celebration of Crow culture, marked by an annual powwow, a rodeo, parades, and other festivities. As many as 1,500 tipis comprise this tribal encampment each year, making it one of the largest Native American gatherings in the United States.
6. The village of Fátima, Portugal, is the location of several reported visitations by Mary to three shepherd children in 1917. The site immediately became a popular place of pilgrimage, and it remains one of the world's most popular religious destinations for Catholic pilgrims today.

Part II

❀

PENTECOSTALISM, CULTURE, AND POLITICS

The four voices in this part are all associated with Pentecostalism on the Crow Reservation. The first two highlight the critical leadership roles that women have played in Crow Pentecostalism from the start. In fact, during the 1920s and 1930s the movement was so dominated by women that some of the oldtimers recall how the men would sit in the back of prayer meetings, openly resigned to the Holy Spirit's apparent preference for women. As active leaders in Crow Pentecostalism today, Pastor Rhea Goes Ahead and Fannie Ward both discuss the challenges of reconciling their strong tribal identity with the movement's condemnation of "Indian religion"—especially those ceremonies associated with medicine bundles, the Sun Dance, and peyote. Drawing on historical accounts and personal encounters alike, they describe the relationship between Christian faith and "Indian religion" in terms of a spiritual war raging beneath the surface of our everyday lives. In this way, it's inaccurate to say that Crow Pentecostals "don't believe" in tribal religions; in many ways, they believe in the power and efficacy of Crow ceremonies more literally than any other Christian community on the reservation. However, their starkly dualistic vision of reality leads them to assign the power of traditional ceremonies to dark spiritual forces that are at enmity with God. This conviction leads many to feel that even peripheral involvement in traditional ceremonies represents a betrayal of their faith in Jesus.

Kenneth Pretty On Top Sr., ministering alongside his wife, Hannah, is senior pastor of the largest Pentecostal church on the reservation. While most Crow Pentecostal churches remain independent, Kenneth's congregation is affiliated with the international Foursquare Church. The denomination was founded by the pioneering preacher Aimee Semple McPherson, whose missionary outreach was responsible for bringing Pentecostalism to the Crow Tribe in the 1920s. Kenneth openly pursues a middle path between judgmentalism and compromise. He holds familiar Pentecostal beliefs about the spiritual dangers of many Native ceremonies, but he rarely preaches against Traditionalism from the pulpit. He even feels comfortable participating in certain Crow ceremonies when only Christians are involved, a practice that attracts the criticism of conservative Pentecostals and Traditionalists alike.

The final voice in this part draws attention to the political impact that Crow Pentecostalism is having among the tribe today. Conrad "CJ" Stewart is a fourth-generation Pentecostal who was an influential tribal legislator from the reservation's Black Lodge District at the time this interview took place. He was instrumental in drafting and securing approval for two resolutions in 2013 that reflect an overtly Christian agenda. One declares Jesus as Lord of the Crow Reservation, while the other formalizes the Crow Tribe's support for the state of Israel. As CJ's interview demonstrates, the motivation behind these symbolic declarations of Christian loyalty is the conviction that spiritual and economic blessings will follow such public, communal expressions of biblical faith. As the interview also makes clear, this religiopolitical trend is at once decidedly eschatological and overtly Zionistic. Today, a growing number of Crow Pentecostal pastors and laypersons are embracing such a biblically based, Israel-centric, end-times-oriented vision for the tribe's future—a trend made manifest by the massive billboard recently erected at Crow Agency declaring, "Jesus Christ Is Lord on the Crow Nation." The hope of socioeconomic improvement driving this campaign is reflected in the Bible verse chosen for the bottom of the sign: "Blessed is the nation whose God is the Lord; and the people whom he hath chosen for his own inheritance" (Psalm 33:12).

5

Demonic Owls and Fraidy Cats

AN INTERVIEW WITH RHEA GOES AHEAD

Rhea Goes Ahead has been the pastor of Full Gospel Revival Tabernacle in Billings, Montana, just north of the Crow Reservation, since 1990. Her grandmother was Margaret "Maggie" Brass, a well-known healer and pioneer of Crow Pentecostalism during the first half of the twentieth century. While Rhea's father was a Traditionalist and devout Catholic who practiced the Crow religious ways, her mother was a Pentecostal who deeply influenced Rhea's own religious formation. In the following narrative, Rhea

Rhea Goes Ahead, pastor of Full Gospel Revival Tabernacle (Billings, Mont.), in the lobby of a Pentecostal church at Crow Agency. *Photo courtesy Rhea Goes Ahead*

recounts the story of her own "glorious conversion" to the Pentecostal faith as a college student, while also offering broader reflections on the history of Pentecostalism among the tribe. In the course of her overview, she addresses the dominant role played by women in Pentecostalism's early years on the reservation, a development all the more remarkable, considering her claim that "women are second-class citizens in Crow culture." She gives particular attention to the central role that fasting in the nearby hills, a practice that has deep roots in traditional Crow religion, has played in the religious lives of Crow Pentecostals. Dreams and visions also figure prominently in her religious narrative, elements that likewise play a conspicuous role in Crow Traditionalism.

Despite emphasizing these points of continuity between pre-Christian Crow Traditionalists and Crow Pentecostals over the years, Rhea fiercely contends that Crow Traditionalism and Crow Pentecostalism are fundamentally incompatible traditions. At the root of her condemnation of "Indian religion" lies a conviction that Crow medicine (baaxpée) is animated by demonic, rather than sacred, powers. For this reason, Rhea regards medicine men and medicine women as practitioners of witchcraft. She explains how medicine spirit beings—such as the animal helpers who frequently appear to Crows during fasts—are actually demonic deceivers masquerading as helpers in order to intercept the well-meaning prayers of misguided Traditionalists.

Rhea likewise repudiates the common Crow practice of "smudging" with sweetgrass, sage, or cedar, regarding it as an invitation for evil spirits. Instead, she encourages the use of anointing oil when offering prayers in accordance with biblical teachings, a long-standing Pentecostal tradition for which early Crow adherents were commonly dubbed Akbaatashée— greasers or oilers. For Rhea, Christian faith begins with losing a desire for "the things of the world," a phrase she freely applies to traditional Crow ceremonies and religious beliefs. In this sense, "the world" includes not only medicine bundle ceremonies, the Sun Dance, and the Peyote Way, but also such cultural events as powwows, arrow-throwing tournaments, and hand games. According to Rhea, true conversion requires a thorough rejection of the false gods of Indian religion in order to worship, in their place, "the true and the living God" of Christianity.

The complex and conflicted relationship that exists between Crow Pentecostalism and Crow Traditionalism is further illustrated in Rhea's discussion about the role that clan uncles and clan aunts play in the lives of Crow Pentecostal church members. While retaining respect for the Crow clan system itself, she explains how many Pentecostals are uncomfortable soliciting prayers and blessings from Traditionalist clan relatives. She joins a growing number of Crow Pentecostals who seek out fellow Christian believers for prayers and blessings rather than turning to clan relatives who may not be Christian believers. As she says below, she "never ran to clan uncles or clan aunts. That's what traditional Crows do if something bad is happening, or if they see something bad," adding, "I always get Christians to come and pray. I always look for Holy Ghost–filled Christians—let *them* be the ones to pray, and give *them* the gifts!"

Rhea's faith, like many other Pentecostals on the Crow Reservation, is influenced by the teachings of nationally known charismatic preachers associated with C. Peter Wagner's New Apostolic Reformation, including Chuck Pierce and Cindy Jacobs. This version of charismatic faith is focused on spiritual warfare, strategic intercessory prayer, the breaking of generational curses, and the "spiritual mapping" of geographic regions believed to be plagued by demonic strongholds. All of these elements appear in her account.

In 2011, Rhea received an honorary Doctor of Divinity degree from the United Graduate College and Seminary International. The following material comes from two interviews conducted at Rhea's home in the western Crow Reservation town of Pryor.

❁

FASTING IN THE HILLS, WOMEN HEALERS, AND CROW PENTECOSTAL HISTORY

My grandmother, my real grandmother, is Angela Brass Iron. She was sickly, and from what my mom told me, her sister, Maggie Brass, is the one who raised my mother. My real grandmother died when she was only thirty-two. Maggie Brass became a Christian, and I think it was because she was trying to get healing for her ill sister. Once Maggie became a Christian, she started working alongside Nellie Stewart. You see, back in the 1920s, a sickly Crow lady named Lucy Morrison Old Horn and her husband went to Angelus Temple in California to see Aimee Semple McPherson for a healing. Nellie Pretty Eagle Stewart, along with Grace and Victor Singer, went to join Lucy while they were there at Angelus Temple. Lucy and Nellie both got the baptism of the Holy Ghost, and Lucy received a healing. After Lucy got that healing, they took her to the beach and she got sick again. But the Christians that were with her gathered around and prayed for her, and she got healed again.[1]

When Nellie came back to the reservation from Los Angeles, she and Maggie Brass, along about that time, joined forces to pray for my grandmother Angela. They lived in St. Xavier because my grandpa Edward Iron is from St. X.[2] So they all gathered around her and prayed for her—Nellie Stewart, my grandma Maggie, and other Christians. Nellie and my grandmother Maggie also went to the hills to fast and pray. See, the Crows are a fasting people. So when those early Crow Pentecostals got the baptism of the Holy Ghost, they went to the hills and they had fasting spots themselves. They were praying for my grandmother Angela Brass Iron, and she was doing well.

So Nellie, my grandma, and some others who were with them all went to the hills of St. Xavier to fast and pray one day. When they came back that evening, my grandma Angela was not doing well. Maggie kept inquiring with my grandfather Edward Iron, "What did you do to her? She was well when we left. Why is she sick again?" Finally, my grandpa Edward Iron said, "I gave her a little peyote button to help her out." My grandmother Angela never got well. She just went downhill after that.

But she died a saved woman. She was only thirty-two years old. My grandmother Angela had seven kids. My mom, Ruby Iron Goes Ahead, was the second-to-youngest of the seven. So Maggie took the four youngest ones and started raising them. She was already born-again, Spirit-filled, and she fasted. She was a fasting woman. My mom told me about how my grandmother Maggie Brass fasted and how the enemy would try to come and intercept her prayers during her fasts.

When my grandmother had gotten saved and filled with the Holy Ghost, she went to the hills to fast and pray. One time, an owl landed by her and talked to her in Crow. The owl said, "What are you doing here?" And so my grandmother, knowing better, said, "What do you *think* I'm doing? I'm here praying. Now you get away in the name of Jesus and don't bother me!" And so that owl flew away. My mom always tells us that story. You see, her prayer was not intercepted because she knew the true and the living God. She knew Jesus. Otherwise, owl would have become her Indian medicine. And my mom hates owls! Because to the Crows, and to most Indian tribes, owl means death. So that is kinda like the beginning of Pentecostalism in our family. My mother tried to find out Maggie's Indian name, but nobody knows.

Maggie had hip problems, and back then, you know, there wasn't a lot of medical help for her. The doctor advised her never to get married and not to have kids. So she never had kids, but she became an Auntie Mom to all her nieces and nephews. She became their mother. She was a single mother, but she's had a lot of beautiful testimonies about her. So that's why the fasting and praying continued with these early Holy Ghost Christians. She's got a fasting place in Wyola.[3] Nellie Stewart has one over by Crow Agency. These women, they all have fasting spots where they went into the hills. So when you hear of these early Pentecostal people, they did a lot of fasting. They did a lot of praying. That's why Pentecostalism started growing on the reservation. That's why I wanted to share the roots of fasting and praying with our tribe. But now, since Pentecostalism came, they got into the true and the living God, the true Spirit of God.

THE ROLE OF WOMEN IN CROW PENTECOSTALISM

At that time, back at the beginning of the Pentecostal movement among the Crow tribe in the 1920s and 1930s, there were all these women in those early prayer meetings, like Nellie Stewart and Maggie Brass. The men would sit back and say, "The Holy Spirit is not for us; it's for the women." My mom said the men would sit in the background while the women enjoyed themselves in the Lord. And then, eventually, the men started getting the Holy Ghost, too, the baptism of the Holy Spirit.

In 2006, the year my mom passed away, we found where my grandmother Maggie fasted up in the hills. My mom said, "I want to do two things: I want to go to where my mother fasted, and I want to go find some land that she had." And so, in August of 2006, my cousins found where my grandmother fasted over in Wyola. It was on the Tuesday before the Jubilee Camp Meeting during Crow Fair that we traveled with my mom up to Wyola and we found her fasting spot. It's about five miles outside of town, towards the Big Horn Mountains, on one of the highest hills. It did something to me. I never met my grandmother Maggie, but as we were going up that hill, I felt just a big lump. I said, "My grandmother fasted here. She prayed here."

We spent the whole afternoon up there, and I started agreeing with the prayers of my grandmother. She fasted and prayed so earnestly for those seven kids, and all seven of them are in heaven today because of our grandmother. But the interesting thing with my grandmother Maggie is that she never saw any of them become Christians until after she died. And so I asked my mom, I said, "What did she do when she came up here? Did she just spend a day?" She said, "No, the men of the Yellowmule family she was staying with at the time would bring her up here with canvases and she would stay here for three days." She started doing this when my mom was a little girl. My mom said she would get lonesome for her mother. Then, after three days, the men would go and take her off that hill again. It's a real high hill, no trees or anything. But my mom said that Maggie had some experiences up there. I guess one time she prayed so much until it was almost like she was in a glory cloud up there.

So my grandmother stayed up there all by herself, a woman. Nowadays, us younger Christians are fraidy cats! We went up there, but I spent the time in my van. Ever since then, we've been going to that place. It's just something about that place. Other people have been finding that spot up there, too. My uncle told my mom about this one white guy who came and said, "I want to know where Maggie Brass does her fasting." They told him where, so he went up there and he came back and said, "I came and got my answer." I guess he wanted a healing. My uncle didn't even ask him who he was or how he knew about the spot.

We once spent a Friday night up there with some intercessors. But we cheated—I took my red van and we spent the night in there! I just didn't want to leave. You know, we began to agree with her prayers for the family. We started joining forces. But that was what she was, a woman who loved the Lord. She was also a preacher, and she had a healing ministry. She worked with a lot of people who had tuberculosis. TB was an epidemic at that time. My mom said that people would come and get her, and they would take her to their homes and she would be like a nurse to them—a spiritual nurse to them.

Our grandmother Maggie never got TB. When someone would get TB, in the summertime, they'd put up a tent outside and they wouldn't let nobody come to see them—even family members. They couldn't touch, couldn't kiss, or anything. It was a very contagious disease. But our grandmother would go in and she'd pray for them. Probably a lot of souls got saved during that time because of my grandmother Maggie.

Pentecostal Fasting Today

Today, us Crow Pentecostals do what we call "shut-ins" to carry on the fasting tradition. See, I think the mantle of my grandmother came on me because the Lord has led me to do shut-ins in the church. That's why I said, we kind of cheat nowadays. But it's like a retreat in the church where we'll do shut-ins, from Friday to Sunday. We just spend time in the church. One day, during one of my fastings at the church, the Lord began to reveal the heart of my grandmother to me, and why she lived the life she did. It was just beautiful. It was like a revelation. I could see the heart of my grandmother, Maggie Brass. The El Shaddai Church in Wyola has shut-ins, too, where they'll stay at the church over the weekend.

We call it shut-ins, you see, because we're a little softer. We're modernized! My mom and them, they would go to the mountains, like when my mother was going to have camp meetings. They had three summers in a row that they had camp meetings in Pryor Gap. She and Jeno Left Hand, May Bird Hat, Amy Hill, Blanche Brown, and that group—they would go, and my sister would drop them off. So the fasting kept on. But this generation I'm talking about, we're the softies. My grandmother, my mother, and my mother's generation—they went to the hills. They'd go off and fast. It still goes on today, but some probably do it in their homes now. And, like I said, we also do our fasting in our churches now. So there is still a lot of fasting. Like Linda Little Owl over at Crow Revival Center in Crow Agency—they have all-night prayer meetings on Friday nights there.

We really push fasting with our spiritual warfare—trying to know our roots and know what strongholds we are up against. We have a team we put together with Jim and Faith Chosa, and we sometimes meet over at Pastor Duane Bull Chief's church.[4] We get together and pray for Crow issues. So there's a lot of prayer going on. For a while there, back in the 1990s, several of us—including the pastor's wife at the Wyola Baptist church—we'd go to Dayton, Wyoming. There's a monastery there, and we'd take a whole Saturday and fast all day. We're always praying for our tribe. Anytime there's prayer and fasting, I'm right in there. 'Cause, to me, that's how things work.

When Maggie's mother was dying, she told Maggie, "You go back to Wyola because that is where your relatives are." So my grandmother, Margaret "Maggie" Brass, went back to Wyola and her ministry was there. They lived above that old Baptist church there in Wyola. My mom said for fifteen years they never missed Sunday school, because Maggie raised them up in Christian ways. That's how the Pentecostals were there in Wyola, having services and everything. But the Baptist Church had Sunday school, so my mother was raised that way, you know.

Azusa Street on the Crow Reservation

After Maggie died in 1949, my aunt, Alice Good Luck, missed her so much she started going to the Pentecostal church herself. Soon she got saved and filled with the Holy Ghost. After our grandmother died and Alice got saved, she and her husband, Alice and Tex Good Luck, they had meetings with Harold Carpenter, one of the Crow Pentecostal forerunners. He's from Lodge Grass.

In 1950, a revival broke out in Wyola here on the Crow Reservation. And I always called that the Azusa Street of the Crow Reservation.[5] My oldest brother Adrian had spinal meningitis at the time. They told my mom, "Why don't you take him to Wyola and get him prayed for, 'cause they're having meetings going on over there." So my mom caught a ride and went to Wyola. When they got there, my mom said it was so powerful, because during the day those Christians would go and fast and pray all day in the hills. Then, at nighttime, they'd come and the Holy Ghost would begin to move and a revival broke out over there. And they couldn't leave! That first night, my mom would be sitting there in church, and her hands would

PENTECOSTALISM, CULTURE, AND POLITICS

automatically go up. She said she'd sit on her hands, or otherwise her arms would just automatically go up. Finally, when they had an altar call, she went up there to the front, and she got saved and filled with the Holy Ghost, all in one shot. This was my mother, Ruby Iron Goes Ahead. That happened May 19, 1950.

So that's when that revival was. She got saved between 7 and 9 P.M. The next day, she always tells me, she got up and told Nancy Jefferson, "Why don't you come pray with me. I think this thing left me." She meant speaking in tongues. Nancy kind of smiled, and said, "Come on. Let's go . . . ," and they went up to the hill. They went to the hill and they started praying, and she said she started speaking in tongues. And that was the beginning of my mom's Christian walk. You see, her mom, Maggie Brass, would always tell them things, but she said it never registered—things about the Bible, revelations she had. But it never registered until then. So my Aunt Alice got saved, and then my mom was coming on the scene that night.

And that generation, they got it good. They got it—I don't know how you say it—"lower than the collarbone." I mean the Holy Ghost. Those women, like my Aunt Alice—ah, man! She was a Holy Ghost–filled woman for the rest of her life. My mom was like that, too. And Nancy Jefferson was like that. It was deeper than the collarbone. It stuck with them. They fasted during the day, my mom told me, and then they'd come back for the evening service. She said it was nothing for them to roll all over the floor, prophesying. This was at my aunt's house when that revival broke out, a couple miles outside of Wyola. My mom said that, back at Pryor, they heard that all those Christians were eating up Alice and Tex Good Luck's chickens! They couldn't leave that place. They had a house service, and it just exploded. That's why I say that was the Azusa Street of the Crow Reservation. That is when people started getting saved. They all got saved.

And that's the atmosphere we grew up under. My mom got saved and filled with the Holy Ghost before I was born. So we were born in the Pentecostal realm. It was nothing for us to hear of speaking in tongues, the laughing in the Spirit—those were things we grew up with. I thought that was the norm.

When my mom got filled with the Holy Ghost and saved, my brother Adrian never got well from spinal meningitis. He was getting all curled up. I never met him. He was the oldest. My mom said that, when they got back from the meetings in Wyola, he just started curling up backwards even worse. So, one day, she said she realized how selfish she was. And so she told the Lord, "If you want to take him home, take him home, if that is your will." And not too long after that, my brother died. Later, when they went to Bullis Mortuary in Hardin and they opened up the coffin, she had a vision of Jesus holding my brother. He had rosy cheeks, and there wasn't even nothing wrong with him. She said she couldn't even cry. She said people probably thought she was heartless, but she didn't even cry. She couldn't cry. But later on, when she missed him, she'd get on her knees and start speaking in tongues, and the Holy Spirit would comfort her. That was the beginning of her walk with the Lord.

SEPARATED LIVES: "THEY CAME OUT OF THEIR INDIAN RELIGION"

My mom lived here in Pryor. She worked closely with Rosie Lincoln, another lady who got saved, and she talked a lot about how they had house meetings here. They didn't have established churches back then. The Pentecostals were kind of freelancing! They didn't have a church, and they were strongly nondenominational. So they would have house meetings. They'd also have camp meetings, and they'd have revivals. This is where Harold Carpenter from Lodge Grass was very instrumental. He was kind of an elder for them. They kind of looked up to him. He would come and have meetings here in Pryor, and then during that time my mom and Rosie Lincoln would have house meetings. Rosie was kind of the leader here in Pryor. They had a lot of house meetings and people started getting saved.

People who would get sick around here in Pryor, they would go and get prayer, and they would get healed and start serving God. So that's how the Pentecostal movement kind of started here in the Pryor District. Harold Carpenter was going to all the districts after that great outpouring in Wyola. People were getting saved left and right, filled with the Holy Ghost, and so a lot of people started coming to the Lord. It was kind of interesting—there were a couple relatives who were strong Catholics who were trying to get my Uncle Tex out of the Pentecostal movement. But when they started praying for him, they ended up both getting saved and filled with the Holy Ghost.

There were a number of elderly people who got saved in these prayer meetings here in Pryor who came out of their Indian religion—Annie Big Day, Julia Rock Above, Cecilia Stands. These are all my grandaunts. Talk about separated lives! Annie Big Day's husband was really into Indian religion and was real traditional, but she just loved the Lord. Nobody could stop her. My mom would tell me how those ladies were hot and on fire for the Lord. All the young people would be having Bible studies and Annie Big Day would be right in there with them, eating popcorn and having Bible studies. Annie was very materialistic, and she liked her blankets and her material for dresses and stuff. But she got saved and got delivered from all that materialism. And she stopped all her Indian religion stuff. It was a separated life for her. And that's the way I grew up. My mother and the others, they lived a very separated life. Hand games, arrow-throwing tournaments, powwows—they put those things aside. And that really helped me when I became a Christian, because they lived very separated lives.

Harold Carpenter was a man that really preached against a lot of things. I think he might have had an influence on them in this way. But they lost their desire for things like that. My mom said that when she got saved she just lost her desire for the world. Her in-laws were into Sun Dance, and my grandma and grandpa were very traditional. They were really into Indian religion, and my grandmother was in the Tobacco Society. But my mom said she just "lost it for the world" when she got saved. So when they would move over to camp at the Sun Dance grounds, she wouldn't go. She just stayed back at the house, and my grandmother would get worried. She'd say, "You're young. You should go!" But my mom said she just lost it. And see, that's what happened to me when I got saved. I just lost it for the world. I think for a lot of these, when they meet that true and living God, they lose it for the world and worldly things.

RHEA'S CONVERSION STORY

I got saved on August 28, 1972, during a convention at Full Gospel Revival Tabernacle in Billings, where I now pastor. That's when I got saved and started sitting under their ministry. I never knew I'd be a pastor down the road. See, what happened, I kind of went my own way for many years. I used to make God promises that, if he'd keep me out of trouble, I would serve him for the rest of my life. I was scared of the end of the world. I was scared of dying. I knew I was going to hell, because of the teachings I heard in Sunday school. I always bring out the illustration of the salt-and-pepper shakers. One represented sin; one represented Jesus. That always stuck with me. I think Sunday school and knowing there is a heaven and hell got me through my teen years. And so for myself, I thought, "I'll get saved when I am forty years old, when all the fun is over." I also thought, "I'm gonna get educated. I'm gonna make lots of money. I'm gonna have a big executive kind of job." I was looking at New York City, Los Angeles, Chicago—you know, I kind of laugh now. For a little girl who grew up on a gravel road, with no telephones, I had these big dreams! But that was my thinking. So, I studied in school. I went to college. When I was still in college, the Lord kept dealing with me. And I had a dream that it was the end of the world. The sky was just lit up orange. I fell on my knees—but it was too late. I felt just terrible in this dream because it seemed so real. When I woke up, I remember looking around and thinking, "I'm still here! I still have a chance to change my life and make it into heaven one day."

That dream haunted me when I went back to college. I tried to be good—to live good and not party or run around, because I was getting into the partying scene like most college students. And I was heading down the wrong road. That next summer, I was living and working in Billings, not far from home. I had an apartment. And I remember I was sitting on the edge of my bed, and in my mind's eye I saw a pure white ladder. And I saw a black ladder going down. And it was like, if I give my heart to the Lord, and serve him, things will work out in my life, and I'll eventually make heaven my home. But if I stay in sin, things are going to get worse, and I'll eventually end up in hell. And today, as I talk to you, I can still see that black ladder and that white ladder.

I was just sitting there on the edge of my bed. I wasn't even a Christian. But the Lord had been dealing with me. I was being crazy and was rebellious. That next summer, I came back from college and I was seventeen, so I thought I'd do my own thing. But my folks put me in my place. My mom caught me drinking, so she took me to Billings and had Brother and Sister Mosley pray for me. I was rebellious! But their prayers haunted me. Finally, the Lord dealt with me and dealt with me, until August of 1972. They had a convention at our church and I remember my mom had gone. Some of us would drop her off at church and then go to Kmart. We were trying not to party; we were trying to live a good life. It was so boring—all we did was movies and Kmart, movies and Kmart!

So we dropped my mom off, and when we came back after her, the windows of the church were opened and people were shouting and having a "hallelujah time." I told my sister and my friend, "It's time for us to serve God. We can't get ready at the last minute." They agreed. The next day we put dresses on and went into church, and I got saved. I had a glorious conversion, because the man was preaching down my back alley. He was from Philadelphia, but he was preaching about living right and loving God. And, see, I was trying to live right—but I was doing it without God. When he had the altar call, I went up. There was a whole bunch of people who went up. But I remember that I just poured my heart out to the Lord. That's the night I surrendered. I said, "Jesus, take me. Use me any way you want. I don't care how hard it gets. Lord, I'll serve you for the rest of my life. I'm tired of going my own way." I just wept and wept. Then I saw a great big, round, yellow light. And it engulfed me. It was just me and Jesus. I prayed and prayed, and when I got done I was the only one up there at the altar.

I got saved and I went out the door never the same. There was a generational curse of alcoholism in our family on my dad's side. A craving for alcohol was starting to get a hold of me. My grandmother used to just weep with my dad and his uncles not to drink. From a young age, that had an influence on me, to see how sad my grandmother was. She would just weep, begging them not to drink. But that night the Lord saved me and delivered me. Ever since then, any desire for alcohol went out the window. The restlessness was gone. And I got gloriously saved that night when I finally surrendered to the Lord. The Lord changed my life.

Medicine Bundles, Smudging, and Evil Spirits

One of my granduncles was a medicine man. And one time he was in Bullis Mortuary all night long when a daughter had died.[6] And all night he saw spirits coming and going. And they did what I call indoctrination. They got him. See, he had a medicine bundle in the family, and my dad really believed in him. 'Cause one time my dad was at my granduncle's house and my elderly grandma was here at home. And he told my dad, "You bet-ter go home, because your mother's coming out of the door." So my dad came home, and my grandma was going out of the house. So my dad really believed in that uncle of his. But when he was dying, some Christians got to him, and he repented and made things right. One day my dad told me, "Did you know that when your granduncle was dying, he told me, 'All that I have been doing is of the devil'?" After that, my dad hasn't really gotten into Indian medicine. That kind of broke it off for him because he really looked up to that man.

A lot of Indians don't realize how medicine attracts evil spirits. There was an aunt I used to visit all the time. When I went in that home as a child, there was a medicine chest there. And her family would say, "Don't sit on that! That's sacred." And they were forever seeing things looking at them in the windows. That house always had an eerie feeling. But at our home, because my mom was Holy Ghost–filled, praying all the time, we never noticed nothing in our house. It was always peaceful. Only later did I find out they had medicine bundles in that chest. After I got saved, I began to realize that medicine bundles attract evil spirits into the home.

It's the same thing with smudging. You know, people do the smudg-ing, but that attracts evil spirits. Then some people pray with cigarettes—tobacco. That also attracts evil spirits, because they are delving into the spirit world. When you use those things, you are connecting into the spirit world. And I've seen people at the hospital that do that, and then spirits bother them. I tell them, "Don't do that! Use the olive oil instead of all that sweetgrass." I call it the gos-pill—that olive oil, that anointing oil.[7] That's the true medicine. In the Catholic Church, they are into form and ritual, and they use incense. So the Catholic churches here on the reservation readily accept all the smudging, too. In the Old Testament, they had incense like that. But in the New Testament, you don't see Jesus smudging, you know? You don't see him doing all that the high priests did in the Old Testament. It is kind of like forming a ritual. In the New Testament, you don't need all that stuff. You go directly to God. That's the way I look at it. You don't need the substitutes like that.

One night when I had already graduated from high school, I was with my cousins—Spooky, Jolene, and Anna. And we were riding around town here. My cousin had this little truck. We were going by Chief Plenty Coups Park, and Spooky—he's a real prankster—was driving.[8] So right when we went by the grave of Plenty Coups, he took a cigarette out and said, "Here, have a smoke!" And right when he did that, there was a big pound on the top of our cab—right on top of the pickup. And I said, "Spooky, don't be doing that." His name is Marlon, but he was born on Halloween, so we all know him as Spooky. And he said, "No, it isn't me. Look!" And I could see that his arms were too short, because the thump was right in the middle.

So we turned around in Plenty Coups Park, and while we were heading towards town we were singing these 49er songs, these Indian lyrical songs. They're in English, but to a powwow beat. And all of a sudden, I heard this woman in a high-pitched voice, like the women that usually sing with the powwow singers, and she was singing with us. I looked at Anna and Jolene—they have bullfrog voices—and I said, "Did you hear that? Somebody was singing with us!" And they said, "Yes!" We told Spooky, "Go to that corner store right here in Pryor, and park." We got out and thought maybe somebody was in the back of the pickup. We jumped off and looked in the back, and nobody was there. I had chills from my head all the way to my feet. After I got saved, I understood that we were connecting into a spirit world with that tobacco because there are medicine bundles over at Plenty Coups Park. Plenty Coups's medicine is the chickadee.

Clan Uncles and Clan Aunts: Pentecostal Revisions

After that, everybody got scared for us. They thought maybe we were going to have a car accident or something bad was going to happen. They wanted us to have a clan feed, and that's when my mom took me to Brother Mosley's home in Billings. She told Brother Mosley, and he right away said, "Those were definitely evil spirits." When he said that, it was a big relief, because somebody understood me.

With my mom being a Holy Ghost–filled Christian, we never smudge. We don't run to clan uncles and aunts, either. My dad, not being a Christian but being a traditional man, he was the one into all that. But we never ran to clan uncles or clan aunts. That's what traditional Crows do if something bad is happening, or if they see something bad—something like we heard while driving that pickup truck and everything. They always say, "Go to your clan uncles and clan aunts." So they'll invite them in, and then they'll usually give them four gifts. They'll have a meal, and then those clan aunts or clan uncles will pray over them. Traditional Crows do that. My dad, not being a Christian, he was always into that stuff. But my mom and her sisters would never do that. If there was ever a need in the house, they would come together, get in a room, and they'd start praying. That's how my mother raised us. She was never into stuff like that. We were never into the smudging, or into the clan uncles and clan aunts. The scriptures say that if you don't have the spirit of Christ, you are none of his. So sometimes these people you bring in to pray might not even be Christians. Their prayers might hit the ceiling and come down. That's the way I look at it. So if they're ever gonna do something like that, I always get Christians to come and pray. I always look for Holy Ghost–filled Christians—let *them* be the ones to pray, and give *them* the gifts!

I believe our traditional ancestors before Christianity had a form of religion, and in their fasting that animal would come in and intercept their prayers. So then the animal became their god. But when you look at Genesis 1:26, God gave us dominion over the fowl of the air, over the things underwater, over things on the land. We're not to worship eagles. Sometimes the traditional people will get excited and say, "Oh, I saw an eagle!" But maybe that eagle was just being nosy and wanted to see why these humans were gathering. They got sharp eyes and are always looking for food. But we make it spiritual. Then the devil works on your superstition. He feeds on that superstition. He really likes that. You know, he's been around a long time, too.

One time when my folks were still alive and I was here at home, in the middle of the night I woke up and heard an owl hooting on top of the house. I didn't even open my mouth, but in the spirit I said, "Now you leave me alone. You know I don't believe in you. You get away in the name of Jesus and stop bothering us!" That's what I said in my spirit, in my heart. And that thing quieted down, and I never heard from him the rest of the night. If you know your authority in the Lord, then those things don't bother you. I don't want my message from an owl; I want my message from the Holy Ghost. That's the way I look at it. If God's gonna show me something, let it be by the Spirit—not by an animal in that way.

Spiritual Strongholds

Some reservations are really strong into their traditional ways. They're really into their Indian medicine, Sun Dances, and peyote. And these are strongholds in terms of spiritual warfare. That's why there's a lot of prayer going up. These strongholds need to be broken. One time I went up in the Pryor Mountains with some of my family. There are medicine bundles being kept up there by our traditional elders. We took my dad's pickup, and we were trying to get firewood. So we went up this little mountain, and my nephew was in the back. He was just a little kid then. And all of a sudden, when we got up to the top, there was a knock on the back window. I said, "Jaris, what'ya doing?" He said, "Auntie, it isn't me." So we went a little bit further, and then more knocking. I said, "Jaris, . . ." but he said, "It's not me!"

He was standing in the middle of the pickup bed when there was a knock on that window. At first, you kind of want to get scared. But then we were like, "Wait a minute!" In the Crow language, *Akbaatashée* means to anoint with oil—or "the greasers." I guess the non-Christian community around here gave that name to the Pentecostal Christians because they used anointing oil so much. So I got out my olive oil, and I started pouring it. "You demons of hell," I said, "this is my mountain!" And I really started binding and rebuking. And we had a really nice day.

NOTES

1. For more on Nellie Pretty Eagle Stewart and the early history of Crow Pentecostalism, see Mark Clatterbuck, "Healing Hills and Sacred Songs: Crow Pentecostalism, Anti-Traditionalism, and Native Religious Identity," *Spiritus* 12 (Fall 2012): 252–56.
2. St. Xavier is a town located in the Big Horn District, roughly in the center of the Crow Reservation.
3. Wyola is a town located in the southeast corner of the Crow Reservation.
4. Jim (Chippewa) and Faith (Crow) Chosa are directors of Day Chief Ministries based in Yellowtail, Montana, on the Crow Reservation. Duane Bull Chief is pastor of The Father's House, a Pentecostal church located at Crow Agency. He has also served as spiritual advisor to the Crow tribal legislature.
5. The Azusa Street Revival was a spiritual movement that began in 1906 in a small, abandoned building in Los Angeles, California, in which participants seeking baptism in the Holy Spirit spoke in tongues and demonstrated other ecstatic

spiritual experiences. It lasted for several years and is widely regarded as the beginning of the modern-day Pentecostal movement.

6. Bullis Mortuary is located in the town of Hardin along I-90 on the northern border of the Crow Reservation.

7. The use of anointing oil was so common among early Crow Pentecostals that they became known as *Akbaatashée*—"the greasers." Still today, anointing with oil for healing, protection, or deliverance is a ubiquitous element in Crow Pentecostal prayer services.

8. Chief Plenty Coups (1848–1932) is widely recognized as the last principal chief of the Crow Tribe. His log home and sacred spring have been incorporated into a Montana State Park and National Historic Landmark named in his honor. The park is located in the Pryor District of the Crow Reservation.

6

Hand Game Demons and Medicine Man Curses

AN INTERVIEW WITH
FANNIE PLAIN FEATHER WARD

For more than twenty years, Fannie Ward served as youth director for a Pentecostal mission church in the reservation town of Pryor. During that time, she also worked as a kindergarten teacher for St. Charles Catholic School, located just a few miles down the road from the church. While her bivocational status reflects the common Crow pattern of multidenominational participation, Fannie's own religious faith is rooted firmly in Pentecostal soil.

In the stories that follow, Fannie refers more than once to Old Man Plain Feather, her great-grandfather who was reportedly 114 years old at the time of his death. Plain Feather was a well-known medicine man who

Fannie Ward in the sanctuary of Mountain Crow Worship Center in Pryor, Crow Reservation. *Photo by Dave Kapferer*

lived in the reservation's Pryor District. In 1949, he hosted a Sun Dance for the healing of his critically ailing wife. When she died within the year, he appeared to lose confidence in the ceremony. This opened the way for his eventual embrace of Christianity, which took place after he experienced a powerful vision of Jesus one winter up in the Pryor Mountains. In 1955, he was among those who received prayer at the hands of Oral Roberts during an evangelistic crusade at Crow Agency. About that same time, his granddaughter Ruby, who would later become Fannie's mother, experienced "speaking in tongues" at a revival led by Harold Carpenter, a well-known Crow Pentecostal preacher. After that experience, Ruby recalls her grandfather telling her, "I've got medicine, but what you have now, that Holy Ghost, is way better than what I have. So I'm not giving it to you kids." In the end, Plain Feather instructed his family to bury him with his medicine bundles, rather than passing them on to his own children and grandchildren.[1]

Old Man Plain Feather's confidence in the superiority of Christian faith over the power of indigenous religion is reflected, three generations later, in Fannie's own decision to choose the teachings of Jesus over traditional Crow practices when she was still a child. Her narrative opens by recalling her first experience at a Crow hand game tournament. Hand games are wildly popular, and fiercely competitive, contests held among the six districts on the Crow Reservation. Teams take turns facing off in a game of chance and deception as players alternate hiding, and then guessing the location of, small bone objects. Each team typically places the task of guessing into the hands of a medicine man known for possessing *xapáaliia*—a specific application of *baaxpée*, or "medicine"—that helps bring success in games of chance.[2]

Being raised by a devout Pentecostal mother, Fannie was strictly forbidden to attend hand games as a child for fear of becoming entangled with such "medicine." As seen elsewhere in this collection of narratives, Crow Pentecostals commonly regard *baaxpée*, as used in Crow ceremonies, to be of demonic origin, and Fannie's experience as described below confirmed her mother's warnings. Her second story follows a similar pattern, although this time she tells of encountering demonic forces at a peyote meeting. The story dates to that same time when, as an adolescent, she was exploring some of the traditional ways that her Pentecostal upbringing had denied her.

She recalls spending the night in a truck outside a peyote meeting, where she watched dark figures circling, entering, and exiting the tipi through the night. The experience convinced her, once again, that traditional Native ceremonies are fraught with demonic forces.

Fannie's third and final story offers yet another critique of traditional Crow medicine, once more linking it to the demonic. The account places the spiritual power of medicine men in open warfare against the power of the Holy Ghost. In the end, Fannie's Pentecostal faith prevails. Her prayers turn back the dark medicine curses that were intended for her, resulting in a tragic demise for each of the four medicine men who sought her harm. The following interview took place at the Mountain Crow Worship Center in Pryor.

Gambling with Death at the Hand Games

During the spring when I was in sixth grade, I was lookin' at whether Christianity was the way, or if it was maybe *not* the way, for me as a Native American. I wanted to experience more of, I guess, the culture. I wanted to look on the religion side of what our culture was mainly about. Growing up in a Christian home, I saw a lot of things that I thought weren't real, that weren't for me. Being young at the time and brought up in a Christian home, my mom forbid us as her children from going to any hand games. We weren't brought up that way.

However, as a young person, I guess we all experience wanting to see whether those places were good or not. So I ended up going to a hand game during the wintertime. I think it was a senior hand game. My older sister and I caught a ride to my aunt's house, and from there I took a ride to the hand game with her, knowing that I wasn't supposed to go. My sister said, "You better not go!" But I ended up going. My aunt was in one of the hand games there. It was the team from Reno District that we were playing.

As soon as we arrived, I got with my friends. And, you know, all Crow children learn how to "hooky bob." That's when you catch onto the outside of cars as they ride along, and that's what we were doing. We were just being kids outside. At one point, several of us were sitting on the trunk of a car.

And as we were facing the west of the Round Hall there at Crow Agency where the hand games were taking place, I happened to see this dark figure. I just wanted to be there hanging out with all of my friends, when all of a sudden I saw this dark figure behind this big tree. At first, I thought I was just seeing things. Then as I watched it, I saw eyes on this figure.

I looked at my friends that were sitting on the car, and they said, "Did you see that?" I thought I was the only one that saw it. So I said, "Yeah, I saw it!" One of them just started screaming, "That's a demon! That's a big demon!" It was a black figure. I couldn't really make it out, but there were eyes there, and it moved several times as we were all standing there. There were at least ten of us and there were other kids on the other side that saw it, too. So we all ran inside the building. Inside, I went straight to my aunt, who was in there with all the crowd. Here, come to find out, the Reno team had won their game within ten minutes. It's usually not like that at all. It sometimes takes hours to win a hand game.

The hand game is actually a game that was adopted from another tribe. And what I was told coming up in a Christian home is what my great-grandfather Old Man Plain Feather told my mom. He told her about an old man who went out on a vision quest. And while he was on this vision quest fasting, he saw these people playing the hand game. As they were playing, there were these buffalo robes lined up there which represented the sticks. It's really just a guessing game, as these bones are hitting your hand. Well, in this vision, that old man saw that these people were gambling. And those buffalo robes represented people that are already dead. Back in the day, the Crow people used to bury their dead in buffalo robes up on these raised platforms. They wouldn't put 'em underground; they had 'em up high. These buffalo robes were laying there as these people were lined up facing each other. In this old man's vision, he ended up seeing that they were gambling over people's lives—the ones that were already dead, and the ones that were about to die. He saw that it wasn't a good type of a cultural game for the Crow people.

So he informed my grandfather about it, and I don't think my grandfather ever participated in this game. And we were told not to participate, either. That's why my mother—not only being Christian, but being told by her grandfather not to participate in this hand game—taught us not to participate. When I was there in that hall as a kid, I wasn't participating, but I was still there. And to be there and to witness that dark figure, it really put a lot of fear in me about what I was told not to do.

So I ran to my aunt and told her, "I wanna get out of here!" And we left right away. I told my sister what happened, and she said, "You shouldn't have been there! I told you not to go." And she really gave me a hard time! When I told my mom about it, she just said, "Well, now you know why I don't want you to be around those places. Because there's spirits there that are not of the Lord, and I just don't want you to be a part of that." So that was a lesson there, and it showed me that there's a good reason we aren't supposed to go to those types of cultural games. She just didn't want me to see or be a part of anything like that. And that's what I experienced firsthand. That was my first and last time ever being at a hand game.

DEMONIC PEYOTE GIANTS

I'm pretty sure it was during that following spring that I went to a peyote meeting with that same aunt. She was really traditional. She was my mom's youngest sister and was raised by traditional people in addition to my grandfather and them. She was raised by other family members. They wanted to adopt her, so they did. So they raised her, basically, and brought her up in that type of environment. I spent a lot of time with her that spring, and we ended up going to a peyote meeting. Again, I just wanted to know more about the traditional ways, and I thought maybe this was the way to go about a religion. I was looking for something to fulfill my religious side. So I went with her. I think it was a peyote meeting put up for someone who just graduated from school, so I ended up going with her that evening.

It was kinda later in the evening, probably toward midnight, when she went into the peyote meeting that was held in the St. Xavier area here on the reservation. I was sitting in the truck after they all went inside the tipi. It was really dark outside, and the only light they had was the fire going inside the tipi that was facing east. Throughout that night I kept seeing little dark figures outside the tipi. I thought I was just seeing things. But they were there! One was on the right-hand side of the tipi from where I was sitting. A second one popped up by the door and went around the side of the tipi. The next one was around the back of it. Another one was on the west side of the tipi, near the back. There were these four figures. I saw them! I wasn't afraid. I just sat there the whole time, letting the belief sink in that I was actually seeing these things.

Just before the sun came up, I saw a dark figure as high as the flaps vanish right into the tipi. As it went in, that's right when the sun came up and they were done. And, see, like each time they were done singin' a song, these figures came out. So from that time on, I just closed my eyes and I asked the Lord to protect me. Because I knew that these figures were not friendly spirits. They were spirits that were demonic. I went home and I told my mom about it. And she said again, "Those are things that I told you not to participate in." She goes, "Well, you had to see for yourself, 'cause you were really wanting to know more about it. Now you saw it for yourself."

Then she asked me, "Well, what did you think of it?" And I told her, I said, "Well, I don't think it's something that I want to participate in 'cause it didn't give me no peace. It showed me that wasn't good." Because all of this was taking place at a really dark time, and these spirits were just the presence of evil. But I didn't fear it. I knew I was protected. So I just allowed myself to accept the fact that these two traditional situations that I experienced weren't for me. These were something that I knew I wasn't supposed to be a part of, and I had to see it for myself. It was more or less comforting for me, knowing that this wasn't the way.

Now, being a Christian looking back on it, I just thank the Lord for giving me that peace and that assurance that whatever I was trying to dabble into wasn't for me. And it's nothing for anybody! Because it never brought me any peace, and I've never been to a peyote ceremony again—except for one that I saw in seventh grade, but I didn't take part in it. I was just there for a moment and I left. But it's just something that my mom brought us up knowing that it's not of God. It's not of the Lord. It's not something that the Lord wants us to participate in. Because her grandfather brought her up in the tradition that those ways are not of the Lord and the only true way is Jesus Christ.

HOLY GHOST POWER VERSUS MEDICINE MEN

I was working as a youth pastor for a Pentecostal church on another reservation in Montana back in the summer of 1991. I worked there for two and a half years. During the second year I was there, we had lot of kids coming for children's church and a lot of youth coming in. And the more youth that we were getting in, it was just really exciting because they were basically getting on fire and wanting to know more about Jesus and the Christian ways compared to what they experienced growing up in a traditional way.

At the time, the pastor, his wife, and I were all living in the basement of the church there. And one night as I was going to bed, getting ready for the next day, I always prayed. So I knelt down and I was gonna pray—when the Holy Spirit spoke to me and said, "Just be ready." Then as I was getting in bed, I could hear drums and I knew where the drums were coming from. They were coming from up the road where this traditional man was living. I didn't think anything more about it. But then, in the middle of the night, the pastor's wife came in and told me, "Don't be afraid—it's me." So I said, "What's going on?" And as she came in, there was like a really cold draft that just now came in with her, and she had a blanket wrapped around her.

And she goes, "Fannie, we have to pray. I don't know what's going on, but we have to pray!" So we just knelt down and we started praying. And we started praying in the Holy Spirit. And the Holy Spirit just said to me, "Put your hand on her. Put your hand on her back." She was shivering—it was cold, it was midwinter. I just put my hand on the small of her back and I started praying for her. And she was just shaking. But as I put my hand on her and we were praying for like an hour or two, we finally felt the release, a breakthrough, as we prayed through.

When she went to close my door on her way out, she saw an angel at the foot of my bed with a sword. Then as she went to check on both of her children, she saw two angels in there. And as she shut her own door before crawling back into bed, she saw an angel at the foot of her bed, too. At the time, the pastor wasn't there at the church. He was at a meeting where he had been invited to speak in the town of Circle in eastern Montana. But, as we found out later, he said the Holy Spirit prompted him to stop and pray because he felt something was going on at home and he did. And that exact time of when he started praying was when his wife came into my room that night.

The next morning, I went to work and these two young girls came running up to me. They were part of the youth group and had been going to our youth group for a while. They basically grew up in that church, because they used to go to children's church and now one was an eighth-grader and the other was a senior in high school. She came running up to me as they saw me pulling up to the school there, and they said, "Are you okay?" and I said, "What do you mean?" And they said, "No, really, are you okay?" And I said, "Yeah, we're okay." Then they asked me about the pastors, and I said they were okay, too.

They said, "Didn't you hear those drums last night?" "Yeah, I heard 'em," I said, "Why?" And they both said, "They were for you." And I said, "What do you mean, they were for us?" And they said, "Because we started goin' to church and our dad didn't like us goin' to church, they put this thing on you—a kind of curse." But those girls even told their father that it wouldn't work on us, because we were the true ones that were there and nothing would happen to us.

Later on I found out that those four men that tried to put a curse on us, that wanted to run us out of there—well, those things basically backfired on them. They were leaders there on that reservation at the time. One had diabetes, one had a stroke, one had a heart attack, and I think one had cancer. All four of them—something happened to them. It just showed that we were covered by the blood of Jesus. The prophet Isaiah says, "no weapon that's formed against me shall prosper," and God's word stands true even to this day.

NOTES

1. Ruby Plain Feather, interview by author, July 17, 2011, Pryor, Montana.
2. For an explanation of *baaxpée* and *xapáaliia* as specifically used in the service of successful gaming, see chapter 7, "Application of *Xapáaliia*" in Frey, *World of the Crow Indians*, 143–49.

PENTECOSTALISM, CULTURE, AND POLITICS

7

The Bible, the Devil, and Crow Blood

AN INTERVIEW WITH
KENNETH PRETTY ON TOP SR.

Spirit of Life Lighthouse for the Nations Foursquare Church is the largest Pentecostal church on the Crow Reservation. And for the past twenty-five years, Kenneth Pretty On Top Sr. has been its pastor. In many ways, Kenneth shares a great deal in common with most other Pentecostal pastors on the reservation. His faith is rooted deeply in the Bible, he refuses to take part in many traditional Crow ceremonies, and he continually oversees a variety of evangelistic and mission-team outreach programs on the reservation in conjunction with churches across the country.

Yet, in other ways, he stands apart from many of his Pentecostal colleagues. His soft-spoken preaching style, his refusal to openly condemn

Kenneth Pretty On Top Sr. preaching during an interdenominational Sunday morning service held at the powwow dance arbor during Crow Fair. *Photo by Dave Kapferer*

traditional Crow religions from the pulpit, and his commitment to working across denominational lines cause some of his peers to question his Pentecostal loyalty or accuse him of "compromise." That he frequently leads sweats in a lodge on his own land generates even more consternation among his Pentecostal critics. Through it all, Kenneth rarely feels the need to defend himself, invariably returning to the Bible and responding to his naysayers with a wry wit and conceding their right to follow their own convictions.

Kenneth's comments highlight a number of key principles that guide his thriving ministry, beginning with his understanding of Crow culture. He rejects the claim that taking part in tribal traditions and ceremonies is a necessary part of being Crow, arguing that Crow traditions are often revered to the point of becoming functional "idols" among Traditionalists committed to protecting the old ways. Instead of placing tradition at the heart of Crow identity, Kenneth insists that one's blood is what truly counts. As he says below, "bein' a Crow is you got that Crow blood."

After Crow blood, core tribal values rank next for Kenneth in establishing one's Crow credentials. These values include hospitality, love of family, and respect for others. In this way, he decenters the role of traditional Crow ceremonies and other religious practices, paving the way for Crow Christians to fully defend their tribal identity, even while rejecting many of the traditions commonly regarded as quintessentially Crow. As he explains below, Kenneth is willing to participate in some traditional rituals by downplaying their religious significance. In the case of the sweat lodge, for example, he emphasizes the health benefits the ritual provides, thereby avoiding conflict with his religious beliefs.

Kenneth likewise challenges what he regards as overly sentimental portrayals of old-time Crows who lived in a romanticized past "back in the day." Like many Crow Pentecostals, he closely identifies traditional tribal religion with the tribe's difficult, nomadic, and unpredictable pre-Christian days. Furthermore, he believes that the tribe's mineral wealth and improved standard of living in modern times is directly attributable to blessings poured upon them by the God of the Bible, blessings that will grow in proportion to the tribe's commitment to honoring Jesus Christ. This interview took place at the Spirit of Life Lighthouse for the Nations

Foursquare Church at Crow Agency, where Kenneth serves as senior pastor.

❁

Hanging On to the Bible "without Hurting People"

In our mission statement here at the church, one of the things we do is look for very different ways of preaching the Gospel without compromising the word of God. Because a lot of times people will accuse you of compromising. But if you stay straight with the Bible—well, one verse in the Bible that really keeps me going is "the truth shall set you free." This is why I really push Bible study—Bible study, and looking at the word when we preach. Study it, and listen to what the Bible says. Because if you use your own words to push the people, then it ain't gonna work. Now the Bible—his word is more powerful than yours. His wisdom is more powerful than yours. So you need to depend on that. You need to depend on his word, and the truth shall set you free.

I think that's one of the things we need to hang on to. We hang on to his word and what the Bible says, without hurting people. Of course, when you go back to the Bible, there are places where it says, "Don't do this" or "Don't do that." And sometimes people use those verses to turn around and push people down. But the Bible is there to bring people to God, to build a relationship with God. But not everybody sees that. The whole story from the beginning to the end is about relationship. We lost that relationship, and God wants to bring that relationship back together again.

God loves people. I think it says somewhere in the Bible, "Love God and love people." You might want to look for that in the Bible. You just might find it there somewhere, you know! [laughing] That's where I'm at, and that's where our convictions are, too. And my convictions are the same way as my wife Hannah's. We're the same way. And if you live this kind of life that I'm talking about, then people will see that. You don't have to go out there and preach, or put out tracts. Just live that life that God has given you. Be an example, walk that walk, and people will see that. You don't have to go cut people down.

One of the things that really gets me is that, as God's people—in different denominations, different churches—we're all God's children. It's just the same way with us and our children. We got children, we got grandchildren. God has children, too. What if somebody says something bad to you about your children, about your son or your daughter? What if they talked bad to you about your children? How would you feel? You'd be a little bit disturbed over that. I believe that God's the same way when we talk bad about his other children. He says, "Hey, these are all my people. I love 'em."

COMPROMISE AND SYNCRETISM

As far as compromising goes, I don't think a lot of people understand that word when they accuse us of compromising. I think they hear it from preachers, from evangelists, and all this talk about how there's compromise in the world, in the church, and all this stuff. But they need to look at it a little closer. Compromising is mixing two beliefs together—syncretism, trying to bring this religion and that religion together to mesh them as one. But there's only one way, and that's through Christ. That's through God, through Jesus Christ. But what some people try to do is mix all this stuff together. I heard one time a guy who said, "Have you ever tried to drink coffee where you take a cup of coffee and put some orange juice in there, put some pop in there, put some grape juice in there, all this stuff, and then drink it? What would it taste like?" I think that's what a lot of people try to do.

There's one individual, and I really enjoyed his story, he was really into the Native tradition and he was being groomed for that, but then he gave his life to the Lord and went to Christianity. When his dad found out about that, he came to him and he gave him one piece of advice. He told him, "You either go one way, or the other way. Don't be playing with it."

When you have a strong conviction, you don't need to force your conviction on other people. Just listen to 'em. Hear what they say first, and then go from there. And I tell people, if you want to read a good book about that, there's four good books you can read that'll really help you. They're called the four Gospels: Matthew, Mark, Luke, and John. Read that and look at Jesus's ministry. After you go through that, then you can go through the Epistles. Look at them. Look how Paul preached. Look how Paul brought out the word. Paul was pretty sharp, but yet he had that heart. He was blunt, but he had that heart. He was strict, but he had that heart.

Those are things we need to be looking at as pastors and as children of God. We need to show that heart, so people see us and say, "Hey, what's this? What do you got?" And then you don't need to argue with them. The Bible, to me, isn't something to be argued over. You need to study it and get your own convictions from it, but I don't have to tell you what to believe or what not to believe. That's one of the things that you need to do. That choice is yours. In everything we do, we make our own choices—whether we go in this direction or that direction.

As Christians, we can be so judgmental. We can be judgmental about everything around us, but what does that do? That just brings the people down. One of our biggest problems in being Christians is that we don't walk that walk. We have a tough time with that. This is why I think a lot of people reject Christianity. That was one of the things I didn't like about Christianity before I got into it. I seen all these people goin' through that and puttin' their convictions on other people and cutting them down. But it shouldn't be that way. The Bible is to bring people together, draw people together. That's what it's for. Give 'em hope that there is eternal life.

So I try to live that life, live what the Bible says, and I have a tough time. Even now, thirty some years later, I still have a tough time doin' it. But we have to keep praying, keep goin' in that direction. And a lot of this stuff gets a little—I wouldn't say easier—but it's a little easier as you go along. It takes time. God can do it overnight, but I think God gives us that experience to find out what's goin' on. And I think if you share your experience with what the Bible says and what God has done for you, then I think people will see that more than anything else. It's the way you live. Be an example. And I think that's what we try to portray here at the church.

Drawing Lines: Medicine Bundles and Smudging

We're open to a lot of things, but there are some areas where I have to put my foot down. But I try to do that in a gentle way. I say, "Lord, give me the right words to say, the right things to say so I don't push 'em away but bring 'em to you, Lord."

One place where I put my foot down is when it comes to some of the traditions, some of the rituals that they have. That's my conviction, and that's one of the things where I'll put my foot down. Say, for example, medicine bundles. Why do you want to look at idols? But then you have that other problem, where some of the churches and denominations get us off track, because people see some of the same things as medicine bundles! These other churches have their own little things—they got their portraits, they got their statues. For us Pentecostals, we got our oil and all that other stuff. But I think you can't mix that stuff together.

The Bible—again, I come back to the Bible—it tells you what you can do. For example, you can have communion. Remember the breaking of the bread at the Last Supper? Jesus said, "Do this until I return." Then the second thing he said was, "Make disciples of all nations, baptize in the name of the Father, the Son, and the Holy Spirit." You know, them two are commandments that we need to really look at. Those are things that can be allowed in church. You know, there's no problem with that. Fasting is another one, you know. Those are things that we need to do.

Then again, we can sometimes take these things the wrong way, too. And you have to really think about that. Like fasting. You know, in the Sun Dance lodge they fast for three days. But in their fasting, what are they looking for? What's the motive behind that? Because the enemy is a mimic. He'll copy a lot of stuff. Even being Pentecostal, even thinkin' about tongues. If that's all you're looking for is speaking in tongues—hey, the devil can give you that! He'll give you tongues. You want to see visions? He'll give you that, too. But we have to be careful. You have to read the Bible. You have to keep going back to the Bible and ask, "What does the Bible say?" To do that, you have to study the Bible. You have to come to the word all the time.

Some of the specific things people want to do, they might have to stop those things as they come into the church. I might have to say, "Hey, I can't do this. We cannot do this." And that's my conviction. It's our church. I talk to 'em and I try to do it in a gentle way, and I believe that a lot of people have more respect if you approach 'em that way than to cut 'em down.

Just like that one lady who asked me about smudging. I think she was from Oregon, you know, up in one of them cities over there. She called me up and we started talking about that. "There's something that I'm really having convictions over," she said. "I work at a kindergarten school on a small reservation in Washington State, and they want to come in and smudge all the kids, including the teachers." And she said, "I don't agree with it. I'm having problems with it. What can I do?" And I told her, "Why don't you just graciously tell them that you don't agree with it, and hope they don't mind if you don't participate in it? Don't say, 'Hey, you people are going to hell!' Don't say that. Say it in a way where you can just pull away."

That's how I feel about smudging and that sort of thing. I have people that sometimes want to have a traditional funeral here at our church. They want to use our building. Like, recently, the Catholic church wanted to hold a funeral here because there was more room. Well, the first thing that I told them is, "I don't agree with that smudging, but I hope you'll have respect for that and not do it inside the church." And they showed a lot of respect, a lot of respect, and they said, "We won't do that." I also jokingly tell them, I said, "Well, we got smoke alarms, too, and I don't want to set them off!" So they waited until after they went out the door, and they did their smudging outside.

Some of the other Pentecostal churches didn't like that, even letting them do their smudging outside. That's when they called us "a compromising church." But we're open to spread the Gospel, and that's what we're here for. So they come and use our church, and they do their thing. I sit there, and I listen. I listen to some of those sermons, including some I don't agree with. But I sit there, and I listen to 'em. And one thing that really helps me in this area is to remember that they're preaching the Gospel. Maybe for the wrong motive, but I'm grateful they're preaching that. They're preaching the Gospel any way they can, even if they need to listen a little more or read a little more. And then the other thing, like Paul talked about, one of the scriptures talks about Barnabas. Those guys were preaching, and they were a little bit off. But Paul said to pray for them that they do preach well. You know the Bible is full of that kind of thing, so you need to look at that. And when you do, you look at people and can say, "Hey, these guys are doin' it. They're helpin' God's work." I think that's one of the things we try to do, too.

SEEKING UNITY AMONG CROW CHURCHES

What I would like to see among the churches on the Crow Reservation is more unity—more unity and working together instead of clashing with each other, battling with each other. And I'd like to see people preachin' more Jesus. We need to look at what the Bible says about spreading his kingdom, not ours. That's what I'd like to see. I'd like to see them be more open, and cooperate, and show the love of Jesus to the people. I believe that's when it's gonna begin. You're gonna see people start doin' that and livin' that life. You know that phrase, "What would Jesus do?" I think when all the churches start doin' that, you're gonna have a revival. You're gonna have an outbreak. There wouldn't be anything like it in the world.

Before I went to church—B.C., before Christ—anyway, we used to camp at Crow Fair right across from the dance arbor. On Sunday mornings, they'd have service there. The Baptist church did that, and there were maybe a few people there. And then the Catholics did one across the arbor, on the other side, separately. That was before I became Christian. After I gave my life to the Lord and was pastoring the church, we kind of got into that, and we started to have services there at the arbor, too. We joined with two other churches, both Baptist, and it got bigger and bigger. We shut our church building down on that Sunday of Crow Fair, and meet there instead. The other two churches shut down for the day, too, and we have our service there, all together.

I meet with a group of guys, pastors from Hardin and then two churches here at Crow Agency, and we've been meeting together for the last twenty-some years, every Friday. We missed some of them, but I would say every Friday we have prayer time. And one of the things I keep harping on them about is that if we, as pastors, don't work together, how do you expect your people to work together? That's one of the things we need to do as an example. Like havin' fellowship together, and Crow Fair is one of those times. There's also a sunrise service on Easter, when all our churches come together. And then Christmas Eve. On Christmas Eve last year, I think we almost filled the place up. We had the balcony full, and that's over 300-some people on Christmas Eve service. We need to work together and try to accomplish what God wants us to do. I know you're gonna have problems when you do that, and the Bible even says we all ain't gonna get together until the end comes. But we'll keep punching away at it.

Redefining the Fundamentals of Crow Culture

You know, the Bible talks in the book of Revelation about how we're all different voices 'til our nations come together, right? A lot of times we try to change our lifestyles, the way we're built, and I don't think we need to do that. Because I'm Crow, and I can't say I'm not Crow. I can't turn white. I can't turn Spanish or anything. I'm a Crow Indian, and that's what I'm gonna be. I cannot play a role. You're unique. God created you the way you are, and I believe that God's gonna use you how he created you to bring his people in. Diversity. I can't change people, and we can't change people. Only God can. And all his workers come together as one. But that's one of the things I need to really be specific about—to talk about the nations, Indian and non-Indian. I tell people, "You're an Indian and you can't change it. That's where you grew up, that's your culture, and that's where you came up."

For example, the Crows are known to be friendly. With all the different reservations, they're the friendliest Indian tribe around. And I do believe God used that to bring people together. There's that big sign out there that says, "Welcome to Crow Country." Several years ago, when we first got our first mission team here at the church, we started a tradition.[1] We said, "Welcome to Crow Country. Hey, welcome to our land. You're more than welcome to be here with us." I think we've lost some of that with our younger generation. We're turnin' more white. We got more education now, and I think we're just gettin' a little more strict about who we welcome. But I think we still need to keep that. That's what God gave us a heart for, to be friendly, to adopt people, to bring people in. And I think God gave us that unique position to do that as Crow Indians with Indian culture.

The other thing I look at is that we respect people, especially family-wise. Family is one of the biggest things that you see in the Bible. You go back in the Old Testament, to the Jewish people. How close are they in family relationship? How close are they in keeping their traditions, their cultures? I think Crows are probably the same way. As an Indian, we try to keep our traditions. And we try to keep our families together. I think that's a plus. We got people that come here to our church from out of state. Out of the country, too. And one thing that we've learned is how to be family. Some of these groups tell us, "We came here to teach about love, but you guys taught us love." We hear that a lot. And those are the things that I think God has blessed us with. That's the Crow culture and tradition. Why don't we use that to spread his kingdom?

Recovering the Tribe's Past, without Sentimentalism

You know, a lot of our young people say, "Oh, we Crows did this, or that, back then . . ." and all this other stuff. Well, I'd like to see 'em live in a tipi at 30 below zero and have nothing to eat! "Back in the day," they say. God has blessed us with a great piece of land here, a great piece of land. And we need to take care of it. We need to be good stewards of it. But we're not. God blessed us with a lot of kids, with a lot of people, with family. We need to respect that, and we need to take care of that. And you see that in the scriptures, talking about bein' stewards of the land that God has given us. Some people are caught up in saying, "This is what we believe in as a culture." Why don't we change that around and say, "What has God given our tribe that we can use to bring the people together?"

I hear stories about the old-time camps. Some of the older people used to talk about this, and some still do. They talk about how the tribe used to move all the time. And the tribe used to have camps, like at Crow Fair. They moved to different areas, and they had what they called a camp leader. The camp leader controls the camp. There comes a time when he comes over and says, "Hey, this place is getting bad." He says, "We're starting to use up the grass, and it's startin' to stink. Let's move." And they kept the land clean by movin' on. Why don't we get that back again? Why don't we follow that practice again, get this place movin' and make a change? This would be a showplace. It'd really be a showplace for God if we'd look at the scriptures and look what it says and use some of the things God blessed us with, and use some of our talents.

There are no dummies here. They're smart—we got some smart kids. You got some guys that are pretty well educated. But we're getting too much education and we're forgetting about all the stuff that God has given us. We got spoiled because we got the reservation. "Hey, you're still a man," I tell 'em. "You haven't changed. Why don't you go out and do some work? Why don't you go out and clean up? Why don't you go out and support your family?" After all, "back in the day" that's what they did! Those are the things in our Crow culture that can be used to bring glory to the Lord and spread his kingdom. And that's not compromising. You're not compromising the word of God when you see culture that way. You're not worshipping any idols or anything.

I heard a guy asking one time, "What makes you a Crow?" Did you ever hear that? "What makes you a Crow?" Some of the answers came back,

"Well, we participate in dancing, and we participate in this, and we participate in that." But that doesn't make you Crow. What makes you Crow? Here's the answer: blood. You got Crow blood. Anybody can dance. Anybody can wear feathers. Anybody can do those things. But bein' a Crow is you got that Crow blood. The blood. And then you can turn that and say, "What makes you a Christian?" The blood of Jesus. You know, those are things to look at.

The Sweat Lodge and Making Idols of Culture

As far as other cultural things, there's the sweat lodge. I don't mind goin' to the sweat. As a matter of fact, we've had maybe three or four conversions in the sweat. We talked about how the tradition is, and how this was set up and passed down generation to generation. What I'm lookin' at is Romans, chapter 1. God gave us all these things, but we turned around and we worshipped those things instead of him.[2] How about the sweat? I see it as a medicinal thing, just like a good cleansing, a good bath, that takes the soreness out. But some turn around and worship that.

Like right now, let's say you get some people from way back when and took 'em to the hospital, or get 'em an X-ray, or have a problem with their teeth, or give em' some pills and they get healed. They'd say, *"Baaxpée!"* But that's a problem when they call these things holy, or they say, "Let's worship it." I think that's what happened with some of these traditions. God gave us some of these things, and we should say, "Thank you, Lord, for this." We don't need to worship it. Just like the plants. Just like the trees. It's not only in Crow culture, but different ethnic groups all over the world do that.

There was a young pastor who went to a sweat lodge. And when he came back and he talked about it to his congregation, they condemned him. So he went and talked to the old pastor that used to be there and asked him, "What can I do? What can I say?" That old pastor said, "What's wrong with a bunch of guys gettin' together and prayin'?" That's what he said. I think it's how you use it, and how you look at it. Just like this church here, you can change this around to a discotheque, or have bingo, or even a casino in here.

My wife, Hannah, and I like to watch ballgames. We were up in Billings waiting for a game, so we went to the mall. And while I was sittin' there, there was a pastor that came by and I said, "You doin' your shoppin'?" And he said, "Yeah." We said, "We're just sittin' here waiting." He said, "Waitin' for what?" I said, "We're goin' to the ballgame." We sat there and talked for a while, and then he said, "I don't go to the ballgames." I said, "Why not?" He said, "Well, there's gamblin' there, there's drinkin' there, there's adultery. All this takes place in a ballgame."

So I sat there, and I didn't say nothin' 'til he got done. Then I looked at him, and I said, "What are you doin' in here?" He said again, "I'm shoppin'." I told him, "You shouldn't be here." "Why?" he asked. So I just pointed around. "Theater over there, bar over there, casino over there, books and pornography over there. Look at all this. I bet there's probably somebody that's runnin' off with somebody's wife or somebody's husband. And somebody's stealing something there." Suddenly he said, "Oh I gotta go!"—and he got up and left.

Sometimes I can get kind of smarty. I don't do it much. A lot of times I just keep my mouth shut. But the reason I got smart with him is because this guy's been in Christianity for a lot of years. And remember who Jesus got after? The religious people. He got after them. They know the word, they know what's goin' on, but he got after them. And you have to do that every now and then.

NOTES

1. Spirit of Life Lighthouse for the Nations Foursquare Church regularly hosts short-term summer mission teams from churches across the United States. Most teams are comprised of non-Indian, high school–age students, many of whom have had no previous contact with reservation communities. Although more active than most, Kenneth's church is not alone in hosting such teams. Off-reservation, short-term Christian mission teams are regularly hosted by many churches on the reservation today.

2. Romans 1:20–25 reads, "Ever since the creation of the world his eternal power and divine nature, invisible though they are, have been understood and seen through the things he has made. So they are without excuse; for though they knew God, they did not honor him as God or give thanks to him, but they became futile in their thinking, and their senseless eyes were darkened. Claiming to be wise, they became fools; and they exchanged the glory of the immortal God for images resembling a mortal human being or four-footed animals or reptiles," and "they exchanged the truth about God for a lie and worshipped and served the creature rather than the Creator, who is blessed for ever!" (New Revised Standard Version).

8

Pentecostal Politics

AN INTERVIEW WITH CONRAD "CJ" STEWART

CJ Stewart is a great-grandson of Nellie Pretty Eagle Stewart, the pioneering founder of Crow Pentecostalism in the 1920s. Until the fall of 2015, he served in the Crow tribal legislature as a senator from the reservation's Black Lodge District. Like his great-grandmother, CJ is a devoted Pentecostal Christian, and he freely blends his religious passion with his political zeal. In March 2013, he sponsored Legislative Resolution 13-02, titled "A Resolution of the Crow Tribal Legislature to Honor God for His Great Blessings upon the Crow Tribe and to Proclaim Jesus Christ as Lord of the Crow Indian Reservation." The bill provides for "a monument to this proclamation" to be publicly displayed in the legislative chamber. It also stipulates that signage be erected along Interstate 90, declaring "Jesus Christ Is Lord of the Crow Reservation"—a provision that received a $23,000 allocation in the tribe's

Conrad "CJ" Stewart, former senator from the Black Lodge District, in the speaker's chamber of the Crow tribal legislature. *Photo by Dave Kapferer*

2014 budget, thanks to CJ's efforts. The promised billboard was completed in December 2014 and now greets drivers who pass through Crow Agency along I-90. Reflecting the considerable influence of Pentecostalism on Crow tribal politics, LR 13-02 passed without a single vote in opposition.

In April 2013, CJ was also instrumental in drafting Joint Action Resolution 13-05, titled "A Crow Tribal Joint Action Resolution to Establish Crow Tribal Policy Officially Supporting the State of Israel on a Nation-to-Nation Basis." The resolution quotes Genesis 12, where God declares to Abraham, "I will bless them that bless thee, and curse him that curseth thee, and in thee shall all families of the Earth be blessed." The resolution passed unanimously. In March 2014, tribal leaders formally presented the resolution to Ron Dermer, Israeli ambassador to the United States, during a ceremony held in Washington, D.C. The resolution reflects a confluence of biblical literalism, pro-Israel politics, and Pentecostal prosperity theology.

Based on his reading of the Bible, along with a number of prophecies spoken about the Crow Tribe by high-profile Pentecostal evangelists passing through the reservation, CJ is confident that God has a bright future in store for the tribe, one marked by sweeping social improvement and great economic prosperity. The rich mineral resources on Crow tribal lands play an important role in this vision. CJ has lobbied aggressively for the expansion of mining operations on the reservation in order to exploit the blessing of mineral wealth he believes God has given to the tribe. These efforts paid off in October 2013, when the National Congress of American Indians passed a landmark resolution supporting the Crow Tribe's efforts to sell significant portions of their enormous coal reserve to an off-reservation energy company. This move was part of an ambitious Coal-to-Liquids program expected to generate millions of dollars for the tribe.

The following interview took place in the speaker's chamber of the Crow legislative branch office in Crow Agency.

❦

The Pentecostal Legacy on the Crow Reservation

My name is Conrad J. Stewart. They know me as CJ Stewart, and I serve as a senator for the Black Lodge District. This is my second term; I was elected in 2007. I'm only thirty-nine years of age. I've been a resident of Crow Reservation all my life.

You see, going back to the old days, when Pentecostalism was introduced to the Crows, it was my [great-]grandmother Nellie Stewart who went to Aimee McPherson at Angelus Temple in Los Angeles and got filled with the Holy Ghost. She didn't know how to read, so my [great-]grandpa, Joe Stewart, would read portions of the Bible to her and she would take it and preach the word to the people. She developed a following, and amongst that following there were various pastors, preachers, ministers—and the word was embedded in everyone's hearts and souls and minds. And there were great preachers that came out of this reservation that have passed on now. Amongst them were apostles such as Harold Carpenter.[1] He went all over Canada, all over America. He shared a platform with A. A. Allen and R. W. Schambach and ministers of that caliber. He was part of that, and he brought the word to a lot of Indian Country. When he would have his camp meeting, they would call it the granddaddy of 'em all—the Crow Camp Meeting. It's still held today, always on the first weekend of August.

It was always a huge camp meeting, where all the Natives came together during that time. Through his study and research of the word of God, he would impart the message unto them at that time. During his camp meetings and services, there were actually healings that went on, where some people had demonic forces in them and they were cast out. There were some that couldn't see that got to see. They were some that couldn't hear that were able to hear. And some that were plagued with diabetes and cancer. Carpenter would lay hands on them and the infirmity, the disease, would leave. There was even an instance where one guy's leg was shorter than the other and he wanted healing 'cause he didn't like the way he walked. So Carpenter said, "You have to believe, and I'm going to believe with you." And he prayed with him and he pulled on his leg, and as he was pulling on his leg the people saw it before their eyes—through the power of God, through the faith of that gentleman, and the assistance of Carpenter—he pulled the leg out to where it was the same length as the other one. Healed him right there. It was the power of God. There were a lot of healings that went on here at the Crow Agency camp meeting site, and that's sacred ground.

Crow Tribal Resolution Declaring "Jesus Christ as Lord of the Crow Indian Reservation"

I'm a believer. I was born-again in 1999, on October 24, and baptized and filled with the Holy Ghost at that time. And so it's always kind of been in my heart to help the people and the Lord. The Lord has shown me to assist the people, and the best way is to get involved, to get in the trenches. So, when I first got elected, I wanted to have something—whether it be a scripture or something else—that we could put in part of a legislation, pass it, and kind of identify it as a seed of faith.

Then I got to thinking, we used to have a sign here on the Crow Reservation that the Crow Revival Center put up under Pastor Larry Little Owl. He's the senior pastor of the Crow Reservation out of all the pastors, and we have great respect for him. He and his church put up a sign along Interstate 90 years ago, which was taken down about two or three administrations ago. It stated, "Jesus Is Lord on the Crow Reservation."

It was located at the park here in Crow Agency, at the Henrietta Park—they also call it Warriors Park. It was right next to the bridge. That's where a lot of the Pentecostal camp meetings are held during the summer time. I don't actually know who took it down. But at some point, it was just taken down, and a new sign was put up that said, "Warriors Park." But I thought that was really great to have that sign put up. It was something for us believers. That's what we believed, you know? That Jesus is the Lord on the Crow Reservation.

The Crow Tribe is a blessed nation. This is where the word of God went out to Indian Country. This is where it started. We have a lot of gospel musicians here, and a lot of ministers. Of course, we still have our problems like every other community: alcoholism, meth, diabetes, cancer, all those things. But what I envisioned with this legislation, what the Lord spoke to me, was that I had to plant a seed of faith. This is what the Lord spoke to me in my heart. I've heard the Bible verse so many times, but this time when it came to me it was so clear. He said, "The requirement to move that mountain is just the portion of a mustard seed, your faith. Now if you plant that faith and it grows to be bigger than that mustard seed, how much more will it do for you if just a small portion of a mustard seed of faith can move the mountain?"

So what that basically said to me was that I didn't want to hide a scripture in any legislation. Instead, I was going to be up-front. I was going to bring it to the senators, and I was going to make that "Jesus is Lord" proclamation throughout the land. Prior to going out there to vote on this legislation, we came in here to the speaker's chambers with Pastor Duane Bull Chief of My Father's House, a church here in Crow Agency, along with the speaker of the house and Senator Duke Goes Ahead from Pryor, and we prayed in here. I told them what I wanted. I said, "This is what's going to have to happen. We're going to make it a declaration. We're going to make a decree. We're going to make a proclamation over the land. Some of the others might not understand the spiritual aspect of what we're doing here, but this is only part of it. This is the beginning."

And so when Pastor Bull Chief prayed at the invocation of the legislative session itself, he made that proclamation supporting the resolution. He made that decree. He spoke it over the land, over the nation. Then we went into the reading of the legislation, and then he came up as a proponent, as well as others. We had one fella speak kind of against it in the audience. He wasn't for it. But overall, it went through. It passed. When we were out there on the floor presenting this, it was kind of a steady calm. I could feel it. It was kind of a strength—a divine strength, you know? You could feel the presence of God. It was powerful. You could feel it in there. And then I told these gentlemen, I said, "If we're not ashamed, he's not going to be ashamed of us. And so we have to go forth."

Crow Tribal Resolution Supporting the State of Israel

We then agreed at that time that the next possible legislation was going to have to be a resolution supporting Israel, because they supported the indigenous rights of the Native people of the United States, as well as other nations, in the United Nations.[2] We all agreed. And when we went out there and everybody voted, they voted "Yes" to support the state of Israel. A lot of the people in there, I don't know if they really understood the dynamics that were at play. You know, we were only tools in that vote. The Lord had something big planned that we needed to establish, and I don't know what's coming or what we're up against, or what blessing there is that is going to come to this nation. But the Lord had a preparation prior to it, and I'm just glad to say that I was part of it. I was chosen. And so, like I said, the Lord spoke to me and he stated, "The measure and requirement to move this mountain is only the size of a mustard seed. Now if you plant this seed and it grows, how much more will it do for you?" So we planted that seed that day.

There was a section set aside in that resolution where we quoted a scripture in there. So we actually have scripture in our law. In Genesis 12, he says, "And I will make thee a great nation and I will bless thee and make thy name great and thou shalt be a blessing. And I will bless them that bless thee, and curse him that curseth thee, and in thee shall all families of Earth be blessed." That was the scripture that was chosen to include in the resolution. When you look at the history of the Crow people, it coincides a lot with the history of the twelve tribes of Israel. You know, like Israel, we were a small nation that was battled from all angles. We're the same way. But like Israel, we've survived 'til now.

And recently, we've been receiving prophecies of the Crow Tribe being a big player in national and international business. R. W. Schambach prophesized this, as well as Chuck Pierce—a prophet based out of Denton, Texas, who goes all over the world. He comes here very often now, and he prophesized. Rod Parsley has even prophesied about the reservation—that the Crow people will be the lender and not the borrower, that we will be the head and not the tail, that we will be leading Indian Nations, and that the United States will be depending on the Crow people and their mineral resources to bring 'em out of dependency. And we're kind of seeing that now, you know, where the nation is looking at the Crow Tribe for the Coal-to-Liquids project and getting away from dependency on oil from nations that don't care for us as Christians.[3] And so there's all of that history and the spiritual content behind it that the Crow people are involved in, and still to this day we're acting in these areas.

On the Relationship between Christianity and Crow Traditionalism

If you're not too sure of yourself, it'd be hard to hold your Christian faith and Crow identity together at the same time. But when you understand who you're praying to, it's easy, because now you know the source of your suppli-cation. As far as dealing with the cultural side of being a Crow, you know, I grew up dancing. I grew up with the hand games, the arrow games, and just the different areas of being Crow. Our clan systems are very important to me. My dad, he's always been a servant of the people as well. He worked with many chairmen from the past. He's got a lot of respect in the district with a lot of people. He's one of the elders now. But he taught us to have respect for our elders. He would even read us the word of God, you know? He was a parish council chairman at St. Dennis Catholic Church in Crow Agency. Being a Christian was very important to him, yet he didn't com-promise any of his cultural beliefs.

He wasn't involved with the Native American Church (peyote). He wasn't involved with the Sun Dance. But he fasted. He would go to the mountains and fast. He was kind of taken in and raised by Frank Takes Gun, who was basically the one who got the Native American Church incorporated. Again, the Crows were at the forefront of that. If you talk to different ones pertaining to the Native American Church, my Grandpa Frank Takes Gun was the one that went to Congress and spoke on the congressional floor. He was the one that got depositions from doctors and different psychologists, talking about peyote, working to get the ceremony recognized.

So it's kinda funny that we never participated in the Native American Church, since Grandpa Frank was always there. He was a well-known man and prominent in that area of Native American Church. So my dad certainly had exposure to those different beliefs, and he would hold dif-ferent cultural rites amongst the tribe. He's a pipe holder, and he gave me that right as a pipe holder. The pipe that he holds is from White Man Runs Him, which is the pipe I have now.[4] He also has the right to speak publicly amongst the tribe. He's given me those rights and passed that on down to me. And different areas of hand game—he's given those rights to me. And so we haven't given anything up. We've just embraced the name of our Lord. We know who he is.

There are some people that hold Christianity and the traditional Crow religions together. But I was never—well, I was taught about the traditional ways. I was taught about the Sun Dance, the sweat lodge, fasting. I didn't really have too much teaching towards the Peyote religion. I have a brother that goes to peyote meetings, and he has certain rights in handling that. Then I have sisters that go into the Sun Dance, and they fast, they pray—you know, they ask for good things for the families and they do their thing. But then again, they call on our Lord. They know who our God is. So it was just never really pressing for me 'cause my dad never really pressed us to go into Sun Dance or the Native American Church. But we grew up going into the sweat lodge, praying, understanding those areas of Native American culture, the Crow culture, and fasting—having the one-on-one with the Lord.

Fasting and praying are things I still do, although I don't always go in the hills. There are times I'm here at work fasting, doing my own thing, but I won't let it be known. Also, I often carry oil with me. I always keep my oil. Before I come in to work, I'll put some on my hand and put it on my arms and my hands, like this. [*Here CJ takes a small vial of anointing oil from his pocket, pours some into his hands, and then rubs it onto his forearms.*] I put on my armor of faith: my helmet of salvation, breastplate of righteousness, my shield of faith, my sword of the Spirit. I shod my feet with the preparation of the Gospel of peace, and I gird my loins with the truth. So I always make sure I'm wearing my armor.[5] I carry this oil with me. You just never know. Some people need it. And they'll need prayer. Not that we need the oil to pray but you know it's just—I carry it with me.[6]

CRITICISM AGAINST THE "JESUS IS LORD" LEGISLATION

While working on the "Jesus is Lord" resolution, we had one gentleman that I thought would stand with me, but he didn't make himself available in the end. And I think, most likely, he was probably afraid of the people. And I understand that. I don't hold nothing against nobody. Everybody has a right to their own opinion. He was kind of thinking that the people would be upset. I think that all of us did. Yet again, I knew that it needed to be done. It was about finding the right timing and talking to individual senators. I just didn't put it out on the floor and hope for them to vote. No, I talked to them, different ones, key senators, talked to them and said, "We need to do this."

We also made sure to put certain language into the resolution. Like we had *Akbaatatdía*—he's the Creator in the Crow language. And *Ischawúuannaukaasua*—the One with the Pierced Hands. That's how we say Jesus in

PENTECOSTALISM, CULTURE, AND POLITICS

Crow. I made sure our attorney put that in there, because that's who we refer to as Jesus. He's not just son of God. He's Jesus, the name above all names. No other name is given under heaven whereby we must be saved. It's very important to recognize his name.

There was some kind of blog critical of the resolution after I put it out there on Facebook. Some people were like, "So, do we give up our ways?"—being sarcastic about it. But then again, you gotta understand that there are people that are not spiritually minded. They kinda want to say things out of spite. But we didn't give up our ways. We just made that recognition that Jesus is Lord here among the tribe. There's a big majority of the reservation that are already Christians. Then again, there's young ones that are still seeking. But there are also young ones that are fully convinced. It depends on who you talk to.

Actually, it was kinda funny. Some of the criticism we got was basically from individuals, different tribal people, who live miles and miles away from Crow Reservation. They're Crow, but maybe just a portion of Crow. And I didn't understand that, you know? We live right here in the heart of everything, and I'm almost full-blood Crow—I'm a little bit over three-quarters Crow, 53/64 Crow—and yet there's some out there that might not even be a quarter Crow, and yet they wanted to say something bad against this declaration. So it's kinda funny how that worked out that way. 'Cause I noticed that some of the criticism was from different members, but they lived elsewhere.

Again, it's not an issue of denouncing or putting away our cultural beliefs. It's an issue of recognizing our Lord and who he is. Our Lord has a name. I think some people have a "we're right and you're wrong" kinda attitude in religion. But religion, all it does is build walls, you know? And so all I was here to do was to establish a seed for our nation and let him do the work. He says, "It's not your battle, it's my battle. All you do is make yourself available." And so that's what I did. That's what we did. I presented the resolution to the body, and by the grace of God everything got done.

And I don't think we can ever reverse it. It's been done. It's part of our history now, and hopefully it leads us to bigger and better things for the Crow people. I just pray that the blessings will come for our people. We have too much meth use. We've got chronic diabetes, alcoholism, cancer.

Oppression and depression have set in to the point where our society is sick and that's where we need the healing. That's where we need the blessing so we can rise up as people and start being fathers to our children, and mothers to the kids, and be a strong family-based people again.

NOTES

1. The late Harold Carpenter grew up in the Crow Reservation town of Lodge Grass. With a youthful reputation for drinking and fighting, he experienced a dramatic encounter with Pentecostal Christianity in 1950, before emerging as the single most influential Crow preacher and healer in the second half of the twentieth century.

2. Here CJ is referring to the United Nations Declaration on the Rights of Indigenous People (2007). Two months before the U.N. vote on the declaration, the Crow Tribe publicly urged the United States "to fully support the adoption of the Declaration" in Joint Action Resolution 07-07, titled "Resolution to Urge Support of the United Nations Declaration on the Rights of Indigenous Peoples." At the vote, however, the United States joined with Canada, New Zealand, and Australia as the only four U.N. member nations to oppose the declaration. Not until 2010 did the United States give its belated endorsement to the declaration. Contrary to CJ's claims here regarding Israel's support of the measure, Israel was among thirty-four U.N. member nations that were absent for the vote.

3. Under the Coal-to-Liquids project, the Crow Tribe would lease more than 1 billion tons of coal to off-reservation energy companies that plan to ship the liquefied fuel primarily to Asian markets.

4. White Man Runs Him famously served as a Crow scout for George Custer during the Battle of Little Bighorn in 1876, on what is now the Crow Indian Reservation.

5. Here CJ is referencing a well-known biblical passage describing the "armor of God" as found in Ephesians 6:13–17.

6. The use of anointing oil for prayer and healing was so common among early Crow Pentecostals that they earned the name *Akbaatashée,* meaning "those who use oil" or "the greasers."

Part III

❀

THE BAPTIST MIDDLE WAY

The American Baptist Home Missionary Society first gained a foothold among the Crow Tribe in 1904 when local tribal leaders reluctantly granted them permission to establish a church. What the community really wanted was a quality day school to provide an alternative to the government boarding school at Crow Agency, since families were naturally loath to part with their children for months at a time. The Baptist Society, which was located just south of the reservation in Sheridan, Wyoming, agreed to establish the school only if granted permission to found a church as well. Significantly, both voices in this part highlight the role that education has played in their own lives, with Angela Russell listing the Crow Baptist emphasis on education among its most important and enduring legacies.

In addition to valuing educational success, both of the following speakers also value participation in traditional Crow ways. Newton Old Crow—a longtime Baptist pastor, substance abuse counselor, and prison chaplain—actively seeks ways to integrate Crow rituals and ceremonies into his various ministry settings, believing that the Christian faith in no way requires him to abandon the traditional ways. In fact, he appears to regard Crow religions and Christianity as equally legitimate spiritual paths, explaining that he feels no compulsion to convert traditional family members and friends to Christianity, including his two sons who practice the Sun Dance religion.

Angela Russell discusses her strong identification with the Baptist Church alongside her participation in both the Sun Dance and peyote traditions. She prays to Jesus Christ, whether she's in church, in the Sun Dance lodge, or in the peyote tipi, and sees no contradiction or incompatibility among the various ways. The primary advantage she sees in the Baptist Church over traditional religions is the sense of fellowship she has found among "the community of believers" in her own church. When specifying the key points of Crow identity, she cites the tribe's attachment to their land, commitment to family, the Crow language, and a strong tradition of sacred songs. All of these, she says, are compatible with her deep Christian faith.

9

Rodeo Man and Reluctant Pastor

AN INTERVIEW WITH NEWTON OLD CROW SR.

Newton Old Crow, former pastor of the historic First Crow Indian Baptist Church in Lodge Grass, spent his youth running away from Christianity. He was raised by parents steeped in Crow traditional ways as well as Catholicism, both of which Newton rejected for much of his life. It was only after observing the role that Christian faith played in his wife's recovery from alcoholism that Newton, in his own words, "asked Jesus to come into my heart" and "got saved." These events took place through the ministry of an American Baptist church. With his wife, he later received seminary training at a theological college in Tempe, Arizona. From there, he spent several years pastoring a Native American congregation in Oklahoma, before returning home to pastor First Crow Indian Baptist Church.

Throughout the reservation, Newton Old Crow is a highly respected

Newton Old Crow Sr. on the grounds of the rodeo grandstand, Crow Agency. *Photo by Dave Kapferer*

rodeo cowboy. One recent story I heard described a sea of aspiring young rodeo cowboys stepping aside, "like the Red Sea parting for Moses," with reverential awe when Newton entered the corral. He also has done extensive alcohol counseling and, for many years, ran a prison ministry for Native inmates. According to Newton, his own experiences with alcohol and drug addiction make him averse to pointing fingers or passing judgment on others who struggle with similar challenges. It's a posture that also carries over into his emphatic rejection of religious judgmentalism. In this regard, he is especially troubled by Pentecostalism's tendency to preach against aspects of Crow culture as well as its reputation for condemning Crow Christians who participate in traditional Indian ceremonies.

Two months after conducting the following interview, I heard Newton deliver a controversial presentation at a Pentecostal conference at Crow Agency, where he spoke openly about his dual participation in Christianity and Crow religious practices. He even defended participating in the Sun Dance when family members have invited him to attend, arguing that a spirit of humility and familial obligation ought always to trump religious legalism.

Newton does not actively seek converts to the Christian faith, even among his own children and grandchildren. Instead, he openly gives his blessing to his two sons who are involved in the Sun Dance; he does the same for other family members who participate in the Native American Church. Newton himself has become very comfortable participating in many of the traditional Crow ways he learned as a child, including praying in the sweat lodge, drumming at Sun Dances, and joining in parades, powwows, and Crow social dances. In his own ministry, he seeks to bring Crow traditional practices into church services to the extent that his congregations embrace them, such as smudging with cedar before communion.

Newton's story demonstrates, once again, the polyreligious diversity that shapes the identity of so many Crow tribal members. In his case, this includes substantial encounters with Crow Traditionalism, the American Baptist Church, the Mennonite Church, and Catholicism. Considering Newton's passion for rodeo, the following interview fittingly took place on the grounds of the Crow Agency rodeo grandstand during the annual festivities of Crow Native Days.

A Childhood in Crow Traditionalism
and Mission Catholicism

My name is Newton Old Crow Sr. I'm a retired minister of the American Baptist Church in Lodge Grass, Montana. I also ministered for a time at the Little Brown Church in Lodge Grass.

My mom and dad were very traditional in the Crow way. They were also very strong Catholics 'cause they were both in the mission schools. We were all brought up Catholic. I was baptized and confirmed and took First Communion and all of that. I went through all of that. But then, I guess at an age of understanding, I just kind of went a different way. I wanted to be a rodeo cowboy. And the things that my father wanted me to do—he wanted me to go to church—he tried to kind of force it on me, and I did not like it. So I did my own thing for many years.

I know all of our Crow traditional ways, but I never did take part in them while growing up. See, that was part of my rebellion against my father because of his alcoholic behavior and verbal abuse. He tried to push us to go in to church. That's when I went completely opposite. So I was not a very religious sort of person then. Back then, as far as church—Christianity, Christian church—I wanted nothing to do with it. Nothing! My first wife was a Pentecostal. I didn't like it, the way they kind of point fingers and that kind of thing. I did not like it.

Alcohol Recovery, Jesus, and Rodeo

Not until my current wife went through alcohol treatment did that change. She was brought up a Christian, in a Christian home. She knew all of that church stuff. She was brought up in a Mennonite home. She was baptized at a very young age.[1] The lady that raised her was a very nice Christian lady, a Mennonite Christian lady. Then, when she was growing up in high school, she went out to the West Coast. She went to high school, then college out there. Then she married and started drinking and took that road. For many years, she was on that road 'til we got married in 1980. And when we got married, she sobered up and she went back to church, which I did not like.

But I guess, in a way, I was watching her. I was watching her and the change that I saw in her. I guess that's when I finally went to church myself.

After that, my wife wanted to go to Bible school in Tempe, Arizona—to Charles Cook Theological School. In the meantime, I was startin' going to church, but I was not really committed. And then, June 7, 1981, is when I got saved. I asked Jesus to come into my heart. But I was still drinkin', still smokin' and all that kinda stuff in the world, very much in the world. Then at this camp meeting, a lady from that Charles Cook School was recruiting, and she talked to my wife about going to school. She kept saying to me, "We gotta go to school." I said, "No, I'm too old. I don't want to do that." My people, the Crow people, we're kinda—well, we criticize each other. Especially the men, we tease. The men, my friends, know that. So that's what I didn't want to do. But she kept saying, "That's it. We're goin' to school." I said, "No, I'm not going to school!" But we went down to Arizona in the end.

See, I'm a rodeo cowboy. So I took my horse down there. My thought was I was going to rope and rodeo in the winter months down in Arizona. I said, "All right, you go to school and I'll support you." I'm a carpenter by trade. So I know that there's a lot of construction work down there with that good weather in the Phoenix area. I was gonna do carpenter work and let her go to school. But she said, "No, we both have to go to school." So we had a big argument right in front of the lady that did the registrations for the school, and then this lady said, "Newton, why don't you go one semester?" One semester turned into more, 'til I finished. So that's how that went.

SEMINARY TRAINING AND EARLY CHRISTIAN MINISTRY

I wanted to be trained in alcohol counseling. That's what I wanted, so I took a lot of training in that area. But then when the time came, at the end of our third year, we got our certificates, but the alcohol counseling program was closed down. I couldn't get in there. Naturally, we wanted to come back here to the Crow Reservation to do ministry 'cause this is where I'm from and I was raised here. But my wife and I, we made this commitment that wherever God wanted us to go we would go. We made that agreement together. So when the time came at the end of our school year, Herschel Daney, our director of Indian ministries, said there's no church openings on the Crow or the Northern Cheyenne reservations.[2] Soon afterward, Herschel Daney was talking to a friend of his, Lawrence Hart, and said to him, "I got these two that are finishing school and I got no place to send them." Lawrence Hart said, "I know two places in Oklahoma where there's two churches that are open."

Lawrence Hart's wife, Betty Hart, was a director of Native Mennonite Ministries. So she called me a couple days later and introduced herself and said, "My husband met Herschel Daney from your American Baptist school, and he said you might be interested in coming to these churches in Oklahoma." "What kind of churches?" I said. "If it's Pentecostal, I don't want to go to no Pentecostal." And she said, "No, it's Mennonite." Mennonite church—I heard about that 'cause my wife was raised in that area. Not being raised around a Christian church setting, and since I got saved in an American Baptist ministry, I wanted to be going to a Baptist church. I guess, in a way, I was gettin' kinda religious right there, getting hung up on the denomination instead of God. But when this lady said "Mennonite," in my mind I saw these pictures about these Mennonites—they got these little straight hats. I said, "Lady, I'm not gonna wear them goofy little hats!" She kinda chuckled and said, "No, we're not that way." Anyway, that's how we got to go to Oklahoma. We were there eight years.

After that, here on the Crow Reservation, First Crow Indian Baptist Church in Lodge Grass, Montana, had an opening. Minnie Allen Fistler, the moderator, kept calling my wife and me, and finally we said, "All right, I guess it's time to go home." But I was afraid. I did not want to come back to my own people 'cause of that verse where Jesus says a missionary is without honor in his own home. And sure enough, we got back and it was all right during that honeymoon stage for a few months, and then people-problems started to pop up. There's where me being in recovery helped me to stay steady through those problems. For when the time comes for me to run, I don't run to church people, but to my sponsors at the Twelve Step program. That's what kept me going.

I was open to the Indian religion, like the Sun Dance and the Native American Church and all of the ways of my people. I knew all about that 'cause my father and my mother are very much into that. I'm comfortable going there. Like I mentioned earlier about my first wife, the Pentecostal deal, they'll put them traditional people down, these people that use our

Crow culture and the Crow religion. They put 'em down. So I kinda had it in my mind that I'm not gonna be that way. 'Cause I think, to me, I'm really nothing. I'm nothing! It's the same way with recovery. When I got sober and I took this road, I'm not gonna turn around and condemn a person that's recovering. I never put nobody down. When I was on the other side, I didn't like it when people started pointing fingers at me, saying, "You should, or should not, do this or that." I'm not that way. I mean, I'm not condoning drinking or drugging or smoking. It's just that when I was on the other side, when people point fingers, I didn't like that. So I never do that. I'm not saying, "It's all right." But I'll just tell 'em why I never put nobody down.

Bringing Traditional Crow Practices into the Church

When we were in Oklahoma, there were these people in our church that were uncomfortable being there. Even though I'm Native American and ministering to Native American people, they're still uncomfortable 'cause the missionaries kind of do everything for them. They know I'm a Native American myself, but still they won't come to church. I got to thinking, "I wonder if I can do something so they'll be comfortable in church?" So I start goin' around to the different families, the church families that are really supportive of that church. This one family said, "We want to try something. We'd like to burn cedar in the church so we can smudge. That's how we are at home, something that we're used to doing."

But bringing smudging into the church, that's what I had questions about. I didn't want to just do it without talking to each family about it first. Finally, they all said, "Yes." So we did it in church, and they really liked it. For example, we burn cedar to purify ourselves before we take communion. We'll purify ourselves in that way so we'll be clean, inside and out. We confess our sins, bless ourselves, and we purify ourselves when we burn cedar, or sage, or bear root. When I did that, they really liked it. That's when I started a little more at a time. Like this young man from another tribe married into that tribe where we were, and I asked him to collect the offering. "No," he said, "next week." So I don't know how many "next weeks" we went through. Finally, I said, "Why don't you pray in your own language?" He was Navajo. He kinda gave me a funny look. "You mean I can pray in my language when I take the offering?" "Yeah," I said. So he did. He always takes this little kid with him to the front of the church when he takes offering—he has the kid stand in front of him, then he'll pray in his own Navajo language, and then he'll take offering. See, that's using something that they know, that they're comfortable with. That's how it starts, how they know they can do that in church. Where, before, the missionaries would say, "No. Doing that's just not right."

Like I mentioned, my mother and father were raised in the Catholic boarding school. And I guess they were really strict. And when they talked in the Crow language, they'll spank them or even wash their mouth with soap. That kinda treatment. And then the missionaries, once a tribal member converted, they'd take their sacred objects—like their medicine bundle or pipe or whatever they used to pray—and they'll take 'em away and say, "That's the work of the devil." So that is something that I did not like. Then, over time, the missionaries started wanting to bring this stuff back into the church, and then the Native people didn't want to do that. They did not want that. In other words, the missionaries are hypocrites! To take the things they said were bad, and now they want them to do them again.

Conversion and Crow Indian Religion

Two of my sons go in the Sun Dance, and I support 'em. I'm not a singer, but I'll sit around the drum with the singers and I'll support them. 'Cause I respect my boys doing that. It's what they want. I never condemned them. I never said, "No." It's their spirituality. God bless 'em. I give 'em my blessing. And same way with Native American Church. I got family members that are Native American Church. I might not go into their ceremonies, but still I support them. And they know. Sun Dance, Native American Church, powwows—these Pentecostals, they say, "No way." But I go there, I parade, and I take part, even in these social dances like the push dance. I dance. That's how I am.

I never try to convert my children or my grandchildren. I don't want them to come to church for me. If you come to church, come for God, not for me. Don't come for Dad or Grandpa. If they get converted, find a church where you're comfortable. I don't ever try to convert them, 'cause that's how I am.

I had a prison ministry. And these Native inmates, they didn't know how to take me. See, there again, they're kinda like me, how I heard from people all the time: "Doing this is bad, you can't do that!" So that way of thinking is kind of in 'em. Then when I went there, since they know I'm a minister, they call me Preacher Man. You know, they're good people. Just a bunch of guys. Sure, they're in prison because they commit some kind of felony—but they're good guys, good people.

But there again I don't try to convert. And they'll ask me things. It's kinda funny what's on their minds. On Tuesdays they have a sweat lodge. And I go in the sweat lodge 'cause that's one of our Crow ways. That's how I was raised. It's a minimum-security prison, so Tuesdays they have a sweat lodge. So I go in with this one guy, he must be kinda the leader, and he pointed at the sweat lodge and said, "Preacher man! If you're a preacher, why do you go in there?" So I start telling him about the way the Crows are. That's the way I was raised. I was raised that way and the way I was taught. I explained it to him, the way I saw it. I cannot speak for other tribes, but only for my own tribe and the way I'm taught.

I explained how you pour water over the heated rocks during a sweat. During the first round, there are four pours. Then they'll raise the door of the lodge, you get a little refreshment, a breath of fresh air, before they close the flap down. Then there are seven pours. And there again, after you'd have seven pours, somebody would pray—something real positive. Then, in the third round, there's ten pours. Then the fourth round, after we raise the door and get a breather, the last one we call 'em "no count"—as many pours as you can go. So I told him that. Then I said, "You have to be given the right to pour and build the lodge." That inmate said, "Well, anybody can do that!" "Not my people," I said, "but I cannot speak for other tribes—only the way I understand. Other tribes, I'll respect them," I said. "I won't change their way. I'll respect them." So after I said that, I guess he was satisfied.

Then he said, "I want to ask you something. Do you worship the pipe?"— meaning the peace pipe. I pulled out a little Bible I always carried. I put that Bible on the table. "This Bible is God's, therefore I respect it. I don't worship it. I do not worship it. Same way with that pipe. That's an instrument of prayer. The way I was taught, you offer the smoke to the four directions and then to the Creator. And we bless ourselves. It's an instrument of prayer, that pipe that you call the peace pipe. Just like I'm an instrument, and just like you're an instrument," I said. "That staff that God gave Moses, God put power in that staff. It's not that staff that's important; it's God's power. That's an instrument of prayer. That's the one that made the sea to part and got water out of that rock. All that power—it's God."

Then they said, "How about the eagle feather?" You know the Plains Indians, we all respect the eagle feathers. When an eagle feather hits the ground, they usually get a veteran to pick up that eagle feather and kinda rub it off and give it back to the owner who dropped it. I told him we don't worship it, but we respect it.

NOTES

1. Amelia (Two Bulls-Petter) Old Crow, Newton's wife since 1980, passed away in January 2016 while this interview was being prepared for publication. Amelia was ordained by the American Baptist Churches USA in 1989, and served on the board of directors for both the American Baptist Churches USA and American Baptist Home Mission Societies. In 1990, she was also ordained in the General Conference Mennonite Church (now Mennonite Church USA), likely the first Native American woman to be ordained in that denomination.
2. The Northern Cheyenne Reservation borders the Crow Reservation to the east.

10

Education, Blended Traditions, and the Crow Baptist Legacy

AN INTERVIEW WITH ANGELA RUSSELL

While sharing her personal story of religious faith and practice, Angela reflects on the history of her family's "home church," known as First Crow Indian Baptist Church, which dates back to the turn of the twentieth century. The mission had its start when local Crow elders in the town of Lodge Grass appealed to the American Baptist Home Missionary Society of Sheridan, Wyoming, to establish a day school as an alternative to the government boarding school located twenty miles to the north at Crow Agency. The Baptist Missionary Society accepted the invitation, but only on the firm condition that they be allowed to establish a church as well. Despite fears that a church would interfere with traditional tribal practices, the elders of Lodge Grass reluctantly agreed to these terms. As Angela notes in her comments, education continues to play an important role in the Crow Baptist

Angela Russell in the Big Horn Mountains. *Photo by Mick Fedulla*

legacy. As an independent attorney and former tribal judge, education has played a critical role in Angela's own life.

Dr. William A. Petzoldt was the founding pastor of that early mission. To this day, he's remembered for persuading converts to publicly dispose of traditional religious paraphernalia in the Lodge Grass Creek, as several voices in this collection recall. In contrast to Petzoldt's hostility to Crow religious practices, the church later served as home to a number of celebrated traditional elders known to be staunch defenders of Crow Traditionalism—including Thomas and Susie Yellowtail and Joe Medicine Crow. The historic First Crow Indian Baptist Church suffered a devastating flood in 2011, resulting in its eventual demolition. Since that time, with rebuilding efforts underway, the congregation has met in the local high school auditorium.

Angela speaks about the importance of "spiritual singing" in Crow religious practice. She believes that the Crow language, combined with sacred singing, creates "a stronger communion" with God, allowing Crow Christians to "really feel the power of the Holy Spirit." For this reason, Angela has been a longtime contributor to the Crow Hymns Ministry (formerly Crow Hymns Project), which, for the past twenty years, has led efforts to discover, record, and perform scores of Crow Christian hymns dating back to the 1920s. These songs are typically received by spiritual supplicants through prayer and fasting, often in the reservation's sacred hills. They're generally "given" in the Crow language and reflect the distinctive musical tradition of Northern Plains tribes. Angela believes these traditional Crow-language songs, which commonly carry biblically themed lyrics steeped in Jesus-centric imagery, illustrate well the compatibility of Crow culture and Christian faith.

One of the striking elements in Angela's narrative is her willingness to name the pain and abuse her tribe has suffered at the hands of Christian missionaries and other "white people," even while expressing gratitude for the Baptist heritage that has been such a defining part of her life. At one point, she implies that the good arising from non-Natives bringing the Gospel of Jesus to the Crows outweighs all the exploitation that has accompanied it. In the end, she regards Crow culture as fully compatible with Christian faith, and regrets those among her tribe who "think negatively" of Christianity. Despite her abiding belief in the complementarity of Native and Christian ways, her closing line betrays a nagging fear that, perhaps, the two paths may not necessarily lead to the same end after all.

The following interview took place outside the Custer Battlefield Café at Crow Agency as a brilliant lightning storm approached.

✿

Deep Family Roots in the Baptist Church

I'm Angela Russell and I live in Lodge Grass. When I was about eight years old, I went to live one summer with my aunt and my uncle in Washington State. This was shortly after my grandmother died. My grandmother had raised me up until that time, because my own mother died when I was a year and a half old. So when my grandmother died, my uncle came and took me back to Washington State with him. He has this really great story, and I have a vague recollection of it. He was working on a master's program at Washington State University in Pullman. Because he had family, we had a really nice house in the faculty housing that we got into.

When we arrived, of course, my uncle and I were very noticeably Indian people, and the neighbors had a name that sounded German. She was not Indian. Well, we became fast friends, and one day she asked me what I was. She said, "What are you?" My uncle happened to be close by, and I said, "I'm a Baptist!" So at eight years of age, and probably even earlier, I was very steeped in the American Baptist Church in our community.

My great-grandmother, I believe, was a strong member of the Baptist Church. Her name was Horse, and then her daughter was Tilly White Man Runs Him. Her daughter, Beth Pease, was my mother. So it's been four generations, starting with my great-grandmother. This was at First Crow Indian Baptist Church in Lodge Grass. That's our home church.

Lodge Grass Baptist Mission History

From what I understand, at the time the Baptist Church was started in Lodge Grass, a lot of the children were sent off to boarding school. Kids were rounded up and brought to a government boarding school here in Crow Agency from Lodge Grass, and probably from other communities, too. There was a brick building right there in the town of Crow, although it's not there anymore. And there was a fence. The story goes that a lot of these children were brought here to town, they would be here all week long, and then they could go home on the weekends.

The one story that really hit my heart was a young grandmother who had raised her child, and the child was brought here to the boarding school. She came and wanted to be with the child, but they said she could not see the child 'til the weekend. So the grandmother brought her bedroll and she just laid out her bedroll right at the fence. That way she could see her child, and then he could come over and talk to her. It's horrible, those kinds of things. I think it was that kind of history, that kind of experience, that led the community in Lodge Grass to say, "Let's bring a school here so our children can be here." Because family is so important. Extended family, too.

So some of the elders in the community—and I'm thinking of White Arm for one, but there were others—they were very dismayed that these children were separated from their parents. So they had a meeting, and they decided that they would go and talk with a minister in Sheridan, Wyoming. Dr. Petzoldt was the minister they talked to. They said, "Would you come and build a school in Lodge Grass?" He was willing to come, but only on the condition that he could build a church. So he came and built the school so the children could go to school in Lodge Grass and didn't have to be separated from their parents. That's around 1904 or 1903—somewhere in there is the date that I have heard about.

In the early years of the mission, the story goes that a lot of people were asked to bring their medicine bundles and then they threw them in the river. Of course, the second chapter of that story is that a lot of them ended up in a museum over in Cody, Wyoming. I don't know for sure, but that's what we've heard. It's probably accurate, because it was a way to bring people into the church in a very strict sense. You either are a Christian, or you're not. And if you're Christian, then you need to give up some of these things like medicine bundles. That's the way they were taught.

An Uncle "Who Was Able to Blend Everything"

As I said, my grandmother is the one who raised me, my older sister, and a first cousin who was raised with us. I call her my sister, too. My grandmother was a very, very strict Christian in the sense that she really followed the dogma that was taught, and there were certain things we couldn't do. Very strict. You couldn't sew on Sunday. You couldn't do any work on Sunday. We had to wear dresses to church and no profanity. So it was very strict, and she believed that.

However, I don't know that she was against our cultural and Native ways, because all of us spoke Crow and she respected the traditions. She had two brothers and she was very involved in their lives and carrying on traditional kinds of things—like giving to sisters-in-law, and having a very special relationship with sisters-in-law. And that's all very traditional.

After my grandmother died and I was with my uncle that one summer, I decided that I wanted to be back here at home with my sisters. So I came back home about the time I turned nine years old and lived here with my aunt and my uncle. My uncle was a strong Native American Church person. He was also a Sun Dancer. He was one of the ones who was in the first Sun Dance that was ever brought here to Crow Country; I think it was in 1941.[1] He was also a very strong Christian, and he grew up in the Baptist Church in Pryor. Yet he was able to blend everything, and he really believed in God and the Creator as one and the same. He didn't feel there were any differences there.

So we grew up with my dad—well, my uncle, who I refer to as my dad. And my mother was accommodating to that. She didn't really participate, but she was very supportive to my father. And because of his history, I was really interested as a young adult to go into the Sun Dance. So, I danced four dances. Then he also often had Native American Church meetings. He would have them at special occasions, like when we graduated from high school or college or some big event. I usually went into those meetings. I usually brought the water in, but I participated in the meetings.

So it's a little bit of everything. I'm not a Tobacco Dance Society member because nobody ever adopted me, and you have to be adopted. I used to tell my parents, my late parents, that it's too bad I never got adopted. Because I'm the most traditional one of the three of us, between my two sisters and me.

A Distinctly Crow Baptist Heritage

My experience probably wasn't very common in my home church. I think a lot of the older members that were in the church when I was growing up were very strict. And they oftentimes really looked down on people who practiced religion in a Native way, I guess is how you would say it. It never really divided the church, but it was just that there was a difference.

I grew up in the church, and the church has been a very, very important part of my life and always will be. In fact, my mother, the aunt that I refer to as my mother, and her two brothers, were very influenced through the Baptist Church and went to Linfield College, which is a Baptist college in Oregon. So there's always been that connection.

I believe one of the real positive things about the Baptist Church in Lodge Grass is that they really did support young people going to college. You've probably heard this before, but I think if you look at the Crow community, that people who have been a part of higher education have some roots back to the Baptist Church in Lodge Grass. If you look at other denominations, I don't think you'll see that. If you look at the Catholic Church, I don't know that that emphasis is as strong as it was with us. And these were early, early people who went on to college and then, therefore, influenced many of us coming along in later generations.

When I think about our church, a few things really come to mind: I believe in Jesus Christ, I really believe in fellowship, and I believe in family. I think that so many times different religions put themselves in boxes. So when they see other people that don't fit into that box, they can be very judgmental. And I really feel good about the fact that I am a Christian. I think I have an open mind about other peoples and that we can all learn from each other.

But if you are a believer in Jesus Christ, I think you need to have fellowship with other believers. I don't think you do it in isolation. I know a lot of people may go into, for instance, the Native American Church. But I don't know that that's a fellowship like in the Baptist Church. I think there's a camaraderie, and I think there is kind of a group spirit, a group relationship there. But I think the Christian fellowship is a little different. I think there's more of a looking toward the future and looking toward other people and kind of a broader perspective on life and human beings. Maybe it's just my focus, but that's kind of how I look at it.

I also believe that Sun Dancing is good, because you can go and fast. I always prayed to Jesus Christ in the Sun Dance. When I go in a peyote meeting—and I haven't gone for years and I probably won't any longer— but, again, I have prayed to Jesus Christ. There are some people who believe that you're praying to something else, but that has never been me. The disadvantage I see in both the Sun Dance and the Native American Church is that there isn't that community of believers like we have in our Baptist Church. As I've said, there's that sort of camaraderie, and they're almost kind of like a sorority or fraternity. They know each other, but it's a little bit different. And I think, as a Christian, we have to have an outreach to other people and to care about the broader population of humanity.

Points of Compatibility:
Land, Language, and Spiritual Songs

I think Christianity and Crow culture are very compatible. Because I think we as Crow people and Native people have always been very, very tied to the land, to creation, and into God—and knowing that God created everything, and that God created us. I guess the difference for me is that he made me an Indian. I know the language, and I have a relationship with people here. I have roots to the land. And all of that is because the Creator, or God, gave that to me.

I remember one of my cousins saying that of all the exploitation that was made on Native people that was extremely negative, she said, "I still always abide with the fact that without white people coming here, we would not have known about Jesus Christ." So that is something that is a really good way to look at it.

I think you can make those separations between Christianity and Native ways, but for me that isn't a problem. I can be Native and do all the things pretty much I want to do, which really are relationships and using the language. And especially the spiritual singing—there's just such a communion with the Holy Spirit with our singing. Even in our prayers, when you use Crow to pray, you just have such a stronger communion and you can really feel the power of the Holy Spirit. And that is so absolutely wonderful.

Some people just think so negatively about Christianity, but many of us don't feel that way. And I would hope that the younger generations will not feel that way. Because we're all looking some day to be in a different place, and we all want to be together up there.

NOTE

1. Angela is referring here to the introduction of the Shoshone Sun Dance to the Crow Tribe in 1941. At the request of William Big Day of Pryor, the Shoshone medicine man John Trehero (sometimes spelled Trujillo) brought the Sun Dance to the Crow Reservation. The Shoshone-Crow Sun Dance continues to be the most widely practiced Sun Dance tradition among Crows today, although Lakota piercing-style Sun Dances are also held on the Crow Reservation. Thomas Yellowtail, who was a lifelong member of the First Crow Indian Baptist Church in Lodge Grass, received the highly coveted honor of being named Trehero's spiritual successor.

Part IV

✽

PEYOTE AND CHRIST

The three voices comprising this part all identify deeply with the Peyote Way, commonly known as the Native American Church. They also identify, to varying degrees, with one of the three historic missionary traditions still active among the Crow Tribe today. Marvin Dawes Sr. identifies deeply with the Catholic Church. He also expresses a strong devotion to Saint Mary, a spiritual proclivity that's mirrored in his admiration for the Water Woman present at the very first peyote meeting, as described in the following narrative. Marlon Passes belongs to a family with deep roots in the American Baptist tradition. His great-grandfather was among those who followed the infamous Dr. Petzoldt into the waters of baptism at the turn of the twentieth century. His description of how peyote has guided his life is accompanied by a steady stream of biblical references, illustrating his conviction that Christianity and the Peyote Way are thoroughly compatible traditions. The final voice in this part is that of Levi Black Eagle. Levi is the grandson of a highly celebrated peyote roadman who adopted President Barack Obama into the Crow Tribe. Levi represents a somewhat rare combination of religious loyalties among the tribe, participating in Pentecostalism and peyote alike. His childhood conviction that love for Jesus demanded a rejection of his family's Traditionalism has recently given way to a deep desire to raise his own children knowing, and respecting, both traditions equally.

11

Our Lady of Guadalupe
Comes to Peyote Roadman

AN INTERVIEW WITH MARVIN DAWES SR.

Marvin Dawes is a roadman in the Peyote Way among the Crow Tribe. His Crow name is *Baa-Xii-Lii-chaa* (Good Red Wing Blackbird). He also identifies himself as "a strong Christian," is activly involved with St. Dennis Catholic Church at Crow Agency, and has a special devotion to Our Lady of Guadalupe. His wide-ranging interview reflects a breadth of knowledge born of his longtime work as a Crow tribal historian and cultural presenter. He holds degrees in liberal arts and Crow cultural studies from Little Big Horn College, where he now serves as chair of the board. He also works as a ranger and interpreter at the Little Bighorn Battlefield National Monument, located on the Crow Reservation.

When discussing the relationship between Christian churches and

Marvin Dawes Sr. in Hardin, Montana, on the northern edge of the Crow Reservation. *Author's photo*

Native American religious practices, Marvin is careful to differentiate "religions" from "ceremonials." He associates the former with Christian denominations that have been recognized by the government and enjoy broad institutional privileges. By contrast, he prefers to designate Native religious practices as ceremonials that are not legitimated by national religious institutions or government bodies, but rather that assert their legitimacy through generational persistence among the tribe. He therefore prefers the label "Peyote Way" to the title Native American Church, arguing that the Native American Church was born of the government's need to force the peyote ceremony into preexisting structures of recognized Christian institutions before granting it formal recognition or legal protection.

With this underlying distinction in place, Marvin's narrative goes on to describe the loosely related, but integrally connected, network of ceremonies and practices that constitute what many regard as Crow Traditionalism. This includes not only the Sun Dance and the Peyote Way, but also medicine bundles, the sweat lodge, clan feeds, giveaways, blessings, naming ceremonies, healing rites, and a host of other cultural events, including powwows. For Marvin, there is a fundamentally Native way of understanding our relationship to the spirit world, to creation, and to the tribal clan system that holds all these practices together in a coherent unity.

The following interview took place at Marvin's home in Hardin, Montana, on the northern edge of the Crow Reservation.

❀

Catholic and Cultural: "There's Nothing Wrong with Doing Both"

My name is Marvin Dawes Sr. I'm a member of the Crow Tribe. Today I'm considered a tribal historian. I always call myself still an apprentice. I'm still learning about our history and ways. I'm fortunate that I've been able to listen to some of the tribal elders, and that I've retained information and stories from my grandfather Joe Ten Bear, my late uncle Tyrone Ten Bear, and also my father, Lloyd Dawes.

As I was growing up, I was really fascinated by history and reading books about Plains Indians. Among the topics talked about was the ceremonial ways among the Crow people. When the white man's way and their religion came into the Crow people back in the 1880s, 1890s, that was when we started to see where tribes were now confined on reservations, which limited some of their traditional ways. The government imposed the white man's law on the Indian people, restricting them from practicing their ceremonial ways, or even banning them. So there was a struggle and confusion. But the Indian people are still trying to hold on to their cultural and belief ways, while also trying to maintain the new ways. So there was a lot of changeover that caused a lot of confusion and heartbreaks. Among the new ways was Christian religion.

As far as I know, the Catholic Church was one of the first ones to come to the Crow Reservation. Then the Baptists, which are nowadays about four branches. Then, more recently, the Pentecostal religion. Now the Indians were forced to submit to the white man's law. They also could no longer practice their ceremonial ways.

Anyway, when I met my wife, she was Catholic. Her father is Crow, and her mother is Mexican. Myself, I'm Crow, brought up the Crow way by my parents and grandparents. I wasn't Catholic until when my wife and I got married. When we got married, my grandfather told me, "It's okay to do both ways—Catholic, since your wife is Catholic, and also your way. There's nothin' wrong with that." I was fortunate that my wife understood, even though she was Catholic. If you think about it, Mexicans are also Natives. And my mother-in-law, who passed away, always talked about her culture—how there was some connection or similarity between their way and the Indian people. So she felt comfortable with my culture, and I was the same with her Catholic religion. My grandfather said, "There's nothing wrong with doing both of them. Because," he said, "when it comes down to it, we all pray to one God. Whether you're Indian, or Mexican, or Chinese or whatever. In religion, all prayers are to one God. The only difference is in the way we conduct our services."

White Religion versus Indian Ceremonials

But the part where I think there's some confusion and misunderstanding is between religion and ceremonials. Like with the peyote religion—if you ask me, I'd say peyote is a ceremonial. The reason why peyote is called a religion—also called the Native American Church—goes back to when peyote was finally being recognized by some of the states, like when Montana finally recognized the peyote ceremonial. The use of peyote among the Crows, the Cheyennes, and other tribes—in order for that to be recognized, of course, it had to go under the authority of the state, and then under the churches. And they also had to give it a name like the other churches. In other words, they told the Indian people, "Okay, now that ceremonial that you're doing, it has to have a name." And that's how the label "Native American Church" comes in. The "peyote religion." But I always tell people that peyote, to me, is a ceremonial. It's a sacred way. And the only reason why it's called the Native American Church is that it has to be put under a structure like the Catholic Church, the Baptist Church, all these. A ceremonial is something that has been practiced for many, many generations, still today.

Because, if you look at it, this ceremonial dates as far back as—well, way before any non-Indians were here. Peyote itself came from the south among the Indian people. It was said that when Cortes and the other Spaniards arrived—the conquistadors, from where they landed in South America and then working up towards this way, from old Mexico and up towards present-day Texas and New Mexico—it was said that the conquistadors always carried peyote and would eat it, not in the ceremonial way. Because of their long travels, they had to stay awake. So they would use peyote to help 'em keep awake. But among the Indian people, they ate peyote in a ceremonial way. There's a story about how the peyote ceremonial came to the Indian people.

Peyote Origin Story

These young boys, these two brothers, were very poor. One day they went out on the hills, and they were hungry because they were so poor, eating whatever they could find, like edible plants. They say it was like fasting. A being came to them in a dream and said, "You boys are very poor. I'm gonna help you. When you wake up, go on top of that hill over there. There's a plant there. Get it, and I'll show you how to use it. When you're there, look around and see the shape of the hill. That's how you build an altar. You've seen the moon, right? The half moon? Put that plant in the middle. And then," he said, "I'll show you the way."

So those boys woke up, and they went and searched, and they found this hill. They climbed up to the top, and right up on top they came upon this peyote there on the ground. So they prayed, and they picked it up, and they did as they were told. They looked around and saw that they were on top of this hill, and the ridge was kind of shaped like that half moon, like a crescent. So they went and took that plant down, and they sat. And that spirit person helped them out, showed them how to do it. And of course, you know, they were singing those songs.

Their mother started to worry about where her boys had gone, and here she came upon them. They were sitting there, and they were singing those songs and taking that peyote. She looked at 'em, and she cried. She felt sorry for these two boys. "Here we are. We don't have nothing. Barely making it. And here's my two boys, and they're doing something good." So she prayed, and she said, "I want to help them." Knowing that they were up all night, and the day before, they needed to drink some water—because water is the essence of our bodies, our souls. So she went and got some water, and asked those boys if they could stop for a minute. So they did.

And the mother told the boys, she said, "What you're doin' here makes me proud. Very proud, and very humble." She said, "My heart feels good 'cause of what you're doin' here, praying to the Creator." So she asked them for some time. She said, "I want to pray for you." So she did. She sat down there, and put the water in front of her. Those two boys were sitting there, and they had that peyote on that crescent there. They also built that fire. And then she prayed. And they say that as she prayed, she cried. It wasn't because she was sad, but because she was very proud, very happy with those kids and what they found. She prayed that, from there, they would prosper. And she prayed that this ceremonial would be carried on.

The Water Woman

Today, when they have those peyote ceremonials, that is the most sacred time of that ceremonial—when that woman brings in the water in the morning, and they sing four songs. The first song is sung, calling for the water and water woman. When that's over, the roadman stops, and they let the woman in. She sits, puts the water in front of her, and makes herself comfortable. Then the roadman starts singing three more songs. During that time, the tobacco is taken and rolled. When all four songs are done, they put their instruments down. They ask someone to pray the cedar—you know, smudge the cedar. When that person's done, then it's time for that woman to pray. A lot of young women today, when their family has meetings and they're asked to bring the water in, especially if it's their first time, they're like, "I'm scared. People will laugh at me, they'll make fun of me!" But I'm told, like by my grandfather who said, "No, that time's yours. That is the most sacred time. That is your time. They aren't gonna make fun of you. We're not gonna laugh at you."

They can pray in their own way, however they choose to pray. Some will pray loud; some always cry. That time, that crying, is the most sacred time of that ceremony. When that woman gets done praying, she holds that smoke four times, and the guy that helps the roadman will come and get that smoke and take it to the front, and he, too, will smoke and pray. Then that water goes around and you drink. They say—even my grandfather and my grandmother used to say—that during that time, either before or after they sing those songs, there's always a woman they could hear. A woman's voice singing, harmonizing songs. They say the spirit of that water woman—the one that started the ceremonial, the first one—is there. I've heard it myself at times.

It was the Creator that gave Indian people the peyote—through prayers, through these visions, through these dreams. This is where a lot of people with different religions don't understand. They say, "The Bible says, 'Thou shalt not worship another idol.' And you peyote people pray to that plant. That is the devil's work!" But the Creator gave this plant to Indian people to help themselves.

Marvin Speaks to Students at the Crow Tribal College

One time I was asked to speak to one of the religion classes over at Little Big Horn College at Crow Agency. And I had a full class, like twenty-five or thirty-some kids. And I asked the instructor, I said, "Do you have a list of who's in the class, a list of their names?" So while I was waiting, I was looking at that list. And sure enough, most of these students came from white religion—from Baptist, Catholic, and Pentecostal families. None came from traditional families.

So they come in, sit down, and I introduce myself, tell 'em I was asked to speak about the Indian way, the cultural way. I said, "I don't know many of you students, but I know your last names from this paper here. Matter of fact, I probably know many of your parents and grandparents. And I know they're Pentecostal, or they're Baptist. And you know what? They respect me, and I respect them. We respect each other, even though the way we pray is different. And some of you don't pray the Indian way anymore, but you're praying the white man's way—which we all do in the white man's church. Nothing wrong with that," I said. "It doesn't matter if you're Indian or white, or how you pray, different churches here and there. But what's true—it's in the Bible, and I even heard it from my elders—is that the true church is right here, *in your heart*. This is the true church, right here. Doesn't matter where you are. Doesn't matter if you have a ten-million-dollar cathedral. It's right here, as long as you're humble."

I told 'em, "This one guy went to church every Sunday. Every Sunday he goes to church. He criticizes people for not going to church, even if they miss one day. He criticizes them. He even embarrasses people, even his own family. Outside the church, he's mean, he's disrespectful, he embarrasses his family. People don't see the inside of that person. But here comes Sunday, and he's right there at church."

Then I said, "Here's this other man. He works hard, but he doesn't go to church. He may go to church once in a while, maybe for some special occasions for his family. He don't go to church, but you know what? That person—wherever he's at, wherever he goes, no matter what time of day—he's always praying. He helps people out, strangers, families, with whatever he has—food, money, he even shelters them. But he always prays in his heart."

My grandfather once told me this story about two old men who were friends since childhood. As elders, they both passed away at the same time. The story goes that the two arrived at the pearly gates of heaven. There they were greeted by Saint Peter. Right away, he lets the kind-hearted man in. The heartless one was told to wait. When he was told to wait, he was furious, expecting to be let in. He asked Saint Peter, "Why does he get to go in? I'm the one that goes to church every Sunday, and he doesn't go to church at all!" Saint Peter then says, "You're right. You go to church every Sunday. But when you leave church, you're a different person. Sorry to say, but you're heartless. The one that went in? Yes, he never hardly goes to church. But he's very humble to people, prays all the time in his heart, no matter who they are—he doesn't ask what religion they belong to. In his eyes, all men, all women, are children of God." Saint Peter told the heartless man, "Go over there"—pointing to purgatory—"and sit awhile, and think about it." So we know, when we die, we're gonna go up there, and God's gonna judge us by our heart. Not who we are, or what we have, or what we did. It's all here—in the heart.

Another thing I taught that class was about the Holy Spirit, the Holy Ghost, other religions, and Indian ceremonial ways. If you open the Bible and look at it, God said that he created the heavens, the stars, the moon. God created the various birds and all the animals, the land and everything on it. Man and wife. God was the one that created those. And in the Bible, it says, "Through these—keep 'em sacred. Respect 'em. Use them. I am the one that made these. You take care of them, and they will take care of you."

"You know," I said, "Indian people, a long time ago, didn't have a Bible. You know where their Bible is? Right here, inside. In the heart, and in the mind. Visions. They knew there was a Creator, a person that made all these things. In Crow, we say *Akbaatadía*. That being, that spirit, came or appeared to these people in dreams, visions, fasting, or apparitions. Just like those two boys I told you about. They came to them and said, 'Use these plants, these birds or feathers, these sacred things. When you pray, you're not praying to them—you're praying through them to me. And they bring your prayers to me. They carry your prayers and thoughts.'"

"Those statues in the Catholic Church," I said, "represent God's chosen ones because of their attributes and powers of intercession. The saints on earth at one time, they were holy. We have statues of the Mother of God, the holiest of all, and many others. We got Our Lady of Guadalupe, Our Lady of Lourdes, Our Lady of the Snows—but all are one Mother of God. We also have saints and angels—like Saint Michael, Saint Jude, and many more. All of these are part of the Holy Ghost and the Holy Spirit. And you can ask your families, your grandparents, at one time they probably saw an angel or felt the presence of an angel, the Holy Spirit. It's the same thing when you have your church meetings. You've heard of the Holy Spirit—that's the same thing. There is no difference. Those things carry prayers to the one and only God, and that's how things are. It doesn't matter how you do it. But like I said, the true church is right here—inside."

Anyways, so after I got done with the class, I had a few minutes left over. So I said, "I'd like all of you, if you don't mind—and you don't have to, and you don't have to write your names—but I'd like you to write a sentence about what you think about the things I said here today." Since class was over, I thought they'd all get up and head out. But you know what? Every one of 'em stayed. Every one of 'em started writing. Once they all left, I started reading them. And you know what the majority of 'em said? "We don't know about these things. My parents, my grandparents, they never told me about these things. All they said was, 'The Indian ceremonial ways today are bad.'" They said, "Now we understand. Now we know the Indian way."

LEARNING THE SACRED WAYS: GRANDFATHER'S TEACHINGS AND *BAAXPÉE*

We're told that you gotta be careful about the cultural way, the Indian way. You have to be very careful with it. Don't play around with it. Don't fool around with it. Because there's always this backfire if you do. My brother— that's his picture right there—he just passed away about February. When we graduated high school in '74, '75, he was already into this ceremonial stuff—the peyote, sweat lodge, naming children, goin' and blessing families. He was already into that stuff. Me, I was just—you know, I went to college a little bit, came back home, met my wife, we dated for about three or four years, then we got married. Sometimes I'd go to the meetings or whatever, but I was like a regular parishioner. Just like in church, where you kind of sit back, just a regular parishioner while you watch these altar boys and people up there really involved. Me, I just sat back. But my brother was already into that.

Finally, in the late '80s and '90s, my grandparents had already passed on, and my dad had passed on, but my mom was there. Some of the families that used to ask my grandfather to pray and to do ceremonial things for them, they said, "He is no longer here. So, Marvin, we feel that, even though your brother was there, and also you have your uncle there, we feel like now it's your time." So after my grandfather had passed away and people started to come to me, I realized what was happening. As I said, at that time, I maybe went to these things, but I wasn't really into it. Before my grandfather passed away, he'd always build a sweat. So when I got home, my wife would say, "Your grandfather called and he's built a sweat. He wants you to go over." And I was like, "I'm tired. I can't go."

Sometimes it would be just me and him, or maybe my brother-in-law. And he gave me the right to pour in there—to be the person that conducts that sweat. He gave that right to me and my brother-in-law. So as we took turns, he was always sitting there, always telling us things—telling us about the Peyote Way, the sacred way, these things. And he'd say, "All these things, there's spiritual power in them—*baaxpée*."[1] People who take care of these things, these spirits, they know. These spirits, they know who to cling to. When a person passes on all his belongings, family often fight over it. Some want this, some want that. "Don't do that," he said. "These things know." And he said, "You know, I passed on a lot of things to your brother and your uncle. But you know what, Marvin? It's going to be different for you. These things are going to come to you in a dream. And, of course, they'll say, 'Grandpa didn't give the right to Marvin, he's just doin' it himself.' But," he said, "when they come to you, you'll see I'm giving you all of what goes to you." Meaning that, when someone has a dream of this thing, it means it wants you. So you already have the right to do that. You don't have to go fasting. They've already chosen you.

When he passed away, I had some people who helped me with the Peyote Way, who helped me with goin' and sweatin'. There's one person that really took me as a brother. He always calls me Little Brother. He always tells me, "You know what, Marvin? Your brother and uncle were already into it, and you were just a bystander. But your grandfather knew that some day it was going to come to you. And that's what he was doing—he was putting things in your head. You didn't know he was doing that, Little Brother, did you?" So after he passed away, sure enough these families started to come and ask me to do things. "We know your grandfather is no longer here," they said, "so we think maybe it's time for you to carry some of this on." From there, I started to get these dreams about certain things.

So I tell people—all the stuff that I got? They came to me. I didn't ask for it. And my grandfather used to say, "You do have the right to accept—or not to accept—these things. If you feel you are not capable of carrying one, do not carry it. Just pray about it, and then let it be. There are some you will

PEYOTE AND CHRIST

be capable of, some that you can handle, and you'll know." And that's what I've been doing all these years.

THE PEYOTE WAY

As for the Peyote Way, you have to be given the right to run that ceremony. Same way with the sweat lodge; you have to be given the right. My father had what we call "the peyote chief." It's a dry peyote button. Every one that runs a peyote meeting—you know, like a priest or father that conducts that meeting—that person who is given the right is also given that plant. So when he runs that meeting—he's called the roadman—he puts that peyote chief in the middle just like those boys did that I told you about in the very beginning. So one day my dad says, "Here, Marvin. I want you to keep this. And some day people might ask you to start running meetings." So I still have that, and that's what I still use.

So when I started doing this Peyote Way, it was *Boom! Boom!* Everything just came at once. And for a time there, like every weekend, I was off going to peyote meetings. People would come and get me, and off we go to peyote meetings. Instead of running the peyote meetings at first, I started by taking care of that fire. When you're asked to run a meeting, conduct a meeting, you ask someone to drum for you—we call that the drum man— and there's that person who takes care of the fire. So I started off taking care of that fire. That was around '92, '93, '94, when I started to kind of get into it.

So I kept going. Sometimes we'd have family plans, and someone comes last minute and asks me to help at a meeting, and I jump in and off we go. One time I was working at the coal mine. I was working night shifts. I was home alone, and I was sitting there, drinking coffee, where there was this knock on the door. Here it was someone from the first family that asked me to run a peyote meeting. So he came in and had some coffee. And he said, "Marvin, I want to tell you something. I've been hearing a lot of good things about you, going to all these peyote meetings. But you know what? Like your grandfather told you, you gotta be careful. You gotta slow down. You need to spend time with your wife, your kids. I know it's hard to say no when someone asks you, but you gotta do it." From then on, I was just kind of like—slow down, slow down, slow down.

Today, I haven't gone to a peyote meeting for five, six years. But I still believe in that way. I still have my stuff there. I'm still asked to go to sweat lodges, to pray for the family, take part in clan feedings and some of those ceremonial things. And my kids, I talk to them about those things.

DEVOTION TO OUR LADY OF GUADALUPE

Nowadays I also go to the Catholic Church. As a matter of fact, in the Catholic Church now I am a strong Christian. I work on Sundays, so I can't always go to church. But I make an effort to go over there on Wednesdays when we have the youth group. I go into Father Charlie's house at St. Dennis to a little room where there's statues in there, and icons and everything. You sit in there, and I'll tell you what! I sometimes feel the presence of the Holy Spirit, the Mother of God, the angels. I've felt their presence.

One night, I was sleeping and I had a dream. I saw Our Lady in a white cloth, and she was holding her hands in front of her, looking at me. And she said, "Pray with me, 'Our Lady, Mother of God, pray for us. Our Lady, Mother of God, pray for us.' Say that!" So I did in my dream. When I woke up, I was still saying that prayer. I told my wife, and she knows that I've had visions and I've had dreams—as a matter of fact, I'm a devoted believer of Our Lady of Guadalupe. So she said, "Our Lady, she gave you that prayer."

I even use that holy oil and pray with families. Whenever I use that oil to pray with families, I can feel the presence of God, or the angels, or the Holy Ghost, or the Holy Spirit, and mostly Our Lady, the Mother of God. Of course, I have my Indian stuff, too. And I also feel the same presence of the spirit with that as I do with my oil and the Catholic religion.

THE ANKO WAY: FROM KIOWA TO CROW

I talk about sacredness and holiness; about the cultural way, the Indian way; about medicine and sacred things; about the way of my grandparents, the Peyote Way. All of these are mentioned in the Bible. The birds, the animals, the plants, they have a spirit in them. And sometimes, as I mentioned, these things are left behind when people pass away, and families will fight over it. But my grandfather said, "If that particular thing wants you to take care of it, you'll know—you'll dream."

Each one that conducts the peyote meeting, they always say "the way." Our way—meaning the way of our family, the Ten Bears—that way comes from Oklahoma. It's called the Anko way.[2] That's Kiowa. My grandparents used to go to Oklahoma during November for hand games. So a long time ago, they met this family down there. That family—well, old man Anko—took my grandmother as his sister. Through this adoption we are also related to the Big Bow family and the Kaulaity family. Then, during spring, they come here to us. The menfolk always call my grandfather "brother-in-law," and they always call my grandmother "sister." So when that old man came, he gave that right of the Oklahoma way, the Anko way, to four Crows. And to each one he gave a water-bird tail-feather fan. My grandfather was one of them.

That's when he gave my grandfather a special water-bird fan to use in the peyote meeting. My uncle was the one that was using it, but he passed away at a very young age. He was a tribal council member. So my grandfather had it. When my grandfather passed away, my uncle, the one that just passed away a few years ago, took care of that fan. So when I started going and gettin' into the Peyote Way as I mentioned, I didn't have nothing. You know, everyone has fans and boxes and stuff. So my uncle gave me a brown box as my first peyote box. Just a plain old box. And I don't have no fan. So he loaned this one to me, just to use during meetings. So I took that fan and I'd go to peyote meetings, and next day I'd come back and return it to him.

Then one night I had a dream. I was standing on the bank of a river. I looked up and there were water birds flying towards me. One of those water birds spoke to me and said, "I'm going to come down into the water, and you grab whatever you want." And the first one came and dove right into the lake, and I grabbed the center tail feather. Then another one came. Pretty soon they're all coming, and I'm like going after the center tail feathers. When I got all the center ones, he said, "Use it. People that are sickly, people that want help—use this. When you use it, call upon my name, *binnakáak-baaxpaa* (holy water bird)." He said, "I give you that."

So next day, I went to my uncle. I said, "Tyrone, last night I had a dream about the water-bird fan"—and I told him about the dream. So, he was sittin' there, kind of quiet. Then pretty soon he got up, you know. He got up, and he went and got his peyote stuff. And he took out that fan and said, "Here"—and he gave me the fan. He said, "They came to you to take care of them. They know. It was meant for you. From now on, you hold it."

It's one of the four fans that was originally given to our tribe by old man Anko. One time I was at a peyote meeting, and I was just in there as a regular parishioner. In the morning we got out, and at noon my wife and kids came. So we were sitting there eating, and this older guy, he's a tribal historian, he was talking to his sister. She was elderly, too. And he was telling his sister about these water-bird fans that came among the Crow—how there was four of 'em that were brought from down below by the Kiowa, by the Anko family. And he said, "I know I've seen two of them, and the other one is still in Pryor. But I always wondered where the fourth one was, because they told me there was four of them. I've never known all these years where the fourth one was. I had a hunch, but I didn't know for sure"—and then he pointed at me—"until last night. That fan rightfully goes to that family."

PERSECUTION OF EARLY CROW PEYOTISTS

Peyote started way back, coming from the south and workin' its way up here. The Cheyennes, just to the east of us, were the ones that got hold of peyote here in Montana. They were already having ceremonials in the 1890s led by a Cheyenne named Leonard Tyler.[3] And here the Crows would go and visit. And it just so happened that a Crow by the name of Frank Bethune went and visited the Cheyennes. He was there in that ceremonial, and he's the one that brought that practice over here to the Crow. He was the first peyote roadman from among the Crow. This was in 1913, 1914.[4] And then, from there, it kind of spread—the Half Moon tradition. Later, some would bring in what we call the Cross Fire tradition. But the majority of Crows here use that Half Moon, the crescent.[5] The Peyote Way was going good, but we started to see where states banned Indians and tribes from using peyote. I always heard that back in the late '50s, '60s, they would hide, they would go to the mountains to do their peyote meetings. There's a point to the west of here that's called Peyote Point. My grandfather told me some stories about that place when they had peyote meetings. You can see it when you're over at Fort Smith. That's how far they went, because if they got caught they'd go to jail.

The Big Sheep Case is one of the historical landmarks for peyote.[6] Right there at my grandparents' old place, inside there they had a peyote meeting.

PEYOTE AND CHRIST

My grandfather Stray Calf was among those that continued the Peyote Way. His brother-in-law, his name was Big Sheep, was the one that was running that meeting. Big Sheep was married to Austin Stray Calf's sister. Night time came, about half way through the meeting, and—*clap!*—the doors open, and here comes the Hardin police.[7] They barged in there, stopped 'em, and they told 'em, "You have broke the law! There are no peyote meetings—peyote is banned, it's outlawed! We'll have to arrest you." Big Sheep, of course, said, "I'm the one. You can take me." But instead of telling him to get up, they literally went over and grabbed him. He was an old man, but they grabbed him, pulled him up, handcuffed him, and drug him out. My grandfather Stray Calf, our grandfather, saw that, and he was furious. The others asked, "Who's going to finish this meeting?" So my grandfather got up, and he went and sat there to finish the meeting.

I talked already about the medicine, the power, in our ceremonies. That's why they always tell us, "Be careful. There's power in that. It may be sacred—it's got the Holy Spirit and everything—but you gotta watch the power of it." Back then, the old folks, as they say, the elderly, they weren't afraid to use ceremonials to kill another person. They weren't afraid. So that night, before my grandfather started that meeting, he rolled a smoke. He was furious about what they did to his brother-in-law. He said, "Those two white people, you'll see. In a few days," he said, "*bahámneetdiio!* They'll be nothing, they'll be gone!" And sure enough, later on one of the officers had a massive heart attack. *Clap!* After that, an escapee from jail here took off. So that other officer went after him. Somehow he caught up with him, but that guy had a gun. Before the officer grabbed him, he turned around and—*boom!*—shot and killed him instantly. Those two went like that.[8]

Peyote's used lots of ways—for school graduations, for health, for well-being, doctoring, or just giving thanks. Because that's the way they've been thanking the Creator through that medicine. So there's many ways of using it—using that power. That's why they always tell me, "Watch what you say at those peyote meetings. Be careful. 'Cause that peyote meeting, it will sometimes do things that you ask which you don't really speak of." But other than that, the peyote is humble. He knows. Like those two boys that found that peyote. They were humble. And their mother cryin' that time, looking for her boys. It felt that holiness, and brought them together.

Relying on Clan Relatives to Share the Load

If anything, this stuff here—like this peyote box, the fans, and all these things—it would normally be my son's. My wife and I were just talking about this a while back. You know, I may give 'em the simple things, things that will help 'em like for health, prosperity, and things like that. But what we call "the heavy duty stuff"—this stuff here like the fans, the staff, the peyote stuff—I don't think I'll pass that on. It's not that they don't know how to do it, but I don't think they'd be able to carry that load. 'Cause when you have those, and families ask you to pray and lead ceremonies, you're carrying a lot of the load. The load of that family is on your shoulders. And whatever you pray—whether in the sweat lodge, or peyote meeting, or even in the Sun Lodge—when you're praying for a family, that whole family's on your shoulders. Because these ceremonials, they're immune to that. They come together, and it's you who's going to have to sort it out.

And that's where, in turn, there's the balance—that's where you replenish yourself by giving one of your clan uncles or clan brothers gifts, or have him or her pray for you. Or you can have a sweat lodge, or have one of your clan uncles come and have him pray. And it's just like my grandfather said one time. He said, "Let's say you got $5 bills, and you have this stuff and every time when you have a family that asks you to pray, it's like you're giving another family one of those $5 bills. And you go on, and finally you'll start to feel that pressure, that stress, that drain. And that's where your clan uncles, clan aunts, the sweat lodge—that's where you need them to help you, have them pray for you, have them use stuff on you. Then, in turn, you get 'em back again. It replenishes you." But he said, "You'll feel it. Don't ever let it drain out. You know your capabilities. You know how much you can do."

The ceremonials, the Peyote Way and sweat lodge—even the powwows or dances—we always talk about the sacred circle. The sacred circle. My grandfather always said, "No matter what the circle is—whether it be the peyote ceremonial, or the sweat lodge, or even the powwow—that circle, inside there, that's sacred, too. There's things inside that circle."

In the powwow circuit today, you'll see dancers in there that if an eagle feather falls, they'll stop and do this ceremonial where they pick it up. That ceremonial originated with the Crows. After World War I, when the Crows came back from overseas, the elders said, "Hey, let's have a celebration.

Let's have a dance." They didn't use the word "powwow" yet. They said, "Let's have a celebration, a dance. We'll all celebrate, thanking the Creator for bringin' our boys home." So they started dancing, and here one of 'em dropped an eagle feather. And they looked at it, and they said, "Hold on here. I'm going to ask one his clan uncles who, in the past, has been a veteran himself"—meaning he was a warrior, he's done many great deeds and had many honors. "I want that veteran to come and pick that feather up and give it back to him. In turn, all that good stuff will be in that fan when the feather is returned." So that old man was called to come forth to pick up that feather, and hand it back to that young man, and say, "Here—may you have a lot of good fortunes, may you have a family, and good stuff." So the family of that young boy gave gifts to that old man. So now that's a tradition. And today, it's a universal thing. Now all tribes do that. We're fortunate that today we still carry on our ways.

HEALING RITES AND HAVING "ONE HEART"

I remember when my kids got sick and were colicky, and we'd be up late at night, I would go and get my grandma. So finally one day she said, "I'm gonna show you, teach you, give you the right to work on children." So she passed that on to me. So even today, families will bring kids to me, their colicky kids or they don't know what's wrong—even adults that need to be rubbed. I have sweet sage, or sometimes I use those coals, ashes, special medicine for kids. Then I have this bag my grandma gave me. She filled it up with cedar, sweet sage, bear root, and sweetgrass. And she said, "Don't ever let this go empty." This was back in the '80s. So every time there's a headache, toothache, whatever, I get that and put it on. It really helps.

We're told not to refuse if someone comes for help, even if they're very sickly and only have a certain time to live. My grandfather used to say, "Don't turn 'em away. Who knows, you might at least extend her or his life a week or two. Just help 'em." And he also said, "When you're going to do these things, don't ever doubt it. Don't ever doubt. Don't ever say, 'I wonder if I can do this.' Even if you don't feel right, don't ever think that way. Don't ever doubt yourself." In Crow we say, *dalúusa dúupasaa*. Meaning, "Don't have two hearts, don't be conflicted." You gotta have one heart. One heart. Go do it. So, no matter what the circumstances are, I try to help whoever comes to me.

NOTES

1. For more on the Crow concept of *baaxpée*, generally referred to as "medicine" or "spiritual power" in English, see Frey, *World of the Crow Indians*, 59–149.
2. Marvin generally spells this Kiowa family name "Ankque." Here I use the spelling adopted by Omer Stewart, a historian of the Peyote Way.
3. Omer Stewart, citing a Mennonite missionary in Montana, offers a date of 1889 for Tyler's introduction of peyote to the Northern Cheyennes. See Omer Stewart, *Peyote Religion: A History* (Norman: University of Oklahoma Press, 1987), 183.
4. For more on the early history of peyote use among the Northern Cheyenne and Crow Tribes of Montana, see Stewart, *Peyote Religion*, 183–89. As Stewart notes, although the two tribes were often unfriendly, their immediate geographical proximity to one another led to the rapid diffusion of peyote from the Northern Cheyennes to the Crows soon after the turn of the twentieth century. Edison Real Bird, as quoted by Omer Stewart, suggests a date similar to the one Marvin gives for the arrival of peyote among the Crows: "My grandfather, Frank Bethune, put up the first peyote tipi on the Crow Reservation about 1910. Before that, he had brought peyotism from the Northern Cheyenne" (184). In documenting the movement of peyote from the Kiowas to the Crows, Stewart cites several of the families and figures referenced by Marvin in his interview. These include Austin Stray Calf, Frank Bethune, the Ten Bears, and the Ankos (188).
5. For a brief description of key ritual differences between the Half Moon and Cross Fire traditions, see Stewart, *Peyote Religion*, 327–30.
6. Omer Stewart gives a date of 1924 for the Big Sheep case. However, it was in 1926 that the Montana Supreme Court issued their ruling in *State v. Big Sheep*, upholding the state's right to prohibit the ceremonial use of peyote. See Larry M. Elison and Fritz Snyder, *The Montana State Constitution: A Reference Guide* (Westport, Conn.: Greenwood Press, 2001), 40. It was not until the 1994 "Amendments" to the American Indian Religious Freedom Act of 1978 that tribally enrolled Native Americans were granted federal protection for the ceremonial use of peyote within the context of "traditional Indian religions for which the sacramental use of peyote is integral to their practice."
7. Hardin is located on the northern boundary of the Crow Reservation, about thirteen miles north of Crow Agency. Its population is roughly 50 percent white and 40 percent American Indian.
8. For more on the events recounted in this story, see Tim McCleary, "A Flash Point in Big Horn County History: The Death of Officer John MacLeod and Sheriff Robert Gilmore," *Big Horn County News* (Hardin, Mont.), April 9, 1997. According to historical records, both officers were killed in the shootout referenced here by Marvin Dawes.

12

Baptists, Bear Medicine, and the Bible

AN INTERVIEW WITH MARLON PASSES

The following interview was conducted beside the sweat lodge where Marlon often prays along the Little Bighorn River near the Crow Reservation town of Garryowen. In the background, the canvas of a peyote tipi was being tested by the stiff winds of a summer thunderstorm that threatened to push us indoors. It was a fitting backdrop for our conversation, beginning with Marlon's opening story of a great-grandfather who had thrown his bear medicine bundle into a nearby river at the urging of a venerated Baptist missionary nearly a century earlier.

Among the central themes of Marlon's interview is a repeated emphasis on the role that nature plays in Crow religious practice—from the reservation's hilltops to the sun, from the wild grizzly to the peyote plant. At

Marlon Passes, sitting beside his sweat lodge and peyote tipi along the Little Bighorn River near Garryowen, Crow Reservation. *Photo by Dave Kapferer*

the same time, he is eager to contrast the tribe's commitment to nature's inherent sanctity with his perception of Christianity as a religion that disparages, and insulates itself against, elements of the natural world. Perhaps this dichotomy is best illustrated in the words he quotes from John Pretty On Top, his clan brother and a Sun Dance chief: "You white men, you have your churches. But my church is this ground. When we fast, we go up to the mountains and we pray to God. And you white men have your cathedrals, your churches, and your steeples with the cross on top. Our cathedrals are the mountains. The highest point of those mountains is our steeple. That's where we go and sit, without food and water, and talk to God."

Despite these difference, Marlon frequently highlights points of complementarity across religious traditions. On more than one occasion, I've heard him refer to the world's religions as different branches of the same tree. While some claim that the Bible condemns Native religions, Marlon cites a variety of passages to argue exactly the opposite. In support of the Sun Dance, Marlon refers to the time that "Moses spoke to God in the form of a fire"—a point that reinforces Marlon's own claim that "God is the sun, and the sun is God." In defense of the sacramental use of peyote in the Native American Church, Marlon cites the New Testament writings of Saint Paul to affirm "everything created by God is good, and nothing is to be rejected." When discussing the spirit helpers who come to the aid of Crows through dreams or while fasting in the hills, Marlon suggests that these are the same beings Christians call angels.

While Marlon emphasizes points of commonality between tribal religious practices and the teachings of the Bible, he does not shy away from drawing attention to the painful colonialist legacy that Christian missionaries have inflicted on the Crow Tribe through the years. In one instance recorded below, he refers to the unnamed wife of a missionary who equated the Sun Dance with devil worship. And then there's the story of his great-grandfather, Deernose Goes Together, whose loyalty to the Baptist church cost the family their bear medicine. "They almost did away with my family's identity," he says, adding: "They used religion to deceive the Indian people." Marlon's explanation of how that lost medicine recently returned to his brother during a fast in the Big Horn Mountains is a testimony to the vitality of Crow traditionalism amid an enduring legacy of Christian evangelism.

While Marlon loosely identifies with the Baptist denomination because of his family's historic relationship with the institution, he primarily regards himself as a practitioner within the Native American Church, a path he has been traveling for the past thirty-five years. As such, he passionately defends the efficacy and sanctity of a host of traditional Crow practices, including the sweat lodge, fasting in the reservation mountains, and the Crow understanding of spiritual power, known as medicine or *baaxpée*, as preserved in sacred objects like the medicine bundle and bear-claw necklace described in the following narrative.

❁

MISSIONARY DISPOSAL OF MEDICINE BUNDLES

One story that I told you about earlier involved Dr. Petzoldt, who was one of the first missionaries to arrive on the Crow Indian Reservation. His thought was to Christianize the Crow people. And some of them people actually took it upon themselves to receive his direction about throwing their medicine bundles into the river. Either to burn 'em, or throw 'em into the river. My great-grandfather's name was Deernose Goes Together. His medicine bundle had something to do with a bear. I don't know what Dr. Petzoldt said to them, but my great-grandfather took that medicine bundle and disposed of it into the river. That was probably in the early 1900s, because my grandfather fought some battles with the enemy tribes back then. He has his story of how he got his name.

But anyway, that happened and my family kind of became strong Baptists, I'll put it that way. They came to believe that the Indian way of praying to God was not right. Their quote was, "Thou shalt have no gods before me." They felt that the traditional Crow way involved praying to various medicine objects instead of praying to God. But the Crows, we believe that these objects were obtained through fasting and self-sacrifice, going without food and water for three or four days. They received these objects either through a dream, or through something of nature that might have occurred while they were out there fasting. They came through an experience that happened between that person and the spirit helpers that we believe in—maybe more commonly known as angels. But to me, they're all the same. They help us, they protect us, they watch over us.

So they revered those objects. They were so sacred that sometimes the holder was prohibited from doing certain things. For example, some people could not eat certain things. There was kind of a restriction in some of those objects. Everybody who has received a power from fasting, or from Sun Dancing, everybody's different, and everybody has their own experience. One good friend of mine just gave a person an Indian name with what he experienced up there in the Big Horn Mountains where he fasted. It's hard to explain. Like I said, the only way you can find out is if you experience the experience itself.

Grizzly Bear and Lost Medicine Returned

Let me tell you about the bear medicine my brother received after fasting up here in the Crazy Mountains a couple years back. He said, "I fasted in front of a waterfall, where I made my circle. And I don't know where that grizzly bear came from"—but he said that grizzly bear came from the north from all those rocks, where there were no trees. Nothing but rock. My brother said, "That bear came about six or seven feet away from me. He looked right at me and, for some reason, I felt that he knew what I was doing. My heart started beating. I was like, 'Boy, this grizzly bear is going to eat me up!' I was scared!" But that grizzly bear just stood there, and then—one time—*ROAR!* Then that bear wandered off.

I told my brother about how, back in the early 1900s, our grandfather's medicine bundle was disposed of in the river. And I said to him, "He gave it back to you. Now you're the owner of that bear medicine because of that experience right there with that grizzly bear." And one of our grandmas, she's gone now, she was the closest of the daughters to our great-grandfather. Before he left, although they had disposed of that medicine bundle due to Dr. Petzoldt, he kept that necklace that was made of bear claw. And before he left, he gave this bear necklace to my grandma in a box.

And she told my brother Robert that, before my father died, my father said to cherish this necklace made out of bear claw. You know those old dimes from the 1800s? Those dimes are tied onto that necklace, too. My brother has that necklace. To me, one plus one, it adds up. I believe they gave that bear medicine back to my brother all these years after it was thrown in the river.

Anyway, my brother became an artist in Santa Fe. He still has that necklace, and I believe the necklace has that power. His business started out slow, but he became a success with his jewelry making. He's made good money doing this work. He's leading a real good life. So that's what I told him. To me, they gave that medicine back to our family, back to my brother.

Peyote, the Bible, and Unknown Tongues

A lot of the peyote people, members of the Native American Church, a lot of 'em have been baptized Christian. Some Pentecostals, some Catholics, some Baptists. They practice both religions. Just like that tree right there, it's got many branches, but there's one seed that started this tree. That's how I perceive the belief in the Creator, God, Jesus.

As for myself, I started using peyote in 1980. My mother who gave birth to me was in a car wreck in 1975. She was in the hospital for years. She was like a wounded animal. It seemed like nothing was helping. People would go in there, and she wasn't getting well. She just lay there day to day. So one day I told myself, "I'm going to go pray for her in a peyote meeting." I even put up a peyote meeting for her.[1]

So we were going to take her to the peyote meeting, but then we found out they were going to have us arrested! We had everything all prepared that night, and the doctor says, "We've been told not to let you take her out." And it was kinda like a blow. She couldn't talk, but she could hear us. So I spoke to her in Crow. I said, "We're having a peyote meeting for you, but they told us not to let you go out." So I said to the doctor that I'm going to talk to her in Crow, and if she nods her head it means she wants to go out with us. I said we'll leave it up to her. But if she says, "No," then we'll just have to go without her. So I said to her, "I'm having a peyote meeting for you, to help you. Do you want to go out with us?" She nodded her head "yes." So we took her out. We took her in a peyote meeting and prayed for her. A medicine man from Oklahoma doctored her that time. We held that meeting in the Two Leggings area.[2]

One time I was going through the Bible and kinda highlighting things that I liked. And somebody told me I was misinterpreting the Bible by saying it supports what we do in the Native American Church. But, to me, we use the peyote as a sacrament. What gives it that feeling when you consume that peyote? Nobody knows. They've tried giving it a name: it's a hallucinogen, it's a narcotic, it's a drug. But what gives you that feeling? It's a natural element that God planted down south, and we bring it north, where it gradually made its way to the northern tribes of the Native American Church in the early 1900s. In the Bible, there's this one chapter that says, "For everything that I have made is good. If you take of it, eat it, and pray to me in that manner, it's all good."[3] But some very staunch Christians who oppose the views of the Native American Church, they don't look at it that way.

They say, "You guys are just praying to a plant." But God made that plant, and he made that plant for a purpose. In the story of the Native American Church, they say a woman and her child were out in the desert. She was thirsty and hungry, and they said while she slept she had a dream. And in this dream, a spirit helper described to her this certain plant. She was supposed to go find that plant, and pray with it, and eat it. She was told, "It's gonna help you make it through your journey, to get to safety." And then he described to her these certain songs that had to be sung. They're always the same songs: the opening song, the midnight water song, the morning water song, and the closing song, as we call it.

You hear people talk about "the unknown tongue."[4] Well, our people still pray in the Crow language. When I pray, I pray in the Apsáalooke language. And people from other tribes don't know what I'm saying. But the Creator knows what I'm saying. It's just like the Cheyennes. They have their own language. And when they pray, they pray in their Cheyenne language. And he listens to them, too. The Navajo, the Kiowa, the Comanches—all different tribes that use peyote, they all pray in their own language.

So when I go to Cheyenne, I might not know what they're saying in their peyote meetings. But they're praying for each other, and we're helping each other out through the power of prayer. A lot of people don't understand that, and they kind of ridicule us for practicing the Native American Church. But like one of my friends always says, "This is a very beautiful way." It's a new way, a new religion to the Crow people. Right here where we're sitting this evening, this is our peyote ground, our sweat ground. This is where we have *our* church. We help each other out here. It's a family. And it's a good way. It's a good way.

"God Is the Sun, and the Sun Is God"

I like the way John Pretty On Top put it. He's my clan brother, and he always talks good to me. He's also a Sun Dance chief. He said, "You white men, you have your churches. But my church is this ground. When we fast, we go up to the mountains and we pray to God. And you white men have your cathedrals, your churches, and your steeples with the cross on top. Our cathedrals are the mountains. The highest point of those mountains is our steeple. That's where we go and sit, without food and water, and talk to God."

I always did like that, you know, the way he expressed it. In the Bible, they say Moses spoke to God in the form of a fire. As I like to say, the sun is God. Man has landed on the moon. They walked up there, but we'll never be able to set foot on the sun. It never goes out. Right now it's dark here in Montana, but it's daybreak on the other side of the world where the sun's serving another group of people. It never goes out. That's my interpretation. That God is the sun.

One time this lady told a missionary's wife, "I'm going to a Sun Dance." The missionary said, "No, don't go! Those things are no good! They're devil-worshipping!" But then that lady told the missionary what I just told you—that they're praying to the sun, that God is the sun, and the sun is God. It never goes out. It helps us. It makes this grass grow after a rain. So that's what I tell people when they ask me about that. I like to go watch the Sun Dance, and listen to the music. It's a beautiful feeling, too, the Sun Dance music—when you hear that eagle whistle.

You know, for us Indian people, nature plays an important role in our beliefs. Everything has a purpose. When you go out and fast, that's when you come to appreciate a blade of grass and a drop of water. This water here in the Little Horn River, God gave this to us, and we use that water for our ceremonies—in the sweat lodge, in the peyote meetings. We pray over that water, and we drink it, and we ask for good things. If it wasn't for water, life would not go on. It won't last very long without water. As I've said before, if the fish ever come to the surface dead, that's when we're in trouble.

NOTES

1. Every peyote meeting has a person who serves as the sponsor. This is what Marlon means when he says that he "put up" a meeting for his mother. The sponsor calls the meeting for a designated purpose (for example, to celebrate the graduation of a child, or to pray for the health of a sick family member, as Marlon did in this case). The sponsor is also responsible for the considerable planning and financial burden associated with each meeting.

2. Two Leggings was a notable Crow warrior of the prereservation days. His story was recorded by ethnologist William Wildschut in the early 1920s. Those notes were later edited and prepared for publication by Peter Nabokov in *Two Leggings: The Making of a Crow Warrior* (1967; reprint, Lincoln: University of Nebraska Press, 1982).

3. Marlon appears to be referencing I Timothy 4:4, "For everything created by God is good, and nothing is to be rejected, provided it is received with thanksgiving; for it is sanctified by God's word and by prayer" (New Revised Standard Version).

4. Here Marlon is referring to the Pentecostal practice of glossolalia, or "speaking in tongues."

13

Peyote, Pentecostalism, and President Obama

AN INTERVIEW WITH LEVI BLACK EAGLE

The comments of Levi Black Eagle illustrate an important shift taking place among young adult Crow Pentecostals today. Since the 1950s, Crow Pentecostalism has consistently condemned traditional Crow ways and exhorted followers to abandon involvement in tribal religious ceremonies. Today, however, a growing number of young Crow Pentecostals are questioning whether such a stark choice is necessary. Levi is among those finding ways to embrace Pentecostalism without rejecting the Traditionalism of the tribe. It's a difficult process, undertaken in the face of sharp opposition from highly revered Crow Pentecostal leaders, all within a tight-knit tribal community where respect for elders is one of the highest values.

Levi Black Eagle on his family's peyote grounds in Lodge Grass, Crow Reservation. *Photo by Dave Kapferer*

Levi grew up in the reservation town of Lodge Grass among a family steeped in the Native American Church. His paternal grandfather, Hartford "Sonny" Black Eagle Jr., was a major figure in the Peyote Way before his death in 2012. When he was just entering high school, however, Levi became deeply affected by a Pentecostal revival in the nearby town of Wyola, which led him to abandon his grandfather's tradition. "After I became a Christian and gave my life to Jesus," he explains, "I thought that my Native American traditional values were bad." For this reason, he refused to attend peyote meetings, including one held in his honor after graduating from high school.

More than ten years later, Levi began looking for ways to overcome this deep religious and cultural divide. He grew increasingly convinced that he could maintain his Christian faith while reclaiming the rich traditions of the Native American Church. He was particularly eager to spare his own children the same agonizing struggle he faced as a child, trying to reconcile his Crow heritage with his Christian faith. To that end, he and his wife decided to leave their reservation congregation for a Pentecostal church in Billings where Levi's multiple religious belongings pose less of a problem. He also began attending peyote meetings. He describes feeling no guilt in practicing both ways and highlights how the two traditions function to complement one another.

The importance of bestowing sacred names within the Crow Tribe is also highlighted in Levi's narrative. He explains how his grandfather gifted him with the name "He Walks to the Drum," a reference to a common practice in the Native American Church. It's clear from Levi's story that a desire to live up to that name was among the factors drawing him back to the Peyote Way, despite Pentecostal pressure to the contrary. It was during a peyote meeting that his grandfather also named Levi's son, bestowing one of his own titles on the young boy: President Adopter. It was back in May 2008 that Levi's grandparents adopted Barack Obama into the Black Eagle family, six months before Obama was elected to his first presidential term. At one point in the narrative, Levi shares his sadness over returning to the Native American Church too late for his deceased grandfather to see him become a full participant in the tradition. As Levi explains, "One of the regrets I have is that my grandpa will never hear me sing. I'll never get to drum for him. And it kind of hurts. It hurts a lot."

Today, Levi continues to attend peyote meetings while remaining active in his Pentecostal church in Billings. In addition to rejecting the kind of anti-Traditionalism that he himself experienced growing up in Crow Pentecostal churches, Levi likewise rejects the strong anti-Christian sentiments he sometimes hears from traditional elders. He believes that the underlying Crow value of respect for all people leaves little room for religious exclusivism, regardless of who's preaching it. The following interview took place on the Black Eagles' peyote grounds in Lodge Grass, beside a tipi set up for a meeting that night.

❀

Balancing Two Cultures as a Youth

My name is Levi Black Eagle. I'm from Lodge Grass, Montana, and I'm Crow Indian. Where we're talking now, we kind of gave this place an informal name after they built this shade arbor. People are calling it Peyote Park, or Peyote Paradise. This little area is kind of specifically used for peyote meetings. Every once in a while they'll use it for some sort of reception, but mainly this is where the peyote meetings happen in my family.

Growing up as a Native American, you're automatically kind of born into the culture. It's so prevalent that you don't even really have a choice in it. You're just kind of in it. I guess that's true for everybody as you grow up. Some people grow up in church, some people grow up in other ways. It just depends on who you are and where you are. So, in a way, I didn't really choose to be who I am. I grew up knowing about clan feeds and giveaways, and everything being passed down through the generations—respect your elders, and values like that. Even small things—for example, we don't look people in the eyes. It's a sign of disrespect. So if someone's talking to you, you'll see a lot of people have their head down, kind of nodding. So that was really hard to break away from when I grew up, left high school, and went out to try to get jobs and stuff. Looking at someone, it's a little uncomfortable. But I know that's what you had to do. It's really hard. If you raise your voice and look someone in the eye, you would only do that if you're kind of being stern and angry at somebody. So, it was a little different growing up.

But it's how I grew up, and I didn't know it was, like, different. You know what I mean?

What was hard was trying to balance two totally different lifestyles. You had the Western civilization come out here, but we already had our thing and we tried to hold on to it the best we could 'cause we never wanted to lose it. Crows traditionally are pretty good about holding on to their tradition. Like with our language, compared to some other tribes, I think Crow has a pretty high percentage of people who still speak their language among tribal high schools. Here in Lodge Grass we actually have a class where they teach our language. A lot of the teachers are Crow, and they try to keep our traditions alive.

Among our tribe, you have your sweat, and you have your peyote meeting, of course, and there's the Sun Dance. A lot of these ceremonies aren't traditionally Crow, since we kind of adopted them from different tribes. But they became traditional, and we made it ours. Another thing is the tipi itself, like the one we have set up here for tonight's peyote meeting. Putting that up is almost like a religion itself. You gotta know a lot in order to do it properly.

Pentecostal Revival in High School: "That Became My Life"

But growing up—how would I say it?—Christianity had a big influence on me. Wyola, a town just south of here on the reservation, is a really, really small town, almost where you'd call it a village. And yet, there's, like, five churches there. Here in Lodge Grass, we also have a number of churches. You got the Catholic church, the Baptist church, and there's also two different Pentecostal churches. Growing up, like during my high school years, I wasn't fully traditional and I wasn't fully into Christianity, either. My one grandpa would make me go to the Catholic church every Sunday. He would kind of wake me up and drag me there. When I got to an age where I could make decisions on my own, me and my whole family got caught up in the revival that broke out in Wyola around '97. I was sixteen years old. That went on for a few months, actually. Every night it was church, church, church, church. It was huge, and it was Pentecostal. It was like a big old revival. People were getting "slain in the Spirit," speaking in tongues. I think I saw a couple exorcisms. It was really weird, and I was in it. I was right in it!

That became my life, and I kind of got caught up in a lot of these fire-and-brimstone teachers. They were saying like—I don't know how to say it without putting anyone down or being disrespectful—but they were really quick to condemn. They're really quick to say, "You can't do this, and you can't do that." A lot of them are pretty extreme, saying, "You can't play sports, and you can't think this way, or you're going to hell." And I was kind of bound by that because those were the people I was under, those were my church elders. So it really veered me away from anything traditional. And it's really hard because my grandpa, who passed away recently—well, the traditional ways were his life. His name was Hartford "Sonny" Black Eagle. This was the way he was raised, and this was what he knew.

He was also—how would I say it?—he had access to the church. He knew who Jesus was. He knew that faith. He gave it a shot, I want to say. He opened that door. He was open to everything. So he went to church for a bit. He got baptized, and he talked about all the things he had to do to be in the church. He once told me the story. He said, "So I did all of those things, and I got that out of the way. But I still ran my peyote meetings." So he was exposed to Christianity, and he retained the whole thing where Jesus said, "Whenever you ask it, ask it in my name." So in the peyote meeting, at the end of all of his prayers, he said, "In Jesus's name." But he used a Crow name for Jesus. I'm not sure what it is, but it translates to "The Man with Holes in His Hands."[1]

Rejecting Native Culture Growing Up— and Regretting the Loss Today

After I became a Christian and gave my life to Jesus, I thought that my Native American traditional values were bad. I thought that if I did those things I was going to hell. I never went out of my way to bash it—I never joined that. I never said, "This is right, and this is wrong." I respected it, because that's who I am. That's my people. That's my tradition. That's who I was born into. I guess the main value I'm taking from my Christianity is love. I think we should love everybody, and I think we should be respectful to everybody. At the same time, for Native Americans, respect is really high up on our values, too. You gotta be really respectful. You gotta be respectful to other people's religions and the way they believe.

But, too many times, it isn't like that. You'll find people around here who are just the exact opposite. There are these preachers who will condemn you to hell for being that way. There's also Native American people who will put you down if you believe in the Western Christianity. I know a lot of them will actually be openly blasphemous, you know what I mean? I don't think that's right, 'cause that's against our traditional values. We're raised to be respectful. So there's polar opposites on both sides.

As I got older, I always skipped the peyote meetings. I would come help set up the tipi and do whatever they needed me to do, but I wouldn't go in. My dad never tried to force it on me, which was really good. He would just kind of let me decide for myself, just the same way my grandpa did with him. They had a meeting for me when I graduated high school, and I didn't even go into that. It was for me, and I didn't even go in. At the beginning of a meeting, there's a part where everybody goes in who's taking part, but then people who kinda want the prayer but don't actually want to be a part of the whole meeting—well, they'll kinda walk them in, they'll smudge while they're in there, and then they'll walk out. So that's what I did at my own meeting, instead of being in there.

My grandpa's been going to the meetings since he was a kid. He grew up that way. So I know, deep down, he always wanted his children to be in there with him. But he never, never said, "Okay, this is the way it's going to be" or "This is how you guys are going to believe." He let them make the choice, and eventually they came back in. They came back around. And that's the same thing that happened to me. Part of me kind of regrets it, thinking that maybe they should've been more forceful. Because now my grandpa's gone, and—how should I say it? I'm still a babe in the Native American Church. I don't know it fully. I just recently started going in. One of the regrets I have is that my grandpa will never hear me sing. I'll never get to drum for him. And it kind of hurts. It hurts a lot. I guess you don't really know what you have until it's gone. He was such a huge presence in the Native American Church.

No Guilt in the Peyote Tipi Now

The first peyote meeting I went to was probably about four or five years ago, I want to say. They were having one for my dad. They were actually having one for all the elected officials. Each one had their own. My dad was having one, and it was in Crow Agency.[2] I said, "Okay, I'll just go to support my dad." I'd never been in there before. And it was like a realization that I didn't want to bash something that I had no idea about. I didn't want to have an opinion on something that I'd never truly experienced. So I walked in with an open mind, and I was totally surprised. It was just like being in my home church, where people go in there to pray and sing. In my church, we sing and worship, we pray for people, we take communion, and things like that. And here in the tipi it was the same thing. We were singing and praying. I didn't really see the difference.

And I didn't feel bad at all. I didn't have any type of negative feelings for it whatsoever. I came out of there feeling like this is a good thing, like there's no way this could be bad. I think we're in there praying for good things, we're in there asking God for good things for these people, making good wishes for whoever the meeting was for. And so when I left I was like, "That's not wrong. I don't want to condemn that. It's something I want to be a part of. I don't want to lose it." 'Cause my grandpa's gone now, so my dad's carrying the torch for him as well as my uncles and my aunts. In the same way, I want him to pass it to me, and I want to pass it to my children. We still go to church every Sunday, and now when the peyote meetings come, we go to our meetings, too.

As far as how I'm raising my children, I'll probably do it the same way I was raised. I'll give them access to the peyote meetings, let them grow up around it. And when the time comes, they will make their own choice. But I want them not to be strangers to it, or them thinking that it's weird or asking, "Why are they going in and just pounding on the drum?" or "Why are they taking peyote?" I want them to know fully what it's all about. And if they want to take part in it, then that would be their choice. I hope that they'll join me in it. Just like my dad never forced me into it, but now I'm going into it. And I'm really making steps to try to learn what it is about and take it in fully and make it a part of my life.

The Legacy of "Sonny" Black Eagle Jr.

My grandpa named me, and for the longest time I had no idea what my name meant. He told me that, translated, my name means, "He Walks to the Drum." I wasn't sure what that means—like, am I "walking to the beat of my own drum" type of thing? But later I learned what it means. My grandpa became known as one of the premier drummers in the Native American Church. You don't just sit there and bang the drum when you're in a meeting. There's a method to it. It's an art form like any other instrument. And he became a really good drummer, as well as a really good singer. So my name, Walks to the Drum, comes from when the drum gets passed around the tipi during a meeting. When you're in there, you don't always have to have the person next to you do the drumming while you sing. You can ask somebody else to drum—you can call their name and ask them to drum, and they'll come walking to you and drum for you. That's where my name came from—He Walks to the Drum. My grandpa's involvement in the Native American Church took him around the world. He's been overseas so many times and has traveled around the world based on his prowess in the Native American Church. He gave credit to his church for all of his accomplishments. He was really a well-known man.

I mean, we're still here today because of him. This is his place. This is where his meetings were held, and we're still trying to keep that alive. He adopted President Obama. The president calls him Dad. The president of the United States calls my grandpa Dad. So that's just—it can't be wrong. I mean, the power of it. There's not many people who can say, "I adopted the president of the United States." My grandpa stayed in the White House. He and my grandma were at the inauguration sitting right behind the president. He would call and check on my grandpa and ask him how he's doing, those types of things. At the end of his life, my grandpa also named my son in the peyote meeting. A lot of people have different styles of naming. Some people give names based on their deeds. One of my grandpa's deeds was that he adopted the president, so he named my son President Adopter. That's the name given to my son right there. He named him in the meeting. It really means a lot to me. It's really an honor.

It's sad because he was such an outstanding presence in the Native American Church, and yet I didn't get to fully experience that because I just started recently going in. That's my only regret for things—that I got started way too late. But it's better late than never, I say. I think I get to keep his legacy alive because I'm a direct descendent. That's where I get my name Black Eagle—from my grandpa and my dad. My hope for my children is that they're gonna know both ways, and they're going to decide for themselves. Maybe they'll be like me and balance the two. I go in there and I pray. I pray to Jesus.

"I Was Made Native American for a Reason"

The church I go to now is Foursquare, and I don't really know what they think of me being in the Native American Church. Not long ago someone at the church asked me if I'm traditional, and I said, "Yeah, I practice my tradition 'cause I don't want to lose it. I think we were given this tradition for a reason. I was made Native American for a reason, and I'm not gonna lose that. I'm gonna pass it on to my children." And they seemed okay with it. "Oh, that's really nice," they said. They thought of it more as neat than anything. But I think you actually have to be in it to fully grasp the whole thing, you know what I mean?

When I first started going into the meetings, there were times when I thought it was going to be an eternal battle, choosing between the two. 'Cause I know my scriptures really well, and I didn't want to do the whole "serving two masters" type of thing.[3] And I used to think that I had to either do *this* one, or I had to do *that* one. But when I actually went into the peyote meeting, I couldn't find anything wrong with it. I wasn't looking for anything wrong—I just went in there with an open mind and I thought, "From where I'm sitting, there's nothing wrong with this. I don't feel bad about it, and I don't need to justify it to myself in any way, shape, or form." I'm not trying to make excuses or talk myself into anything—like when people say, "Whatever helps you sleep at night." I've never had that type of conversation with myself. I went in there and thought, "This is love." You go in there and you love somebody, you pray for them, and you wish them good things. I think that, above all, that's what's important. Jesus loved people. That's what his greatest message was—to love.

NOTES

1. The title for Jesus that Levi is referencing here is *Ischawúuannaukaasua,* a familiar name for Jesus among Crow Pentecostals today. In an effort to demonstrate the extent to which the tribe has embraced Christianity, the Crow tribal legislature invoked this Crow language name for Jesus (followed by the translation "The One with Pierced Hands") in a 2013 legislative resolution titled, "A Resolution of the Crow Tribal Legislature to Honor God for His Great Blessings upon the Crow Tribe and to Proclaim Jesus Christ as Lord of the Crow Indian Reservation" (LR 13-02).
2. Cedric Black Eagle, Levi's father, served as Crow tribal chairman from 2009 to 2012.
3. Here Levi is referring to Matthew 6:24, where Jesus says, "No one can serve two masters; for a slave will either hate the one and love the other, or be devoted to the one and despise the other. You cannot serve God and wealth" (New Revised Standard Version).

Part V

❁

HEALING HYMNS

Crows have long retreated to the hills of southeast Montana, fasting in solitude to seek visions, dreams, and sacred songs of healing power. When Pentecostalism swept into Crow country in the 1920s, the tribe's long-established tradition of spiritual songs was readily transposed into Christian terms by Crow Pentecostals seeking the power of the Holy Spirit in those same hills, giving birth to a new kind of sacred song. Like the earlier songs of medicine elders and Sun Dance leaders, Crow hymns "received" by Pentecostal seekers contain Crow-language lyrics, bear the musical style of the Plains tribes, and are believed to possess healing power when sung, in faith, for supplicants in need. In contrast to the old songs, however, these Christian hymns are steeped in biblical imagery and a fervent expectation of Jesus's second coming. Additionally, when performed, they are invariably accompanied by tambourines rather than hand drums in a conscious effort to distinguish them from "Indian religion."

Though rooted in Crow Pentecostalism, the Crow hymns are now a truly ecumenical tradition among the tribe today. Groups of Crow hymn singers regularly offer these songs in Catholic Masses, Baptist services, and Pentecostal camp meetings across the reservation. These songs have become especially popular at Crow funerals, regardless of the deceased's religious affiliation. Joe Bear Cloud, whose narrative opens this part, has been working closely with ethnomusicologist Dave Graber for almost thirty years to identify, record, transcribe, and perform these songs as part of the Crow Hymns Ministry (formerly called the Crow Hymns Project). He describes the first time he encountered Crows hymns as a boy, and affirms their power to change lives almost a century after the earliest songs were received. Joe does not regard these songs as the product of human inspiration, but rather as gifts given directly by God. Georgine Falls Down, whose interview follows Bear Cloud's, is also a longtime member of the Crow Hymns Ministry. In addition to her work preserving existing sacred songs, she is among those who continue to receive new healing hymns today. She carries her songs with her like a medicine woman might carry *baaxpée*—spiritual power—in a medicine bundle, releasing her musical gift through ritual performance to those seeking its healing power.

14

From Hill Fasting to Radio Broadcasting

AN INTERVIEW WITH JOE BEAR CLOUD SR.

Every Sunday afternoon, Joe Bear Cloud Sr. can be heard emceeing Crow hymns on a local radio station out of Billings, Montana. Joe is a member of the Crow Hymns Ministry that seeks to preserve and popularize these sacred Crow-language songs for future generations of tribal members. The organization (formerly called the Crow Hymns Project) sprang from the combined research efforts of Joe Bear Cloud and Dave Graber, a retired music teacher who has been living and working on the Crow Reservation since the 1980s. The two began identifying members of the tribe who had either received hymns themselves or knew hymns that had been received by others. They audio-recorded these songs and, for the first time, transcribed them to sheet music for a collection that was published in the early 1990s. While many of the songs preserved in this collection date to the

Joe Bear Cloud in the Big Horn Canyon, Crow Reservation.
Author's photo

1920s, Crow hymns continue to be received by tribal members today.

The Crow Hymns Ministry is a loose affiliation of roughly twenty singers who regularly offer these songs for Sunday services, special Masses,
summer Pentecostal camp meetings, and, increasingly, at funerals on the
reservation. They also sing these songs in homes all across the reservation,
often at the request of someone seeking healing for a family member or
loved one. As Joe often explains, "These songs are not man-made written.
These songs are directly from God. They're spiritual and there's everything
in it. There's healing, and we're expecting something to happen."

Although Joe has long been a guest preacher in independent Pentecostal churches across the reservation, he was recently appointed pastor
of an American Baptist church at Crow Agency. In a similar way, Crow
hymns freely cross denominational boundaries among the tribe. Commit-
tee members of the Crow Hymns Ministry come from Baptist, Catholic,
and Pentecostal churches, all seeking the preservation and promotion of
this rich musical tradition. The movement also enjoys broad support from
tribal leaders, as when the Little Big Horn College provided key support for
publication of the first booklet containing Crow hymns transcriptions. Joe's
interview took place at a campsite in the Big Horn Canyon, located in the
southwestern corner of the Crow Reservation.

❀

Early Encounters with Crow Hymns

When I first heard Crow hymns, it was from the Pentecostal movement
when I was about twelve years old. Now I'm seventy-three. It was over at
St. Xavier, that little town you just drove through. That's where I used to
live. The Big Horn Valley, around St. X area, is my hometown. That little
place used to be bigger than what it is today now. That little town used to be
a bank, meat market, a hotel, five filling stations, two grocery stores, pool
hall, a theater. That's when that oil struck in the Soap Creek oil fields for the
tribe. But anyway, that's where I was raised.

When I was about twelve years old, I came across a field and heard some
noise. It was a summer like this, and there was a tent and the sides were
kinda pulled up. And there were some people there singin', and I was kinda

lying on my belly, watching these people singin' at that camp meeting. I listened to it and they sang different ones, and finally this one song they sang, I kinda picked it up while I was watching. That's the first song that I knew when I was twelve years old.

That's when I first seen the Pentecostal movement. That must have been around the early 1950s, somewhere in that area. About two or three years later, I started going to some of these Pentecostal meetings and they

"Jesus, Jesus, *Bíi Baa Díalahcheesh*." Mae House and Philip White Clay remember Fanny Butterfly singing this song, and Joe Bear Cloud sang it during his interview. *Music courtesy Crow Hymns Ministry*

were singin' these Crow hymns again—different ones. These were house meetings. They didn't have no church like today. There weren't hardly any churches in the Pentecostal movement until the '60s. It was all house meetings. At that time, I kinda was goin' in and out of the church. I wasn't a full-time Christian. I didn't even know yet what Christianity and all that stuff was. All I knew is that it's something to do with the church. And they were doin' meetings continually, summer and winter. Finally, I started comin' to the meetings and listening to these hymns. It was there that I picked up this one song that I learned. It's called "Jesus, Jesus, *Bíi Baa Díalahcheesh*." [*Here Joe sings the song.*]

A TRADITION OF INDIGENOUS SPIRITUAL SONGS

But anyway, along the way as I grew up with the Pentecostal movement, I started pickin' up songs. I learned by hearing. These songs were not man-made written. They're given directly from God. Either through a dream at night while you're asleep, or maybe a sound like these timbers blowing in the wind—the wind makes noise, the water makes noise. That's how God moves—by the sound. He gives songs to our people. Along the way, I would say that he poured songs upon the Crow Nation. To every tribe—all the tribes in the United States—they have their own ways of singin'. I was in Oklahoma, with the Cheyennes, and they sing their own ways. They have their own hymns, their own songs, their own understanding.

So each one has their own language. And I'm pretty sure just about all the tribes have their own tradition of songs. And these songs are still out there. If you just go up on top of these hills here and fast there for a few days, the gifts are there. Anywhere! The songs are there. It's still there. It hasn't quit. Some of our people, they go out fasting without food and water for three days. They receive songs just like people in the Sun Dance. They receive songs by fasting.

CROW HYMNS ON THE RADIO

Along the way, I kinda went along with the Pentecostal movement and I picked up songs here and there. Finally, somewhere around the '60s, I kinda backed out of church for about twenty-two years. And during the time while I was gone, the songs haven't quit. They're still goin' on. Then in 1985,

I came back and started doin' the things that I used to do. In them days there's some new Crow hymns that I picked up.

This one lady from our tribe, her name's Dorothy Hoops, I don't know how many songs she knew. But she recorded a ninety-minute cassette tape, and both sides were full of Crow hymns. So I started playin' these songs. I listened to it and listened to it. And I started learning the songs again, by hearing, playing, listening to these tapes. I started workin' on it. I started goin' to church, singing these songs.

I never figured that I'd be in the radio business, broadcasting these Crow hymns. But we have been, and it still goes on today. We've been broadcasting these Crow hymns over the radio in Billings. It's been over eight years now, and we're still goin'. Our broadcast time for today is already over—our program was on from 3:30 to 4:00. I enjoy it, and I'm not ashamed to sing these songs or do anything for Christ. That's my work, and I'm just very pleased that I have been chosen to do this. God has blessed me to do this, so I enjoy it.

THE CROW HYMNS PROJECT

In about 1986, me and Dave Graber, who was a music teacher for many years down in Lodge Grass, began a research project where we started goin' around, visiting different ones who knew these old songs and asking them, "When did you first hear the songs?" A lot of these songs go back to around 1920. So these songs just didn't come out yesterday. They came way back, way before me. Nellie Stewart, one of the founders of the Crow Pentecostal movement, she was blessed with five songs from God. Nellie passed away in 1937, and for fifty years hardly anyone sang the last song she ever received until I started singing it again in churches. And it's still anointed. Her family has asked me to sing it for them on their get-togethers because it's from Nellie Pretty Eagle Stewart. The Stewart and the White Clay family—that's their grandmother. She has five songs, and one of the most popular is the one they asked me to sing. It goes like this. [*Here Joe sings "Akbaatatdía Díssawoók."*]

That's one of the songs that was never sang for fifty years until I came and started singin' it. There's a lot of them songs that haven't been sang for forty, thirty, fifty years until we started digging into the history and started

E - LE - A -HE HE - LE, E - LE A - HE

A -HE - A -HE - A -HE- HE - LE

Ak - baa - tat - dí - a - kaa - ta WE - LE
Dear God

dií - ssee___ boók. A -HE - A -HE - A -HE - HE - LE
To you I am coming.

Ak - baa - tat - dí - a - kaa - ta WE - LE
Dear God

tát - che baa - lée - wia- waak. A -HE - A -HE- HE - LE
I will go straight.

"*Akbaatatdía Díssawoók*" as sung by Dorothy Hoops circa 1970, starting pitch = C. Words and music attributed to Nellie Stewart (d. 1937), widely recognized as the founder of Crow Pentecostalism. Joe Bear Cloud sang this song during his interview. *Music courtesy Crow Hymns Ministry*

singin' it again. And they're still a blessing. A blessing's still there. And it's the same God, same Jesus, same Spirit. Nothing changes except people. People can be changed in many, many ways. But God has never changed. His word is still the same. "Heaven and earth shall pass away, but my word shall never pass away." It's all in the Bible.

15

Singer, Healer, and Powwow Dancer

AN INTERVIEW WITH
GEORGINE TAKES GUN FALLS DOWN

The following interview took place at Georgine's encampment during Crow Fair. Earlier in the morning, she was among the small group of singers riding on the Crow Hymns Ministry parade float, which took first place in its category. Later in the day, she danced in the hugely popular Crow Fair powwow, eventually earning top honors in traditional dancing among female Crow elders. In these ways, she illustrates her conviction that a passionate celebration of Crow culture is fully compatible with Christian faith.

Georgine Falls Down at her Crow Fair encampment, Crow Agency.
Photo by Dave Kapferer

Georgine has long contributed to the Crow Hymns Ministry, volunteering her time and energy to learn, preserve, and perform a growing corpus of Crow sacred songs dating back to the 1920s. Her involvement in Crow hymns, however, extends well beyond historical interest alone, for Georgine is among those who still receive sacred songs today in the traditional Crow way. She describes receiving these Crow-language songs through prayer and regards them as repositories of spiritual power, power that's released through ritual performance. She "carries" these sacred songs much like one might carry a medicine bundle, singing them in homes and churches at the request of those seeking a healing. Her songs are marked by a mournful, haunting beauty, with lyrics expressing deep personal devotion to Jesus. She shared two of her songs with me at the close of our interview.

Like so many others on the Crow Reservation, Georgine has been influenced by all three of the historic Christian denominations among the tribe. She was baptized and raised in the Roman Catholic Church as a child; married a Baptist man, despite strong opposition from her Catholic family; and later experienced a life-changing encounter with healing prayer at the hands of her Pentecostal neighbors. Today she considers herself nondenominational and welcomes the opportunity to pray and sing for "anyone that believes in Jesus Christ."

Georgine has faced many hardships through the years. In addition to battling rheumatoid arthritis and supporting her husband through two kidney transplants, she has also grieved the deaths of two daughters—one to a rare kidney disease, and the other to a train-pedestrian fatality. Since this interview took place, she has also endured the death of her husband. Through it all, she credits a life of prayer and the singing of sacred songs for giving her the strength to carry on, dancing as she goes.

❁

CATHOLIC UPBRINGING, BAPTIST HUSBAND

My name is Georgine Takes Gun Falls Down. Takes Gun is my maiden name; Falls Down is my married name. We're at Crow Fair. It's Friday, right after the parade, and I'm here to share my experiences and how I found the Lord—and how I came about receiving my songs. My mother had rheumatoid arthritis, and she couldn't move around much, but she always went to church. I was born Catholic. I was baptized in the Catholic Church, grew up Catholic, went through catechism, and had my First Communion at twelve years old. And that was my Christian faith. Catholic.

Then I met my husband forty years ago, and he's a Baptist. So when we got married, there was some church members—mainly women, mostly my family—they were criticizing me because I married out of the Catholic faith. And with their Crow beliefs and Catholic beliefs, they figured that I had married into the wrong congregation, I guess. So with my husband being Baptist, I got so much criticism that I quit going to church and just started praying on my own. And my husband was the same way. And before we knew it, ten years went by, and the only time I was in church was at a funeral or a wedding. That was the only time. But since I knew the Lord, I would just pray. Everything I do, I pray. Before I eat, I pray. Before going to bed, putting the kids to bed, I pray.

Then my husband developed strep throat. We took him to the clinic, and they gave him some antibiotics, but he had an allergic reaction that nobody expected. Instead of surfacing, it went inside. It was eating up his insides. And anyhow, he had a failed kidney, a damaged kidney, after that. So I was just devastated because daily my husband was dying, and he was losing a lot of weight. He's big—he's 6 feet 3 inches tall, and he was chunky. He was my macho man! And here he was, losing weight. And I was going around in circles. I took him to the hospital in Sheridan, Wyoming, which is about seventy-five miles from here. I'd take him there, but they wouldn't know what to do. Then I'd take him to Billings, and they wouldn't know, either. From there, I'd take him back to Crow Agency, and it was like a big triangle, searching and searching. I even had a Crow medicine man work on him. My in-laws wanted to have that medicine man, and since I just wanted him well again, I agreed. So I went ahead and had them come over. While all this was going on, I was praying within myself. I knew the Lord, and I was praying. This was in 1983.

GEORGINE RECEIVES HER FIRST SONG

A year before that, on Sunday afternoons, I would always go to my mom after she came back from church. She went to Our Lady of Loretto Catholic

Church in Lodge Grass, and she would share with me what was going on at church. On one particular Sunday, she said, "I sure wanted you in church today!" And I said, "Well, why? What was so special about today?" And she said, "This one lady, the Lord gave her a song. She sang it, and it was so beautiful that I wanted you to be there to listen at how the Lord worked in that woman's life." That stayed with me. After I cleaned house for her, had dinner with her, and then went home, it still stayed with me.

That night when I went to bed, I thought to myself, "Wow, I wonder what it would be like for the Lord to give you a song?" I'd just wonder, and I was just reaching out to the Lord. So a couple days went by, and here this one song—I just kept singing in my heart. It was this one melody, and it was just singing in my heart. And then I would hum it all day. I worked at the Medical Records Department [at the Indian Health Service] at the time, so I was busy taking charts here and there. But at the same time, I heard this tune. I mean, I was constantly singing in my heart. And I thought, "Well, I wonder what this is?"

That evening I went home and I cooked for the family. After that, I was free for the evening. So I just laid back on my bed, trying to relax for a little bit, and that song was really coming strong. I said, "Lord, what is this?" And then I heard some words coming. And I thought, "Lord, am I supposed to be putting the two together—these words that you're sending and this tune?" So I did. I put them together, and as I lay there, I was singing the song, and I couldn't believe this week of experience and how this song was coming.

So I was all excited, but I was all alone 'cause my kids were outside playing and my husband was off playing basketball. So I just laid back and thought to myself, "People will criticize me because, even now, I'm not really accepted in the Catholic Church, and if I were to go to them, they'll say that I'm a sinner and they won't believe me." So I had that song for one whole year without really telling anyone.

HEALING THROUGH RITUAL PERFORMANCE OF SONGS

But I would sing it to myself. I would sing it when I'm driving to work. Then, when my husband, Ronald, started experiencing all the health problems that he did, one of my neighbors came by, and she brought some sisters over to pray for Ronald. They were Pentecostal. They came and they laid hands on him and prayed for him. When they left, my one neighbor—we were pretty close—she stayed behind. She was kind of giving me support, and I said, "You know, when you ladies came and prayed for Ronald, I remembered something. A year ago," I said, "this one song came to me. It was exactly a year ago. This song came to me and I was afraid of people. I should be afraid of the Lord, and here I am afraid of people, of what they would say. So I've kept this for one whole year." So I started sharing with her. Then I told her, "I'll sing it for you." And I did.

And she said, "No wonder your husband's going through a lot! 'Cause that needs to come out, and you're holding onto it." So, I started sharing that one song. It seemed like right there the Lord started working on my husband after I started singing and letting others hear that song. I thought to myself, "Well, if my husband is okay after this, I'll stand up with this song and I'll sing in churches." It was just a thought within my heart, you know.

A couple months went by, and Ronald was doing really good. They learned that it was an allergic reaction, and they were able to help him. But his kidney was damaged, so they still had to send him to a urologist to follow and to watch him. He eventually got on dialysis, and he was on there for about five years before he received a kidney transplant. But the first time he was okay, my mother-in-law said, "Come to church for me. I don't want you to do anything—just come. Right after church I'm going to feed the congregation. Since my son is well, I want to feed the congregation."

So I went to the Baptist church with Ronald, and there we sat. The minister kept saying, "Are there any testimonies out there? Did someone experience anything?" I was just looking around, and then it felt like the Lord just nudged me—"Here's your opportunity." I had made a promise within my heart, and the Lord nudged me to help me remember what I had said. I was fidgeting right there, and I didn't know what to do. Then this minister—the Lord must have had him keep asking, since I had to get up. I finally stood up and said, "I do. I have a testimony." Then I told 'em that I had received the song, but that I had kept it and was afraid to sing it in public. I told 'em if Ronald was well that I would stand up with the song, and today he is. "He's here and he's well," I said, "so I need to share this song." So I got up, and I sang it. The first time I sang it, I cried all the way through. Then the second time I sang it, the words were clearer. That's how I received my first song.

Then I started visiting with this Pentecostal group, the one that came to my house to pray for Ronald. That's how I met Larry Plain Bull and Jerome Hugs. They were with the [Wycliffe] Crow Bible Translation Project out of Pryor. I also met Hugh Matthews, who was working with Dave Graber on Crow hymns. Hugh Matthews was ministering with Larry Plain Bull and Jerome Hugs and translating the Bible. And they had Crow hymns. They had a little radio station, too, in Pryor. So they were singing these, and the Lord put us all together—this group of ladies that I was sharing with, plus that group in Pryor. We started going around house to house. We had house services, and we were invited to almost every house on the reservation. It was like nonstop, every other evening. If it wasn't in Crow Agency here, it was in Lodge Grass. And if it wasn't in Lodge Grass, it was way out in Pryor. We would all jump into the car, and we would go and just uplift the name of Jesus through song and through our testimonies.

GEORGINE RECEIVES MORE SONGS

In 1978 was when I first worked for the Indian Health Service. I was diagnosed in 1980 as having rheumatoid arthritis, the same disease my mom had. I was so devastated; I just gave up, because I knew what she went through. Finally, I prayed one evening when I was all alone, and said, "If this is how I'm going to turn out, at least give me ten years. I just started working, so if I can get medical retirement, then I'll be okay and have something available for living expenses." So I prayed that silent prayer, and then I started following what the doctors had told me. When Ronald had that disease it was in '82. So I gave my life to the Lord, October 17, 1983, in my home. I just got on my knees and said, "Here I am. Whatever you want me to do, I'll do it." That's when I stood up with that song. I had only one song, but I sang it at every house meeting. I would sing it, and I would share with them how I experienced this song.

That Christmas, I was going shopping about December 20. We were traveling to Billings, and as I was driving with Ronald, here another song came. I just yelled, "Lord, I know this is from you!" So I got my second song. After I was helping people with this one song and with my testimony,

I was taking Motrin every four hours, just to get by with my arthritis. Over the next three months—I don't know when exactly—but I didn't need that medication anymore. So the Lord healed me of my illness as I stood up for him, ministering to people. Then these songs, they just kept coming. They just kept coming, and I would get all excited. Then I would have it recorded.

Some of 'em are in English, the words are in English, and I'm trying to get a CD together. It seems like when I'm meditating—when I'm real busy cooking, driving, at full concentration—that's when I receive 'em. People receive 'em in different ways, often through fasting and being all alone. But me, I'm just with my four children. They were small, and I was really occupied with them, but I would just get on my knees when I'm home and just cry out to the Lord. And that's how I was receiving them—when I was concentrating on something, either cooking or when I'm alone driving. That's when they'd come. They just come like, "Here's another one!"

I'd be humming inside, or trying to sing one of my songs, and I would let it out—and it would be a new one, and I would know it's a new one. Then I would thank the Lord. I would remember them, to where I can go ahead and record 'em or share them. I was constantly sharing, sharing them. So I've been into different churches. Anymore, I just pray with anyone. I say I'm nondenominational now because I share with anyone. Anyone that believes in Jesus Christ, I share with them.

I sing 'em mainly in house meetings, with traditional folks, too. They always have house meetings, and they invite a minister and whoever they want. They call upon certain individuals to come share their testimony, so that's how I got my strength and that's how I was able to talk in front of people. The Lord even took my shyness away. When I was in high school I couldn't even give a speech. I couldn't even speak in front of anyone, and I got a really poor grade in speech when I was in high school! But today, if I'm called upon, I just share what the Lord has done for me and I share my songs.

When I sing, I don't sing to the people. I sing to the Lord. I give it my all. I sing to him, to please him. And it's a beautiful feeling within my soul. It's like I'm doing something for the Lord. Even though I don't see him, I trust him. I believe that there's an Almighty God that's watching over us and that's why we're on the Mother Earth. When I was healed from rheumatoid arthritis, it just happened so quick, and I was enjoying what I was doing for the Lord so much that I didn't know when that healing took place. One minute I was singing these songs and going to house meetings, and then in December I realized I had been healed. We were heading to Pryor to a house meeting, and I took four other ladies with me in my car. We were driving down the road, and I was crying, and I said, "Praise the Lord! I don't know when it happened, but I haven't taken the Motrin in a while." I would be in so much pain and wouldn't be able to walk. I was so stiff in the morning that I couldn't bend my fingers—my hands wouldn't work until I got into hot water or something to loosen them up. "But I'm not like that anymore," I said. "I just trust God has done something great for me—that he's healed me and I claim it." That was in 1983.

Her Husband's Healing and Her Children's Faith

My husband was cured when he had his first transplant, but then that kidney failed five years later, and he was back on the kidney machine. Then he received another kidney. In the process, he started serving the Lord, too—in his own way. He's really silent. He doesn't say much, but within I could tell that he was starting to pray. And I said, "You need to ask God directly—ask for that kidney, it's yours. You're a child of God, and you have to ask for that kidney." And here in 2007, October 4, we got a phone call and they found a kidney for him. We had to go to Seattle. This individual was in a car accident. He was a person of Christian faith, and when they opened his wallet he was a donor. So right away they worked to preserve his organs. Right after they got the kidney and preserved it, they looked on the national list, and Ronald was the only recipient to receive that kidney. He had rare antibodies that Ronald had, exact same, so it was a perfect match. So when we got there, they put it in and today he does everything he's been doing. He's healthy, and he said, "I thank God every day for my kidney." So we missed Crow Fair that year in 2007. But I said, "Well, there's always next year. We'll be there again." It was pretty rough 'cause he had some difficulties and he went into surgery about nine times before he was properly healed. But we finally came home in October. He's an accountant and he's been working for the tribe for over thirty-seven years now.

We pray together, even my kids. They're in their thirties now. They amaze me because I thought they weren't listening to me! But when they're having a personal crisis, they always tell me afterwards, "Mom, thanks for what you showed us." And they thank me for raising them in a Christian home, and that they can reach out to the Lord themselves. I lost my oldest daughter to a train-pedestrian accident, just right here in Crow Agency. And my baby, she died from rare kidney disease like her Dad had. They said it wasn't hereditary, but yet she had it. I gave her my left kidney to extend her life, but she was with us another two years, and then she passed on in April of the year 2000. But I know where they both are, and that's my testimony—that my two kids are waiting for me in heaven. And if I want to see them, I have to make it in. So that's how I go on—I talk about my life story and my testimony and all the Lord has done for me. I just share my story with whomever the Lord brings in my path.

Part VI

❁

MISSIONARY VOICES

While this collection of personal narratives is focused on Crow Christian voices, the study would surely be deficient if it failed to consider the ongoing influence of non-Native Christian ministers and missionaries working among the tribe today. All of the priests currently serving the Crow Reservation's five Roman Catholic parishes are white. Of the seven Baptist churches active on the Crow Reservation, five are led by non-Native pastors. And while all of the roughly twenty Pentecostal churches on the reservation are led by Crow pastors, those churches invite a steady, year-round stream of non-Native evangelists, preachers, mission teams, and other off-reservation ministers to preach in their pulpits, run camp meetings, organize vacation Bible schools, host prayer meetings, give seminars, and perform Gospel music for thousands of Crow churchgoers every year. Indeed, non-Native, short-term missionaries are a ministry staple of every denomination represented among the tribe, exercising enormous influence on the nature of Christianity on the Crow Reservation.

The first voice in this part is that of Father Randolph Graczyk. Though a non-Native originally from Milwaukee, Wisconsin, Randolph has become deeply enmeshed in the social and religious life of the tribe over his forty years living among them. He was formally adopted into a Crow family, oversees a grade school for Crow children, and actively participates in a host of traditional Crow ceremonies. His ministry reflects the enormous shift that has taken place in Catholic missionary strategy over the past fifty years since the Second Vatican Council—a strategy that has moved from open condemnation to warm embrace of indigenous religious practices.

The second non-Native minister included in this part is Jonathan Lawton, a Southern Baptist minister who has lived and worked on the Crow Reservation for twenty years. In contrast to Randolph, Jonathan is deeply reticent about the permissibility of Christians attending traditional Indian ceremonies. His comments are striking for the candor with which he expresses uncertainty—even anxiety—about the extent to which his Christian faith might be compromised by participation in cultural events. Another engaging aspect of his narrative is the extent to which his Crow Baptist congregants are likewise conflicted over the same issue.

The third and final interview in this part belongs to Barry Moen, an itinerant Pentecostal evangelist based in Wyoming. For two decades, he has been proselytizing among various tribal communities in Montana and Wyoming, claiming a spectacular number of Native Christian "conversions" through his evangelistic tent ministry. Barry's memorable testimony gives voice to the hundreds of off-reservation missionaries and evangelists whose passion, preaching, prayers, and theological vision have a profound impact on the Crow community, year in and year out.

16

The Sun-Dancing Franciscan Linguist

AN INTERVIEW WITH
RANDOLPH GRACZYK (CATHOLIC)

Father Randolph Graczyk, a Capuchin Franciscan friar, has been working as a Catholic priest among the Crow Tribe for nearly four decades. He currently serves St. Charles Catholic Parish in the western reservation town of Pryor. He also helps to oversee St. Charles School, attended by more than a hundred Crow children from preschool through eighth grade. The school is one of three run by St. Labre, based in Ashland, Montana, an organization with a stated mission "to proclaim the Gospel of Jesus Christ according to Catholic Tradition by providing quality education which celebrates our Catholic faith and embraces Native American cultures."

Randolph's arrival on the Crow Reservation coincided with the freshly unveiled reforms of the Second Vatican Council, which included a more

Randolph Graczyk at St. Charles School in Pryor, Crow Reservation. *Photo by Dave Kapferer*

open posture toward non-Christian religions. He describes the religious behavior of many pre-Vatican II Crow Catholics as "compartmentalized," explaining that "one of the goals of my ministry was to try and break that down, and to let people know that you can be a good Catholic and a good Crow. And I think, to a large extent, that we succeeded."

Even a cursory look at Randolph's time among the Crows adds weight to his claim of a successful integration of Crow culture and Catholic faith. Over the years, he has been deeply affected by traditional Crow ceremonies and ways of understanding the sacred. He prays regularly in the sweat lodge and has participated in the Shoshone-Crow Sun Dance seven times. He has also dedicated considerable time and energy to the study of the Crow language. In the late 1980s, he earned a doctorate in linguistics from the University of Chicago, writing his dissertation on the Crow language. Those efforts culminated in the publication of his nearly five-hundred-page *A Grammar of Crow* (University of Nebraska Press, 2007), a project Randolph describes as his "life's work" as a linguist. He is currently in the process of establishing a Crow-language program for students of the St. Charles Mission School as part of a broad effort by the tribe to preserve and revitalize this endangered Siouan language.

As Crow churchgoers shared hundreds of stories over the past four years for this project, few names were mentioned more often than Father Randolph's. Transcripts reveal Catholic, Pentecostal, Baptist, and Crow Traditionalist participants all speaking of him with near-universal respect, sometimes despite sharp theological differences. Reflective of the way in which traditions converge in this Capuchin priest, one Catholic interviewee even describes a Sun Dance vision in which a spirit helper instructs him to seek Randolph's advice on spiritual matters.

The following interview took place at St. Charles Mission School in Pryor on the Crow Reservation.

From Milwaukee to Montana

I'm a Capuchin priest, and I've been a pastor here at St. Charles Parish for close to forty years.[1] I first came to Pryor in 1975. I'm originally from

Milwaukee. In grade school I was interested in going to seminary to look at the possibility of becoming a priest. The priest in our parish was familiar with St. Lawrence Seminary boarding school, which was run by the Capuchins, and he encouraged me to go there. So I went to high school there for four years and joined the Capuchin Order right out of high school.

After college seminary, we were sent out for summer experiences in different missions and ministries of the Capuchins. I got sent to Montana in 1965 and ended up working in Birney on the Cheyenne Reservation.[2] And, I don't know—something just clicked, and I kind of felt that this is where I wanted to be. I also spent a summer or two on the Crow Reservation. And so after I was ordained in 1968, a year later I was sent out to the Crow Reservation town of Lodge Grass as pastor. And that was really my introduction to Indian ministry.

CROW LANGUAGE STUDY

In 1975, I was transferred here to Pryor and was at Pryor for seven years. I had already started learning the language when I was in Lodge Grass. At the time, pretty much everyone spoke Crow, from babies on up. And I would find myself in situations when I was the only non-Indian, and all this talk was swirling around me, and I had no idea what people were saying.

So I started asking questions of some of the high school kids from our youth group. I asked them, "What's the word for arm? What's the word for eye?" Same thing for colors. And gradually, I just started learning some Crow.

At that time, there was a fellow named Ray Gordon, who worked with Wycliffe Bible Translators, and he was working on the Crow New Testament. He gave me some language help learning Crow. Then, in 1982, I thought maybe I'd like to take a year off and get a little linguistic background. I went to the University of Chicago, took some introductory courses, and was encouraged to stay and pursue a degree.

So I spent the next six or eight years, off and on, working on a Ph.D. in linguistics. My dissertation was on the grammar of Crow. Then I came back to Pryor in 1990 and have been here ever since. I finally got my dissertation revised and published as *A Grammar of Crow* in 2007. In a sense, that's kind of my life's work as far as linguistics goes. Crows have told me that they really appreciate the effort I took to learn the language. That really meant a lot to them, that a non-Indian would do that.

It's the only real comprehensive modern grammar of the Crow language. The early Jesuit missionaries did quite a bit of work on Crow, but it's pretty dated. And there's an anthropologist by the name of Robert Lowie who has written extensively on the Crow, and he did quite a bit of language work, too. But his work suffered because he basically died before he could get it all published, so other people worked on it, not knowing what he knew. So there were a lot of errors in it.

CROW CATHOLICISM

I came to the reservation at a very interesting time. It was in the aftermath of the Second Vatican Council.[3] And at that point, I think there was increasing openness to other religious experiences. I remember in the seminary we had an opportunity to visit a college in Indiana run by the Church of the Brethren, and to meet the people there and have an experience of another faith tradition. But as I grew up and went through grade school, I did not have a single friend who was not Catholic. You know, it was really sort of a ghetto—and the same thing in high school, because I went to an all-boys boarding school. And I think the University of Chicago kind of opened me up there because I met Jewish people—I had never known any Jewish people!—and made some good friends there who are Jewish. But getting back to the Crows, as I said, I came at a time when there was this spirit of openness. So I think I was out here with a number of young priests of my generation, and we were all looking to experience some of what was really going on.

I think up until that point, Crow Catholics sort of compartmentalized. There was one side of them that was traditional Indian religion, and there was the Catholic side. But there was sort of a line there. And they didn't want to mix them at all. And of course the Jesuit priests, in earlier years, did not encourage them to really take part in the Indian religion. But on the other hand, I'm not sure they discouraged them all that much. Because Catholics on the reservation, as far as I can tell, from way back, have done both. Still today, when you go to a Sun Dance, there's gonna be a lot of Crow Catholics in there.

I think Catholic priests on the Crow Reservation over the years looked the other way a lot when it came to practicing Indian religion. And the Baptists, too, were very open. There are a lot of very traditional people who were Baptist in Lodge Grass and Crow Agency. Tom Yellowtail, who was a famous Crow Sun Dance leader, when he was home, he went to the Baptist church on Sunday. At his funeral, I was asked to take part, one of the Baptist ministers took part, there was an Episcopalian priest there, and then traditional people, too. All of us together. And that was his funeral.

"Many Ways to God"

That's one thing I did learn from the Crows—that we need to be open. They'll all tell you, "There are many ways to God, and they're all good." There was this one woman who went to grade school here at St. Charles, probably back in the 1940s. And I remember her telling me how the Sisters who were here at the time were telling them, "You shouldn't go to any Protestant services. That's forbidden. Catholics don't do that." So she went home and told her father, and her father said to his daughter, "What the Sisters tell you is good. But in this, they are wrong." That whole attitude of respect is one thing I have learned very strongly from the Crows.

I think another thing that has broadened me spiritually is to be open to spiritual realities that I may not have been aware of—for example, the existence of spirits. We tend to call them angels and devils, but maybe there are more spirits. I mean, the Crows believe in spirits in natural things and animals and stuff, and I'm not saying there are, but I'm open to the possibility of different kinds of spiritual experiences.

I think for me, now, it's a matter of seamlessly moving from one tradition to the other. And, you know, there are a lot of commonalities. Take, for example, the sweat lodge. In the Catholic Mass we have what we call the "Prayers of the Faithful," which is different petitions: for the church, for peace in the world, for the people who are sick, for those who are in mourning. And that's exactly what happens in the sweat lodge.

And I think one of the things that I've appreciated, that has meant a lot to me personally, is that I get prayed for a lot in Crow ceremonies. Like if I go in the sweat, and say I'm going on a trip some place, everybody in there will pray for me, that I'll have a safe trip—I think much more so than I would get in an average white congregation. There's this deep concern, that we're all part of this community. So we take care of each other, we pray for each other. If I'm praying in a sweat, sometimes people interrupt me and say, "Don't forget to pray for so-and-so." Maybe they're sick, or something else. They'll bring these things out. And that has enriched my spiritual life, just to be prayed for a lot.

CROW RITUALS AT ST. CHARLES

The first obvious thing when you look inside our church is that it looks a little different than your average white congregation in terms of the decorations, the symbols, use of Pendleton blankets and star quilts, and the Crow designs on our altar furniture. So that's kind of the background. Even the shape of the church is more or less round. Like somebody told me in the sweat once, there are no straight lines in God. It's round.[4]

We generally use cedar at the beginning of Mass. We take it around so that everyone can use it. It's a blessing. And Catholics have always kind of interpreted the use of incense to mean "as the smoke rises, our prayer rises to God." It's in one of the Psalms. And Crow people see it as a blessing, too. They'll use cedar in their houses, and we also use it in the sweat lodge.

So to use cedar in church is meaningful to people. Sometimes people who come late and don't get it, they'll do it after Mass. It's an important part of the ritual. We also use Crow language in our services. I read the gospel in Crow every Sunday, and we have some small acclamations in Crow.

After communion, we ordinarily have Crow hymns. Someone will sing these Crow spiritual songs, which people will tell you have been given to them in dreams, you know. It's not something somebody made up. They have a spiritual source.[5] So those are important to people. And those are pretty well shared, as far as I can tell, among all the different churches. That's a common element. And there are other ways we bring in Crow traditions. On special occasions, for example, I have a buckskin vestment that I wear, like on Christmas. So I think those are kind of the main things we do at the Mass.

We're also planning to institute a fairly intensive program of Crow-language learning for the youngest kids in our school here at St. Charles, for kindergarten and preschool. A number of teachers went to a workshop this summer, and materials are being prepared to help them with that. Research shows that kids at that age can learn languages almost overnight. They're really, really receptive and are able to do it.

So our hope is that if we can get some of these younger kids talking Crow, it will help to preserve the language. Last year, I don't know if there were any Crow speakers in this school. And that's with having over a hundred kids, the vast majority of whom are Crow. Sure, there are kids who understand a little, and a lot of the teachers will say real simple things to the kids in Crow, and they'll understand that. But to really carry on a conversation? No. So we're hopeful, although there's no guarantee of success, and it might take a while to get the program off the ground. But we're hopeful it'll be something we can do to help preserve the language.

THE SUN DANCE

I haven't said anything yet about the Sun Dance. I participated in the Sun Dance for the first time back in 1973. A family that I was very close to—the family that later adopted me—had a little boy, an infant, who was very, very sick. He was being treated at St. Vincent's Hospital in Billings. At that point, I went into the chapel and prayed, and promised that I would go into the Sun Dance for him. He got better, and I still remember his mother bringing him to Christmas Mass in her arms after he got out of the hospital. So that next summer, this little boy's grandfather was sponsoring a Sun Dance. And I thought, "Well, this is my opportunity." So, he kind of was my mentor and told me what I needed to do. And other people helped me to make the skirts that you wear in the Sun Dance.

So I went into the Sun Dance. I was a little apprehensive, because it was something no other priest here had ever done. The other priests who were around here at the time supported me. They encouraged me. I remember one saying, "Well, it's not something I would do myself, but. . . ." As far as the reaction of the Crow people, I heard very little negative response. There were a few with an attitude, Traditionalists who don't want anything to do with Christianity. But that was very, very small—at least the remarks that came back to me.

You know, fasting is a very Christian thing, although the Crows during their Sun Dance do it a little different. Theirs is a total fast from all food and drink. But there's still a sense in which fasting helps you to pray. It gets you into the spiritual climate, into the spiritual world. So I was grateful I did that. Including that first time, I've been in a total of seven times for the Sun Dance.

My mentor, who I mentioned earlier, and his family were Catholics. I remember asking the grandfather some questions after the Sun Dance one time. There's a doll, a little effigy, that they fasten to the center pole during the ceremony. I asked him what that was all about, what it represents. He said there was another man who was nailed to a tree. That answered my question.

In his interpretation, the twelve poles that form the circle of the lodge are the twelve apostles. So my impression is that every individual who goes into the Sun Dance brings their own theology with them. And once you get in there, your theology is not the important thing as long as you perform the ritual. I even know Crows who bring their rosaries in there to the Sun Dance. If you do what you're supposed to do and perform the ritual, if you do what everyone else is doing, you can interpret it almost any way you want. That's been my experience.

EPILOGUE

I guess the only way I can respond to those who feel Christianity has no place on the reservation is that there are an awful lot of Crow people for whom Christianity is completely integrated into their spiritual life, along with the Crow values and traditions. So, that's all I can say.

As I was talking earlier, when I first came here, I got the sense that, for many Crow Catholics, there was this compartmentalization. So one of the goals of my ministry was to try and break that down, and to let people know that you can be a good Catholic and a good Crow. And I think, to a large extent, that we succeeded.

There's always a group that really feels Christianity is incompatible with being a Native American. But, as I said, I think for an awful lot of people, they really don't see any conflict. To varying degrees, as in any society, some people join this, and some people join that. So not everybody feels comfortable going in the sweat lodge or the Sun Dance. But I would say that the Crow Catholics all, to some extent, are pretty comfortable with both.

NOTES

1. The Order of Friars Minor Capuchin (O.F.M.Cap.) was founded in 1520 by Matteo da Bascio, an Observant Franciscan friar, who wanted to imitate more strictly the life of Saint Francis of Assisi. Similar to members of other religious communities, Capuchin friars take vows of poverty, chastity, and obedience. Additionally, their work is marked by advancing the two primary ministries of Saint Francis: caring for the poor and preaching.

2. The town of Birney is located on the southeastern edge of the Northern Cheyenne Reservation, which is located immediately to the east of the Crow Reservation in Montana.

3. The Second Vatican Council (1962–65) was a major ecumenical council of Roman Catholic Church leaders who met in Rome to discuss pastoral, liturgical, and theological matters around the theme of Church renewal in the modern world. Among the many important developments that came out of the Council was a more conciliatory posture toward non-Christian religions—one urging dialogue, cooperation, and an affirmation of shared values and beliefs. The key Council document in this regard is the "Declaration on the Relation of the Church to Non-Christian Religions" *(Nostra Aetate)*, which asserts: "The Catholic Church rejects nothing that is true and holy in these religions" (para. 2). The Council had a significant impact on how Catholic missionaries conduct their work in indigenous contexts, triggering interreligious liturgical experimentation and the participation of missionary priests in traditional Native ceremonies.

4. As Nicholas Black Elk famously says in John Neihardt's *Black Elk Speaks*: "You have noticed that everything an Indian does is in a circle, and that is because the Power of the World always works in circles, and everything tries to be round." John G. Neihardt, *Black Elk Speaks: Being the Life Story of a Holy Man of the Oglala Sioux* (1932; reprint, Lincoln: University of Nebraska Press, 2004), 150.

5. As discussed elsewhere in this volume, including in the interviews of Joe Bear Cloud and Georgine Falls Down, the reception of spiritual songs in the Crow language is a long-standing tradition among the tribe, long predating the arrival of Christianity. When Pentecostalism came to the reservation in the 1920s, the reception of sacred songs continued among Crow converts who received biblical-themed, Crow-language hymns while fasting and praying in the reservation's hills. Over time, the tradition spread to Catholic, Baptist, and other Christian communities on the reservation, until the singing of Crow spiritual songs became a thoroughly ecumenical practice.

17

Church Hopping and Bible Sweating

AN INTERVIEW WITH
JONATHAN LAWTON (SOUTHERN BAPTIST)

Jonathan Lawton has been the pastor of Apsáalooke Baptist Church at Crow Agency for twenty years. He was raised on the Navajo Reservation, where his father was a Southern Baptist missionary, and much of his interview draws on that experience as he compares Navajo and Crow expressions of the Christian faith.

Jonathan discusses how one of the key differences between Navajo and Crow Christianity is the freedom with which many Crow churchgoers continue to participate in traditional Native ceremonies, in contrast to Navajo congregants who, he observes, are generally much more circumspect in separating Christian and indigenous practices. This has provided an enormous ministerial challenge for Jonathan among the Crow Tribe, leading

Jonathan Lawton in the sanctuary of Apsáalooke Baptist Church, Crow Agency. *Author's photo*

him to reexamine his own assumptions about the proper role of Crow cultural practices in the lives of his parishioners. He discusses the ways he has navigated the fault lines with his own congregation on this issue—fault lines which, he observes, fall largely along generational lines.

Lack of denominational loyalty among Crow church attendees is another recurring theme of this narrative. At points, Jonathan appears to embrace this phenomenon. For example, he warmly describes the longtime mentoring role that a local Pentecostal pastor has played for him over the years, despite the significant differences separating their theologies. At other times, however, we encounter his open frustration with the disregard that many Crow churchgoers have for denominational labels. He notes, for example, members of his congregation who travel the country to hear a big-name Pentecostal evangelist, or who spend night after night attending summer Pentecostal camp meetings across the reservation, yet seldom make it to Sunday services at their own Baptist church. At one point, he lists "church-hopping" among his greatest frustrations as a reservation pastor.

The openness with which Jonathan discusses his own wrestling with matters of Christian faith and indigenous identity is both disarming and refreshing. The interview that follows took place in the sanctuary of Apsáa-looke Baptist Church immediately following a Sunday morning service as the tribe was preparing for Crow Fair with its famous powwow, rodeo, tribal games, and celebration of traditional Crow culture.

❁

Native Christian Missions: Navajo versus Crow

We're affiliated here at Apsáalooke Baptist Church with the Southern Baptists. My background is that my parents are Southern Baptists. My dad was a pastor and missionary to the Navajo Indians in New Mexico and Arizona. I was seven years old when we moved to New Mexico and to the Navajo Reservation. I was married and had a family when I left the reservation. So that's kind of the background. I knew at a young age that God wanted me to be a pastor, but I had my answer, and it was "No, I'll do anything else!"

Anyway, long story short, I ended up in ministry to Native Americans. I've been here in Crow Agency for twenty years at this church. Prior to that,

I was in Billings for five years. Four of those years were spent pastoring a church on the south side of Billings called All Tribes Baptist Church. We had kind of a mix, about fourteen different tribes represented in our congregation there. That was a real learning experience in urban ministry. Like I said, I grew up in small towns, and reservation life is pretty much all I know. But in the period between there and here, I've been other places.

A lot of times people just say "Native American," as if we can kinda group all the tribes into one. But there are some very significant differences among the various tribes when it comes to the interaction between Christianity and traditional ways. I gave a little bit of background on where I came from, and I can say that living on the Navajo Reservation is quite different than living on the Crow Reservation. For example, Navajo Christians did one thing and non-Christian Navajos did another, and the two paths did not cross. You didn't intermingle, and you didn't bring stuff from your culture in, except maybe language. It was clear-cut.

Then I come here to Crow Agency, and it's all mixed together! How do you figure out what's what and what's right? And so it's been a real learning experience for me. One of the things that I'm thankful to God for is the relationship I have with Pastor Kenneth Pretty On Top.[1] He and his wife adopted me and my wife, so we're actually their children. They are our Crow parents. We've spent lots of time together around coffee and a table, with me asking, "How about this?" and "Okay, how about that?"—or, "This is my struggle, where does this fit in?" He's listened, he's given advice, and sometimes he's been quiet. We had an elderly woman in our church here who has since gone to be with the Lord, but I spent time with her on some things. I'd say, "I don't understand. What should I do here?" I was just trying to figure this out on how things work here.

CROW FAIR

For example, this is Crow Fair week here on the reservation. Well, I went to Arizona for a quick trip to visit our parents and family there 'cause all of our family is in Arizona. I just happened to have a T-shirt on that said, "Crow Fair: Tipi Capital of the World." It had feathers and tipis on it, just a beautiful shirt, you know? Within a couple of hours, I saw a guy I went to school with who was not Christian. He's now runnin' a tire shop, and we just stopped in for something. He said, "Hey, Jonathan, how's it goin'?" Then, when he saw my shirt, he backed away and said, "You're a Christian. You're a pastor. What are you doin' wearin' that shirt?" Well, needless to say, my shirt went back into my suitcase, and I didn't wear it again while I was there.

That's just a different world down there. Different culture. Different everything! This week's Crow Fair around here. We got tipis galore everywhere by the end of the week. But on the Navajo Reservation, the only time you see a tipi is if there's a peyote meeting. So here at Crow, I'm kinda caught in the middle, coming from various backgrounds and then trying to figure this out.

A Generational Divide

But I'm also caught in the middle here because we have older people in our congregation that were brought up basically King James Bible only, with very strict ideas about what Christians do and don't do. You don't do pow-wows. You don't go in the sweat lodge. You don't go to the Sun Dance. You don't do any of that. You quit being—well, basically, you quit being Indian.

On the other hand, we have the younger generation who are seeking an identity and are looking into these things and trying to figure out stuff and what makes them who they are. And I'm caught in the middle, trying to pacify both sides, to work out what's right and what's not. We've got kids and we've got grandkids, and they've got questions, too. So trying to work all this out is an ongoing thing. It's not just like—*clap!* "Oh, yeah, got it!"

Here at our church, it's definitely an ongoing thing. I mean, we've got some people at church that are very vocal. But it's the ones that aren't vocal that I'm more concerned about. I just try to work things out. The guy that actually started Southern Baptist ministry here on this reservation came up with a good analogy, I think. One of the older people were really struggling with just going to a powwow. The minister listened to her concerns, and basically she was wantin' to know, "Is it okay to go to the powwow, because I've been taught not to. But in your opinion, is it okay?" And what he used as an example was going to a basketball game. The crowd is gathered to watch the game, the teams go in the locker room, they put on uniforms, they come out, they entertain us. They play the game. Then they go back in to the locker rooms, take off the uniforms, put on their street clothes, and come back out and join us. Same way with a powwow. It's a social thing, and it's to entertain us. 'Course in Indian Country, spiritual things are attached to everything. So there's that side of it, too. But, in general, he was saying, "It's okay, it's okay. You're just going to be entertained, to watch."

But as far as bringing Crow culture into Christian faith—I mean, to me it's really split down a generational line. The older folks are like, "No way!" And the younger folks are like, "Why not? Let's see." But then there's another line in the whole thing. You have reservation Natives and you have urban Natives. And, you know, we have some in our country that they bring the drums, and they have a grand entry coming in the church just like a grand entry to a powwow—beating the drum and singing and dancing in. Talk about redeeming culture! That might work somewhere else. But here in this church? No way.

The Sweat Lodge

When it comes to the sweat lodge, again the line's kinda drawn—yes and no. Many of our folks here at church will not go to a sweat. As I see it, it's more the older folks than the younger folks. As for me, I participate. I go in a sweat lodge. Most of the time it's with the Pretty On Top family. It's kind of interesting. At Little Big Horn College here at Crow Agency, each student has to take some required classes just like anywhere else, with the exception that they have to have something like two years of the Crow language. They also have to take other Crow studies and Native American studies. And they have a dictionary, and in the dictionary it uses pictures and words. In that dictionary the word "church" can mean a building like this—a church as you and I might think of it: steeple, congregation, that type thing. But it could also be a tipi for a Native American Church peyote meeting, or it could be a sweat lodge. For some, especially the older people, the rituals in the sweat lodge, the prayers, it becomes like that's their church. So a lot of those folks here at church have the idea that they've come out of that, and we don't need to go back to it. But the sweat lodge is different for the younger folks. It's basically just like a sauna; you go there and you relax.

I've had some great Bible studies in the sweat lodge, which sounds funny because it's dark and everybody's sweating! We don't have an actual Bible in there, but we're just talking from what we know. Somebody asks a question. I mean, I know guys that have gotten saved because they asked the question in the sweat lodge, and somebody took the time to answer it, and that led them to the Lord. Prayer time, too—some prayer times in the sweat lodge are just awesome. Some of it's more just an opening and closing prayer type thing. You know, "Lord protect us." Some people still carry into the sweat lodge the rituals, the traditions, and all of this kind of thing. But to others, it's just a good time to relax. You saw some of this going on earlier today as the men were talking during Sunday school, how there's a couple of 'em that are just, "No, don't talk about it. Don't bring it up. This is the way it is. We're Christians!" And the rest of 'em say, "Come meet me at the sweat and we'll have a good time relaxing and talking things over." It's just like guys getting together in a locker room, basically, or a sauna. You sit, you joke, you talk. Maybe you got a problem you ask about.

COMPETING LOYALTIES:
CHRISTIAN FAITH VERSUS FAMILY OBLIGATIONS

Prior to being here on the Crow Reservation, I grew up and had most of my experience on the Navajo Reservation. They have sweat lodges, but I've never seen one there. They build their sweat lodge, do their thing, and then tear it down. Whereas here, among the Crow, they build their sweat lodge and use it year-round. So it's very different here. As for peyote, the Navajos were probably the last tribe to allow the peyote religion to come into their reservation, so it's not really native. It's also not native here among the Crow Tribe, but it's been here longer so it's a little bit different. The Sun Dance, too, came from another reservation to the Crow Tribe, but they've really made it their own over the years. The Navajos don't have a Sun Dance of their own.

So I had to sit and ask questions about these things once I arrived here at Crow Agency. I asked about the Sun Dance, about peyote. I was told, "Stay away. As a pastor, as a Christian, just stay away from these things." But then I have to face people here with questions, people that are trying to follow Christ. Peer pressure's a big thing here, and it's not so much the teens. It's the adults, it's family. I mean, there's some good and bad in every culture. Some of the things I like here about Crow culture is respect for elders, respect for family, respect for spiritual leaders. I want to say that I'm very well respected here in this community, by young and old alike, and that's awesome.

But sometimes this commitment to family causes dilemmas for people in the church. Like with the Native American Church—when they're done with their peyote ceremony, after they sit all night and do their thing— when it's over in the morning, one of the things that's done is that a meal is provided. Breakfast is cooked for everybody, and a lot of pressure's put on family to help provide the food and to help serve. What do you do if you're Christian and you're following Jesus Christ, but your family's got this thing goin' on? What do you do here?

What would Jesus do? I know that's a cliché. But what would he do? Could you not bring food over there and leave? I mean, you didn't partic- ipate in things. What's wrong with that? Jesus got in trouble all the time for sitting and eating with sinners and prostitutes and whatever, you know, whoever. And the Pharisees and religious leaders were always gettin' after him about things he did like that. What about us? Same way with the Sun Dance. While they do their thing, there's meals provided—participants need Gatorade or water or popsicles or whatever when they're done. What do you do when your family asks you, "Hey, we need your help." Do you say, "No, I'm following Jesus. I can't help you"? You don't have to participate, but it's still an issue. Where do you go with it? Can you provide money? Can you provide the food? Can you cook and take food? But then, what does your presence say about being there?

There's a lot to think about. When I first came here, those were my questions: "What's the Sun Dance? What's this? What's that?" And I was told just to back off, to not go. Same thing with hand games. Some of these things have got to do not so much with the activities themselves, but with the outside influences. These are the things that were shared with me, and that's the reason they told me not to go. So I haven't gone. Now arrow games are a little different. I think the arrow throwin' would be more like playin' horseshoes for non-Indian people. Although some people will say they use medicine to help their arrow fly true, or hit the target, or win, or whatever. But for the hand games, I was told to stay away.

The Evolution and Confluence
of Crow Religious Traditions

As far as whether or not Indian religion is redemptive, that's a loaded question. As soon as I begin to talk that way, I hear people say, "Oh, that's white man's religion! That's the Jesus guy!" So you have to come at it from a little bit different angle. I think that Crow religion today is not what it was in the past. I think it's been added to, taken from, mixed together. I think that's what concerns some of our older folks. Because the younger people are searching, like I said, for identity, and stuff gets kinda mixed together. So what actually is Crow religion, what's Indian religion, and what's not? Some of the leaders a long time ago, like Chief Pretty Eagle, used to go up in the hills and fast and pray. Well, we find that in the Bible. I wonder what he prayed for? You know, the Native people are different than white folks because of the spiritual side of things. They grow up with spiritual things from birth to death. Spiritual 24/7. Whereas white people can kinda say, "I go to church Sunday and that's it. I did my time."

So they know about a Creator. But also, being spiritual people, they know about spirit, and so they can begin to identify with the Holy Spirit and with God as Creator. In fact, the Crows use a word that means First Maker, which is Creator, which is God. I mean, call it what you want. But you can kinda begin to use those things. You don't want to hit 'em over the head with a Bible or preach at 'em, but get talking and asking questions. One of the things I find remarkable about the Crow people is that, in their history, they've pretty much always been friendly toward white people. Custer's scouts were Crows. So you can ask questions. You can ask about anything, and you'll get an answer. They're open and you won't offend 'em. It's a teaching time. It's good to ask these questions and get people's view on it.

Is there anything in Crow religion that we can redeem, bring into Christianity? You know, some churches have tried. The Catholic Church, for example, with the incense—they sometimes replace the incense with cedar or sweetgrass or sage, which is what's used with the Crow people. What's wrong with that? The Bible talks about incense. The Bible talks about a bowl of incense and that representing our prayers. You can look at the Old Testament and the Jewish people, and you can look and make some comparisons and you'll see Native American ways in the Bible. Some of the foods they ate, customs they kept, festivals and things like this.

We had a guy one time, a Messianic Jew, who came from back East, from New Jersey. This happened before I got here, but I've met him, and he's told me the story since he's usually here at Crow Fair. The first time he came, somebody took him across to where Crow Fair is held where they have all the tipis and brush arbors and stuff. Well, it was the week before Crow Fair, and they were just in the process of setting up, so they just had the frames up and were starting to make the brush arbors. Well, his mouth was hanging open, his eyes were wide open, and he was like, "What's going on here? This looks like the Feast of Tabernacles, just like when I'm home among my own people, the Jews!" I mean, there are a lot of similarities you can see. For example, numbers are a big thing for the Crows. Four, seven, ten, twelve—these numbers have significance in both the Jewish and Crow cultures. Twelve, for example—the twelve tribes of Israel. You can look for these things to use, and begin to share with people.

We had another guy from back East visit here at the church one time. He walked in, and after service, I said, "What do you think?" And he said, "Well, I could've found this anywhere." And I agree! Like I said, my background was the Navajo. And they have a Bible that's been translated into Navajo, and they have a songbook that has a lot of hymns that have just been put into their language. I grew up with services that would last two or three hours. There would be lots of singing. When I was a teenager, our church had a paid interpreter who sat on the front row. He was soft-spoken, but he had a microphone. And while my dad was preaching, George would talk and repeat what's being said in their language. On that particular side of the church, they had little boxes and headsets. And if you didn't understand English or you preferred Navajo, you just got one and plugged it in, and you sat there and enjoyed it. But almost all the music was done in their language—the prayers, the testimonies. I grew up with that.

And then I come here, and it's like we sing hymns in English and that's it. I have a voice and I can sing—I've never had any lessons, but I can sing. And so, what I did with one of the ladies here is, I sat down with her, and she taught me a couple of songs. I even took a cassette recorder, and I recorded it and then listened. Some of the people know the song but there's nobody that really will step up and lead, so I've just kind of done that because I want to see it continue. I want the language to continue, and I want it to be part of the service.

DENOMINATIONS, EVANGELIZATION, AND WHITE PASTORS

One of the frustrating things that I deal with here among Crow Christians is an "anything goes" mindset. And I'm not just talking about going out and sinning, or doing whatever. What I'm talking about is—well, I've given it a term: "church hopping." Hop from Pentecostal to Baptist to Catholic to whatever. Everything gets mixed, and some of the traditional beliefs, too. And there's no clear-cut path to follow. There's no clear-cut distinction. We have some that will travel 1,500 miles to hear Benny Hinn, and yet they can't walk across the street to come to church. We have some that come to the camp meetings, because here in our community, every week during the summer, somebody's having a camp meeting. All week long, you know? They'll go to the camp meeting. That becomes their church. They'll go to the camp meeting, but for the rest of the year?

One guy told me when I came here, he said, "These people have been evangelized to death. They can probably quote the evangelistic scriptures and tools that you have been trained with. They know these things. What they need to see is somebody live it out for 'em in front of their eyes." And so I've hung onto that. That's what I want to do. And so my big thing, my big push, has been discipleship. Know who you are, and what you believe, and why. And so, to do that, we're just back to the Bible. What does the Bible say? Hopefully, by doing that, you begin to get a distinction about what a Christian looks like here in Crow country. I'm just now beginning to understand this, and I've been here twenty years!

Kenneth Pretty On Top did a survey one time in our community. He asked a bunch of questions. But one of the questions I remember was, "What does your church do well?" And what surprised me was the answer here at our church. The answer our church gave was, "Eat." Of course, now that's a Baptist thing anywhere in the world, you know? Potluck, eat, fellowship. But a thing that really got me on one of his other surveys was the question, "Would you prefer to have a white person as your pastor, or a

Native person?" And the response in the whole community was 50/50. So it really didn't matter. The only thing that bothers me, and I have to really check myself, is this: if they see a white person willing to do something, the Native person backs up and you get to do it. It's like, "The white man's here, the white man will do stuff." And so for twenty years, what I have fought to teach is "This is your church. God has given this to you. Make it yours. It's not me." I don't know how good a job I've done on that, but that's my hope, anyway.

NOTE

1. Kenneth Pretty On Top Sr. is the long-serving pastor of Spirit of Life Lighthouse for the Nations Foursquare Church at Crow Agency; his wife's name is Hannah. An interview with Kenneth is included in this collection of narratives.

18

Powwow Evangelism and American Revival

AN INTERVIEW WITH
BARRY MOEN (PENTECOSTAL)

Barry Moen is the founder of Third Day Ministry, a Pentecostal Christian outreach focused on evangelizing Native communities in Montana, Wyoming, and South Dakota. The ministry draws its name from an experience Barry had during the third day of a solo camping trip up in the Big Horn Mountains, where he was praying for a clear, new direction in life. The chief tool of this itinerant ministry is a "prayer and healing tent" that Barry sets up at tribal powwows all across the region. The distribution of balloons, water bottles, and religious CDs and literature is accompanied by a personal invitation to pray for salvation through Jesus Christ. Although Barry has been involved in ministry to the Crow tribe for nearly twenty years,

Barry Moen beside his prayer and healing tent at Crow Fair, Crow Agency. *Photo by Dave Kapferer*

he was marking the third year of setting up his prayer tent at Crow Fair when we met for this interview. According to his count, his powwow tent ministry across the state of Montana had led over sixteen thousand Native people to make a commitment to Jesus in the previous three years alone.

In 1992, Barry graduated from Rhema Bible Training College in Oklahoma. The school was started by Kenneth E. Hagin (died 2003), an influential founding force in the "Word of Faith" movement that emphasizes health and prosperity through positive, faith-filled confessions. As a Vietnam veteran and former member of the Twelfth Special Forces Group (Airborne) of the U.S. Army Reserves, Barry regularly appropriates military language when describing his evangelistic mission. He refers to his time in Bible college as "spiritual Special Forces training," speaks of being on "God's A-Team," and describes the mission of Third Day Ministry in terms of the Green Beret motto, *De Oppresso Liber*, or "Liberate the Oppressed." He has even assigned a military-style designator (ODA-777, for "Operation Detachment Alpha") to his evangelistic efforts, employing "weapons of spiritual warfare" to liberate others from the "tyranny of the Devil."

A self-described revivalist, Barry bases his ministry to the Crow Tribe on two closely related convictions: (1) that an end-times Pentecostal revival in the United States is imminent, and (2) that a mass religious conversion of Native Americans is the requisite trigger for unleashing this national revival. Among Pentecostal Crows today, this second point is gaining a considerable following, a trend being fueled by numerous off-reservation revivalists much like Barry. He also believes that a nation's prosperity is dependent upon spiritual realities, leading him to explain that wealthy nations are being blessed by God, while the suffering of poor and struggling nations—including tribal nations—suggests an urgent need to accept the Gospel of Jesus. But even as nationalism plays an important part in Barry's spiritual topography, racial constructs play an even larger role. Based on a vision of "five cups" he received during a church service on the Crow Reservation, Barry believes God has appointed a distinctive "gift" to each of the five cultures symbolized, in his vision, by a different colored cup. To the "red" cup—"the Indian culture"—God gave "spiritualness," fueling Barry's evangelistic fervor to see the spiritual power of Native people brought into the service of Christian faith and American revival.

Third Day Ministry is no anomaly among the Crows. Indeed, there are dozens of off-reservation Pentecostal outreach programs exercising significant influence among tribal members today. And, just like Barry's ministry, most are marked by a similar blend of prophetic proclamations, a heavy reliance on visions and dreams, frequent appeals to spiritual warfare, and a relentless end-times urgency. Most are also fiercely independent.

The following interview took place at Barry's prayer and healing tent during Crow Fair, with the steady beating of powwow drums reverberating in the background.

❀

PREACHING ON THE POWWOW TRAIL

My name is Barry Moen. I'm a minister of the gospel at Third Day Ministry out of Sheridan, Wyoming. We've been coming to the Native American nations since 1985. We went to the Apache and Navajo Reservations, and after that my wife, Beth, and I went to Rhema Bible College in Oklahoma.

The Lord led us to come up to Sheridan, Wyoming, and pioneer a church there. During that time, we began outreaches to the Northern Cheyenne Nation and the Crow Nation, both in Montana. We've been coming here to the Crow Nation for the last eighteen years, and we've been working with the Northern Cheyenne people for the last eight years.

Three years ago, we felt in our heart to begin going to the powwows of the different Native nations, and we set up this prayer and healing tent in order to share the Gospel of Jesus Christ—that God loves all people, that he's got good plans for their lives, that there is a God that loves them and cares very much about them. In a nutshell, that's what led us here to the Crow Fair powwow with you today.

PRAYER AND HEALING TENT AT CROW FAIR

As our banner hanging there behind us states, we have a prayer and healing tent. We believe in the fullness of the Gospel, that Jesus not only died for our sins but that he took sickness and disease upon himself in the stripes that he bore on the cross. And so we not only reach out with the salvation message of God's love for these people, that Jesus died for mankind's sins, but that he also took sickness and disease upon himself, so that they can be set free. We just trust our Lord through the anointing that he gives us to bring forth healing manifestations as well as salvation.

At our tent, we give out a CD called "Father's Love Letter." It's an excellent tool, and it just simply talks about God's love for all mankind, from Genesis to Revelation. We teach that when God created man in his image, in his likeness, that eventually man sinned and did wrong—all mankind has, and so we present that to the people. Nobody is perfect, none of us are perfect. But Jesus gave us the way to find intimacy with Father God, and to come into his family and discover that God truly is a God of love.

I'm God's favorite little rascal, and I know that I am! One of the biggest things I have found in my life is that God's love for mankind isn't based upon your performance. God is love. When you find that out, it takes all the religion out of it. Because it's not about religion. It's about a relationship with a heavenly father that created us for fellowship. So that's what we bring to these children. And I think we see more children than adults because they're innocent. They haven't been—how can I put this? They haven't been taught things in a negative way yet, and it keeps them more open to the simplicity of the gospel. They're very receptive. But we've also seen that the Lord has really opened up the young adults and the adults, too. It's a genuine move of God that we've seen taking place, especially in the last three years.

Barry's Vision of "the Five Cups"

About fifteen years ago, we were here in Crow Agency having a church meeting in a home. And a Crow praise-and-worship team was there. And the Lord gave me a vision of five different cups. There was a red cup, a white cup, a black cup, a brown cup, and a yellow cup. And those cups represented the cultures of the world. And he showed me that the white cup were very industrious. That's what we're doing here—we're spreading the gospel, we're industrious, we're telling people. The black culture is music, rhythm, praise, and worship. The brown cup, they're very hard workers—Latinos, of Spanish descent, very dedicated hard workers. And, of course Asians, the yellow cup, they're very technical: cameras, computers, phones, those kinds of things.

But the red cup, the Indian culture, the red culture, is very, very spiritual.

That's why the enemy, the devil, has oppressed and ostracized the red culture, drawing them out from the others. Because once they come in, the fullness of the body will come together and will be complete. We saw this many years ago. But three years ago, there was a prophecy that was given, stating that revival would come to the nations of Montana, and that they'd take that revival to the world.

Native Converts the Key to America's Revival

When we heard that, and knowing God's call on our life, we began following the powwow trails of the nine different Native Nations of Montana and Wyoming. 'Cause there's seven here in Montana, two in Wyoming, and those are the ones that the Lord put on our heart. Over the past three summers, since that prophecy was given, we have seen over sixteen thousand First Americans come to the Lord through our powwow ministry in these nine nations. Sixteen thousand!

We feel like we're forerunners to that revival—helping to plow this ground and plant the seeds in the hearts of the people. So when the revival comes, these people will rise up and take their rightful places. I also feel in my heart that we'll be a part of that revival, however God wants to use us in that. We're open to him, we're open to anyone that would have us come and share. 'Cause I love to preach and to share what we're sharing now, and just loving people. We really feel we'll be a part of that. But the end of that prophecy declared that when revival comes to the nations of Montana, they would literally take that revival to the world.

There's a young Navajo minister who had the vision of a man on the ground. He was lying there, and at first the minister thought the man was sleeping. But when he walked up to him, he saw that he had no eyes. And immediately he knew that it was the Native Americans, the First Americans, that were missing those eyes. As soon as I heard that, I realized that when those eyes open up, the revival comes. It has to come to the First Americans. It's only right for God to do that—to bring revival to the First Americans first. And that will bring an awakening to America.

Among the Shoshone earlier this year, we led over eight hundred people to the Lord in a single powwow. At Rocky Boy Reservation (Chippewa Cree), seven hundred and fifty came to the Lord. Here at Crow Fair, we'll probably share with very close to a thousand people this weekend. And it just keeps escalating and climbing.

Now, because the Crow Nation really has been evangelized quite a bit, if you walk around this powwow you'll see there's a lot of ministries here. But we're the only ones that I see actually evangelizing these people. At some of the others, people come in, and they'll have water, and they'll give coffee and these kind of things. Maybe pick up garbage, and that's really good. Everyone likes a clean powwow. But to share the Gospel and see these people come out of darkness into God's light—that should be the goal of every Christian.

The Native American Nations are a forgotten people. We send missionaries to India, Africa, China, and all these places, and that's all good. But these people here are in our own backyard. I mean, they're right here. You don't have to spend thousands of dollars to come here, and you can share that love with all these people. So we feel very honored to be here, to be used by the Lord. In that sense, I'm kinda glad we're the only ones. But that's selfish, because we know that we're not. There are so many more that the Lord wants to use and bring to these wonderful people in order to see that body of Christ become complete.

Native Religion, Idolatry, and a "Spiritual People"

You know, I really believe in my heart that all of the red culture had an understanding that the Creator was God. But just like you see in every religion, when man gets involved, you begin to get off course from truth. So I believe that some idolatry has come in, because of the traditions of man. Instead of worshipping him as the creator of all things, it's almost as though they began worshipping Father Sky and Mother Earth. The Sun Dance should be the S-o-n Dance, not the S-u-n Dance.

From what I've seen, I believe they had a truth that just got twisted a little bit. But the Spirit of God is moving; he is opening their eyes to that truth and unraveling it, so to speak. Because the truth must point to the cross and to Jesus Christ. I think every religion in the world—whether it's Buddhism, Hinduism, whatever it might be—has some truth to it. But they've wandered away from *the* truth.

I want people to know that we don't force anyone. If a child comes up here, and he says, "No, I don't want to pray"—or if we feel he comes up here because we give balloons, and we give bracelets, and we give 'em things—we don't want them praying to get a balloon. We don't want to say, "You have to do this." We say to them, "You need to believe in your heart what I'm saying to you. Because if you don't believe this in your heart, you're just speaking words. This is something you have to know and feel in your heart that you need to do."

We honor them. We're not here to change them as a person. God created them special. He created each one of those cups special. Each one has their own talents and gifts and wonderful things that God's given 'em. But when we all come together, then we're full. When we're separate, we're separate. And so we see the Lord doing these things and just bringing the body of Christ together. Because the word of God tells us that he's coming back for a glorious church—one that is without spot [or] wrinkle, holy and without blemish. Again, it's not about works. It's about a God that loves people.

One thing that I can say about these Indian kids is they are a spiritual people. When we talk to them, we ask them, "Do you pray?" And they say, "Yes." Then we ask, "Well, when you pray, does the heavenly father speak back to you?" And most of them say, "Yes"—and they'll tell you what they prayed and what he said. It's because of who they are. They are different than the white kids. They're different than the black kids, the brown kids, the yellow kids. Because they're a spiritual people. So when they see the truth, they hang on to the truth.

There was a time where Native American Christians looked at the church as Eden, and this world—like here at this powwow—was Egypt. And you don't go to Egypt. Why would you want to go back to Egypt? But what I would say to them is "Where would Jesus be?" Would he be sitting around listening to another sermon? Or would he be out sharin' God's love, his Father's love, with the people that need it? And that's where my heart is.

I don't get moved by so-called spirits or by what's going on here at the powwow grounds. I'm focused. I'm on a mission here to share God's love with these people. As for Traditionalists who are really into the Native culture, or white people that think Native Americans have it all together with their medicine and stuff—again, I'm not coming against the culture. But I look at them, and I say to them, "If you look at the nations that have truly made God their God, like America, they're blessed. But the ones that don't, aren't. What's happened here?"

Most of the First American Nations that you go into are in poverty. They're in poverty because they've wandered away from who the Creator truly is. But he wants 'em back. He loves 'em. He's not mad at 'em, he loves 'em. And he's drawing them back. And I pray that we're part of that—part of his arm, his feet, his mouth that is helping to do that.

American Indian Reservations a Part of God's Plan

When the Lord gave me that vision of the five cultures, at the end of that he also opened up my eyes to a revelation. He told me to tell the people that he created the reservations to preserve the red culture as a nation. Because when you look back at history, and when you look at nations that went in and conquered other nations, the nations that were conquered were absorbed into the nation that conquered them.

So God created the reservations *not* as a prison, but as a way to preserve them as a people. And the reason he did that is because of their spiritualness—so that their culture, their spiritualness, would not be lost. But the day will come when they would be grafted into the body of Christ, and the body of Christ will become whole. I think we're seeing that right now with what's been going on with the numbers coming in at these powwows. God kept them and used the reservations to preserve them, not to harm them—not to take away from them, but to preserve them as a people.

That's a good part to know. That's an important part. Because it'll help set them free. They'll go, "Wow, we're *that* special?" They are, they really are. They are that special because of the spiritualness of their heart. There's a kingdom of light versus a kingdom of darkness. That's why—and I don't mind saying this—most Native Americans are either really, really good, or really, really bad. Being a spiritual people, if they're not adhering to light they'll be drawn to that darkness. You can't straddle the two. The Lord said, "Choose you this day who you're gonna serve."

Once they come into the light, that's probably part of the reason why they say, "Don't go back to Egypt. Stay in Eden." And maybe, for a season, that's a good thing for them to do, until they overcome that. Because we all know that the temptation to go back is strong for anyone, once they're set free. So God has a great plan for these people.

Conclusion

EMERGING TRENDS IN CROW CHRISTIANITY

A number of emerging trends in Crow religious practice and self-understanding are suggested by the preceding narratives. Perhaps the three most dominant among them are (1) the ascendancy of Pentecostalism, (2) the rising influence of Traditionalism on Crow Christianity, and (3) the simultaneous Christianization of Crow ceremonies and customs.

THE RISING TIDE OF CROW PENTECOSTALISM

An important study of Crow Pentecostalism, published in 2000, contends that, in terms of sociopolitical power, the movement peaked in the 1980s and early 1990s.[1] After a noticeable decline through the 1990s and early 2000s, the movement is clearly experiencing a resurgence as it approaches its ninetieth anniversary among the Apsáalooke Nation. Nowhere is this more evident than in recent tribal politics. The alignment of key Pentecostal legislators, led by Conrad "CJ" Stewart and Carlson "Duke" Goes Ahead, with influential Pentecostal preachers, led by Duane Bull Chief, who functions as the legislature's chaplain, has recently passed two remarkable pieces of tribal legislation, as discussed earlier. The first declares Jesus as Lord of the Crow Tribe; the second expresses formal support for the State of Israel on a nation-to-nation basis.

Both resolutions combine an evangelical zeal with the pursuit of socioeconomic blessings. More specifically, each reflects an underlying conviction that earnest, public declarations of faith in Jesus Christ and a literalist commitment to the Bible will deliver spiritual and material blessings to the tribe. Even more telling than the legislative victories themselves may be the vote tallies behind them. Despite expressions of concern and opposition on the floor during debate, not a single "nay" vote was ultimately recorded for either action. It appears that the political cost of openly challenging the Pentecostal agenda was higher than anyone was willing to pay.

The resolution on Israel reflects a trend among Crow Pentecostalism that deserves special note, for one of the distinctive characteristics of the current wave of Pentecostal revivalism among the Crow Tribe is a decidedly pro-Israel theology. It's a theology driven by an eschatological vision in which nations of the world rise or fall according to their support or neglect of Israel. To be sure, a fascination for the people of Israel has long marked Pentecostalism on the Crow Reservation, as reflected in such church names as Lion of Judah, El Bethel, Zion, El Shaddai, and Rose of Sharon. The logo of Day Chief Ministries, a nationally recognized full-Gospel outreach to Native communities based on the Crow Reservation, features a Star of David inscribed in a dream catcher.

Solidarity with the people of Israel goes well beyond logos and church names, however, as the integration of traditional Jewish symbols and rituals is a common trademark of Pentecostal services. The donning of fringed prayer shawls, the blowing of shofar horns, the performance of Davidic dances, and references to Yahweh and Jeshua are common elements of Crow Pentecostal liturgies. At least one congregation displays the menorah on its altar; another displays a huge altar banner featuring the Lion of Judah between the pillars of a stylized temple. Pastor Myron Falls Down of Wyola is overseeing construction of a large new sanctuary that he's calling "a tabernacle for Davidic worship." When construction is complete, a replica of the ancient Hebrew Ark of the Covenant will permanently rest in a specially designed niche behind the altar.

This passion for ancient Jewish rituals, rooted for many Crow Pentecostal churchgoers in a literal reading of the Old Testament, has given rise to enthusiastic support for the modern state of Israel in a number of ways. The recent resolution noted above may be the most dramatic, but it is hardly the only sign. Other examples include Crow Pentecostal pilgrimages to Israel, prayers offered in support of Israel during church services, and the rising influence within Crow Pentecostal circles of high-profile, national-level, non-Native ministries known for their Messianic Jewish agenda and overt Zionist tendencies.[2]

Finally, when assessing the prevalence of Pentecostalism among the Crow Tribe today, it is important to consider the ways that the movement is exerting influence beyond the walls of its own churches. For example, the depth of charismatic practice among many Crow Catholics today is well demonstrated by the reflections of Gloria Goes Ahead Cummins contained in this volume. So is the fact that at least three pastors of Crow Baptist churches participate deeply in Pentecostal practices, including speaking in tongues. Indeed, many trademarks of Pentecostalism—including healing prayer, prophecies, the reception of sacred dreams and visions, fasting, and speaking in tongues—can be found in abundance among those who attend Catholic, Baptist, and other denominational churches on the reservation. Of course, many of these same practices are also found in Crow Traditionalism (for example, fasting, dreams, visions), complicating efforts to trace their presence in Crow Catholic or Baptist churches to a single source. Even so, the increasingly conspicuous presence of Pentecostalism in Crow society likely accounts for much of this bleed-over into churches of every denomination on the reservation.

THE TRADITIONALIZATION OF CROW CHRISTIANITY

There is a certain irony in the fact that the rise of Pentecostalism, known for its anti-traditional tendencies, is taking place alongside the second major trend suggested by this collection of voices—namely, that there is an unmistakable indigenization of Christianity occurring among the Apsáalooke Nation, and it appears to be affecting every major Christian denomination on the reservation. While Catholic, Baptist, and Pentecostal churchgoers clearly reflect different degrees of acceptance when it comes to Crow Traditionalism, they nonetheless share in this unifying trend: relative to their own missionary histories among the tribe, the religious beliefs and practices of Crow Christians are becoming increasingly influenced by Crow Traditionalism.

For the most part, all three major missionary endeavors on the Crow Reservation were marked by open hostility toward Crow Traditionalism in their early years. Stories capturing missionary attempts at cultural erad-ication are well preserved in tribal memory. Some of these are contained in the preceding narratives. Reflecting widespread attitudes among white Americans in the early 1900s, Catholic missionaries regularly identified Crow ceremonies as "savage customs," expressing particular contempt for the Peyote Way. In 1920, an official gathering of Catholics on the Crow

Reservation—called a "Catholic Congress"—formally "condemned the evil of peyote."[3] A few years later, Crow spiritual leader William Big Day was excommunicated by the Catholic Church for taking part in peyote meetings.[4] In her interview, Geneva Whiteman likewise speaks of Catholic threats of excommunication for those participating in Crow religious ceremonies during the first half of the twentieth century.

But, even then, there were hints of a coming change. At least two voices in this collection speak of priests at midcentury who "turned a blind eye" to Native parishioners who continued practicing the old ways. These priestly exceptions became the norm after the reforms of Vatican II. Sporadic priestly tolerance for Native ceremonies gave way to open respect—and, sometimes, even to active participation. This has certainly been the case among Crow Catholic parishes over the past forty years, as demonstrated by Father Randolph Graczyk, whose comments reflect a deep, intentional immersion in Crow ceremonial life.

The Baptist embrace of Crow Traditionalism has been somewhat more gradual, and certainly more uneven. At the historic American Baptist mission in Lodge Grass, Dr. Petzoldt's notorious medicine-bundle scheme in the early 1900s had, by midcentury, given way to more permissive attitudes toward Crow Traditionalism. For more than seventy years, the church served as a spiritual home for the famous Sun Dance chief Thomas Yellowtail and his wife, Susie, as it did for the celebrated Crow historian and traditionalist Joe Medicine Crow (1913–2016). The interviews with Angela Russell and Pastor Newton Old Crow, both of whom identify with the American Baptist tradition today and actively embrace Crow Traditionalism, illustrate a continuing pattern of multireligious practice within the Baptist tradition.

Southern Baptist and independent Baptist congregations are more recent arrivals on the reservation, and both demonstrate more reluctance to embrace traditional Crow ways. Southern Baptist pastor Jonathan Lawton describes the conflict many of his congregants experience with regard to this issue, with roughly equal numbers in his church opting for and against participation in Crow ceremonies.[5]

In contrast to these prevailing trends among Catholic and Baptist congregations, condemnation of traditional ceremonies has been a more enduring trademark of Crow Pentecostalism through most of its history. It was in the

1950s, as primary leadership of the movement shifted from women to men, that Crow Pentecostalism experienced a notable turn to anti-Traditionalism, a turn most forcibly expressed in the legendary preaching ministry of Harold Carpenter. For the past six decades, Carpenter's style of uncompromising, anticultural Pentecostalism dominated the movement. Only very recently, as the generation of Crow preachers trained by Carpenter has begun passing the reins of leadership to the next generation, has a discernible shift begun to take place.

A number of voices in this volume hint at this softening posture. Prominent Pentecostal pastor Kenneth Pretty On Top Sr. describes leading sweat ceremonies, as well as participating in Sunday services held in the powwow dance arbor of Crow Fair each year. Sweats and powwows were both anathema in Carpenter's brand of Pentecostalism. Levi Black Eagle's pursuit of a workable synthesis between Pentecostalism and the Peyote Way is even more striking in this regard. Additionally, as Pentecostalism gains increasing political influence, the pressure on Crow Pentecostals to publicly demonstrate their Crow identity in order to maintain broad tribal support appears to be prompting greater Pentecostal participation in parades, pow-wows, giveaways, and other public ceremonies among the tribe.

And there are other signs that the trend may be gaining momentum. For more than a year now, one energetic group of young Crow Pentecostals has been meeting, praying, and strategizing about a new approach to Christian ministry on the reservation. While demonstrating a deep respect for their Crow Pentecostal heritage, including research into the movement's history among the tribe, members of the group express an eagerness to break with the anti-Traditionalism of their predecessors. It's too soon to know what impact this group will have on long-established attitudes of Pentecostal churchgoers, but its presence alone suggests the rumblings of a shift underway to revision the movement's relationship with Crow religion in the coming years.

The Christianization of Crow Traditionalism

As Crow churchgoers of all denominations become more willing to practice the traditional ways alongside Christianity, Crow Traditionalism is inevitably absorbing the effects of this dialectic process. While most multireligious

Crows tend to practice their Traditionalism and Christianity in distinct ritual contexts, the conscious blending of beliefs and practices is becoming an increasingly frequent pattern of religious behavior. Furthermore, even when multireligious practitioners have no intention of mixing traditions, a mutual transformation is simply unavoidable.

Of course, Christianity's influence on Crow Traditionalism is nothing new. Joe Medicine Crow reflected on this phenomenon in the life of the Baptist Sun Dance chief Thomas Yellowtail more than twenty years ago, writing:

> this man has admirably blended and synthesized the two systems into an integrated, meaningful, and spiritually comfortable way of life. In his prayers he interchanges the Christian words "God" and "Christ" with the Crow expression "Above Old Man" without conflict of feelings. He understands the meaning of Jesus's fasting forty days as he understands a Sun Dance man's fasting four days in the "big lodge." He understands Jesus's telling his disciples to lay hands on a person for healing as he understands the Sun Dance chief's touching a person with feathers for healing.[6]

What appears to be new, however, is the extent to which Christianity is reshaping traditional Crow religion today. The stories contained in this collection are filled with such examples. When Larry Hogan embarked on a series of traditional Crow Sun Dance fasts, he did so in self-conscious imitation of Jesus's suffering, as recorded in the New Testament. When Hogan Sun Dances, he believes that God is drawing the tribe to "the Catholic way" through the spiritual power at work in the lodge's center pole. Angela Russell says that her prayers in both the peyote tipi and sweat lodge are raised to Jesus. Levi Black Eagle recalls how his own grandfather, a widely known peyote roadman, always ended his peyote meeting prayers "in the name of Jesus." Kenneth Pretty On Top Sr., among others, speaks of Crows holding impromptu Bible studies—and even "getting saved"—in the sweat lodge.

While Medicine Crow regards Yellowtail's ability to blend and synthesize Christianity and Indian religions as a positive development, other observers regard Christianity's encroachment into Native ceremonies with grave concerns. The American Indian scholar George Tinker (Osage) is among them. He associates the influence of Christianity on Native communities with a rise in a consumerist and individualistic attitude toward traditional ceremonies. He writes, "This shift to individualism, marked by a person's participation in a ceremony with the intention of gaining personal power, is what I refer to as the christianizing of Indian religious traditions." He continues by adding, "It represents the newest and most insidious colonization of the American Indian mind, one that may or may not be immediately recognizable by the person whose mind is so affected."[7]

Tinker's comments here are specifically addressing the persistent incursion of non-Natives into Native ceremonies, a practice he claims is yielding "a tragic loss" for Natives and non-Natives alike. As mentioned briefly in the general introduction, Tinker blames this costly pattern, at least in part, on what he calls the "dysfunctional virtue" of generosity that "afflicts" so many Indian spiritual leaders who have a hard time saying "no" to white spiritual supplicants.[8] However, the Crow situation has moved decidedly beyond the context described by Tinker. For today, the heaviest Christianizing influence entering the sweat lodge, the Sun Dance lodge, and the peyote tipi among the Crow comes from enrolled tribal members themselves. This observation adds weight to the suggestion that the Crow Tribe has truly entered what might be called a postmissionary era. With more than half the pastors on the reservation now being Crow, and considering the expansive influence of Pentecostalism on tribal politics, this reality is becoming increasingly self-evident.

This phenomenon of a Crow-driven Christianization of Traditionalism raises a number of critical questions. Does the Christianization of traditional ceremonies represent an extension of the colonial legacy among the tribe? Is this "synthesis" of Christian and traditional ways, a trend largely led by well-intentioned Crows, a declaration of Christianity's final triumph over "Indian religion"?

Regardless of how one assesses the merits or dangers of this process, one thing seems sure: if current trends hold steady, a tribally driven Christianization of the old Crow ceremonies is gradually asserting itself as the new Traditionalism, in much the same way that an imported Shoshone Sun Dance has become an indispensable part of traditional Crow culture in a matter of decades. While the affirmation of a conspicuously Christianized

Crow identity—like the one proclaimed in the tribe's new billboard along I-90—is surely led by the evangelistic fervor of Pentecostals, it is no less the product of current Catholic and Baptist religious behavior, as the preceding stories make clear. Challenging familiar characterizations of who's a Christian and who's a Traditionalist, the Crow encounter with Jesus has created a "new indigeneity" born of the widespread Crow conviction that "all prayer is good." Whether the indigenous generosity contained in that multireligious vision proves capable of defying Christianity's legacy of conquest—and creating a new, truly Crow version of multireligious belonging in its place—remains to be seen. But given the tribe's history of dynamic religious pragmatism and ritual reinvention, the odds appear to be in the Crows' favor.

NOTES

1. Timothy P. McCleary, "An Ethnohistory of Pentecostalism among the Crow Indians of Montana," *Wicazo Sa Review* 15, no. 1 (Spring 2000): 117–36.
2. For a detailed study of Zionist tendencies among contemporary Crow and Navajo Pentecostalism, see Mark Clatterbuck, "Tribal Alliances: The State of Israel and Native American Christianity," *Journal of Ecumenical Studies* 49, no. 3 (Summer 2014): 384–404.
3. William J. Downey, "Christmas at St. Xavier Mission," *The Indian Sentinel* 2, no. 6 (April 1921): 290.
4. Voget, *Shoshoni-Crow Sun Dance,* 131. Big Day was largely responsible for the arrival of the Shoshone-Crow Sun Dance among the Crow Tribe in 1941.
5. Independent Baptist churches on the reservation tend to be more hard-line than either American or Southern Baptist churches in terms of their approach to Crow ceremonies, sometimes openly condemning them.
6. Joseph Medicine Crow, *From the Heart of Crow Country: The Crow Indians' Own Stories* (New York: Orion Books, 1992), 54–55.
7. George E. Tinker, *Spirit and Resistance: Political Theology and American Indian Liberation* (Minneapolis: Fortress Press, 2004), 63.
8. Ibid., 67–69.

Bibliography

Books and Articles

Ammerman, Nancy Tatom. *Spiritual Stories, Spiritual Tribes: Finding Religion in Everyday Life.* Oxford: Oxford University Press, 2014.

Charleston, Steven, and Elaine Robinson, eds. *Coming Full Circle: Constructing Native Theology.* Minneapolis: Fortress Press, 2015.

Chosa, Jim, and Faith Chosa. *Thy Kingdom Come: A First Nations Perspective on Strategic Keys for Territorial Deliverance and Transformation.* Yellowtail, Mont.: Day Chief Ministries, 2004.

Clatterbuck, Mark. "Healing Hills and Sacred Songs: Crow Pentecostalism, Anti-Traditionalism, and Native Religious Identity." *Spiritus: A Journal of Christian Spirituality* 12, no. 2 (2012): 248–77.

———. "In Native Tongues: Catholic Charismatic Renewal and Montana's Eastern Tribes (1975–Today)." *U.S. Catholic Historian* 28, no. 2 (Spring 2010): 153–80.

———. "Tribal Alliances: The State of Israel and Native American Christianity." *Journal of Ecumenical Studies* 49, no. 3 (Summer 2014): 384–404.

Cornille, Catherine, ed. *Many Mansions? Multiple Religious Belonging and Christian Identity.* Reprint, Eugene, Ore.: Wipf and Stock, 2010.

Crow Hymns: Draft Sample Transcription of Hymns of 35 Elders. Crow Agency, Mont.: Little Big Horn College, 1997.

Deloria, Vine, Jr. *Custer Died for Your Sins: An Indian Manifesto.* New York: Macmillan, 1969.

Dombrowski, Kirk. *Against Culture: Development, Politics, and Religion in Indian Alaska.* Lincoln: University of Nebraska Press, 2001.

Downey, William J. "Christmas at St. Xavier Mission." *The Indian Sentinel* 2, no. 6 (April 1921), 290.

Elison, Larry M., and Fritz Snyder. *The Montana State Constitution: A Reference Guide.* Westport, Conn.: Greenwood Press, 2001.

Frey, Rodney. *The World of the Crow Indians: As Driftwood Lodges.* Norman: University of Oklahoma Press, 1987.

Graczyk, Randolph. *A Grammar of Crow.* Lincoln: University of Nebraska Press, 2007.

Hoxie, Frederick E. *Parading through History: The Making of the Crow Nation in America, 1805–1935.* Cambridge: Cambridge University Press, 1995.

Indian Sentinel. Multiple issues. Department of Special Collections and University Archives, Raynor Memorial Libraries, Marquette University.

Jones, E. Stanley. *The Christ of the Indian Road.* New York: Abingdon Press, 1925.

Jorgensen, Joseph G. *The Sun Dance Religion: Power for the Powerless.* Chicago: University of Chicago Press, 1972.

Kidwell, Clara Sue, Homer Noley, and George E. Tinker. *A Native American Theology.* Maryknoll, N.Y.: Orbis Books, 2001.

Kovach, Margaret. *Indigenous Methodologies: Characteristics, Conversations, and Contexts.* Toronto: University of Toronto Press, 2009.

Linderman, Frank B. *Pretty-shield: Medicine Woman of the Crows.* 2nd ed. Lincoln: University of Nebraska Press, 2003.

Lowie, Robert H. *The Crow Indians.* Reprint, Lincoln: University of Nebraska Press, 1983.

Martin, Joel. "Introduction." In *Native Americans, Christianity, and the Reshaping of the American Landscape.* Edited by Joel W. Martin and Mark A. Nicholas. Chapel Hill: University of North Carolina Press, 2010.

Matthews, Becky. "Changing Lives: Baptist Women, Benevolence, and Community on the Crow Reservation, 1904–60." *Montana The Magazine of Western History* (Summer 2011): 3–29.

McCleary, Tim. "A Flash Point in Big Horn County History: The Death of Officer John MacLeod and Sheriff Robert Gilmore." *Big Horn County News* (Hardin, Mont.), April 9, 1997.

McCleary, Timothy P. "An Ethnohistory of Pentecostalism among the Crow Indians of Montana." *Wicazo Sa Review* 15, no. 1 (Spring 2000): 117–35.

Medicine Crow, Joseph. *From the Heart of Crow Country: The Crow Indians' Own Stories.* New York: Orion Books, 1992.

Nabokov, Peter. *Two Leggings: The Making of a Crow Warrior.* Reprint, Lincoln: University of Nebraska Press, 1982.

Neihardt, John G. *Black Elk Speaks: Being the Life Story of a Holy Man of the Oglala Sioux.* Reprint, Lincoln: University of Nebraska Press, 2004.

Nicholas, Mark A. "Conclusion." In *Native Americans, Christianity, and the Reshaping of the American Landscape.* Edited by Joel W. Martin and Mark A. Nicholas. Chapel Hill: University of North Carolina Press, 2010.

Noley, Homer. *First White Frost: Native Americans and United Methodism.* Nashville, Tenn.: Abingdon Press, 1991.

Pesantubbee, Michelene. "Foreword." In *Native Americans, Christianity, and the Reshaping of the American Landscape.* Edited by Joel W. Martin and Mark A. Nicholas. Chapel Hill: University of North Carolina Press, 2010.

Shay, Becky. "Vision Fulfilled: Presbyterians Help Catholics Erect Highly Visible Symbol." *Billings (Mont.) Gazette,* July 28, 2007.

Smith, Andrea. *Native Americans and the Christian Right: The Gendered Politics of Unlikely Alliances.* Durham, N.C.: Duke University Press, 2008.

Snell, Alma Hogan. *Grandmother's Grandchild: My Crow Indian Life.* Edited by Becky Matthews. Lincoln: University of Nebraska Press, 2000.

Stewart, Omer. *Peyote Religion: A History.* Norman: University of Oklahoma Press, 1987.

Tarango, Angela. *Choosing the Jesus Way: American Indian Pentecostals and the Fight for the Indigenous Principle.* Chapel Hill: University of North Carolina Press, 2014.

Thackeray, Lorna, and Dory Owens. "Rain Mixes with Tears as 'Spirit' Heals." *Billings (Mont.) Gazette,* July 29, 1979.

Tinker, George E. *Missionary Conquest: The Gospel and Native American Cultural Genocide.* Minneapolis: Fortress Press, 1993.

————. *Spirit and Resistance: Political Theology and American Indian Liberation.* Minneapolis: Fortress Press, 2004.

Treat, James, ed. *Native and Christian: Voices on Religious Identity in the United States and Canada.* Abingdon, Eng.: Routledge, 1996.

Voget, Fred W. *The Shoshoni-Crow Sun Dance.* Norman: University of Oklahoma Press, 1984.

Watembach, Karen. "The History of the Catechesis of the Catholic Church on the Crow Reservation." Master's thesis, Montana State University, 1983.

Yellowtail, Thomas, and Michel Oren Fitzgerald. *Yellowtail: Crow Medicine Man and Sun Dance Chief.* Norman: University of Oklahoma Press, 1991.

Wildschut, William. *Crow Indian Medicine Bundles,* 2nd ed. New York: Museum of the American Indian, 1975.

Legislation

A Crow Tribal Joint Action Resolution to Establish Crow Tribal Policy Officially Supporting the State of Israel on a Nation-to-Nation Basis. JAR No. 13-05 (April 8, 2013).

A Crow Tribal Joint Action Resolution to Urge Support of the United Nations Declaration on the Rights of Indigenous Peoples. JAR No. 07-07 (July 18, 2007).

A Resolution of the Crow Tribal Legislature to Honor God for His Great Blessings upon the Crow Tribe and to Proclaim Jesus Christ as Lord of the Crow Indian Reservation. LR No. 13-02 (March 6, 2013).

Interviews by Author

Anonymous. Crow Reservation, Mont., July 10, 2011.

Antoine, Jim, O.F.M.Cap. Lodge Grass, Mont., June 13, 2012.

Bear Cloud, Joe, Sr. Bighorn Canyon, Mont., July 22, 2012.

Black Eagle, Levi. Lodge Grass, Mont., June 20, 2013.

Cummins, Gloria Goes Ahead. Lodge Grass, Mont., August 11, 2009.

Dawes, Marvin, Sr. Hardin, Mont., June 11, 2012.

Falls Down, Georgine Takes Gun. Crow Agency, Mont., August 17, 2012.

Goes Ahead, Rhea. Pryor, Mont., July 13 and 15, 2011.

Graczyk, Randolph, O.F.M.Cap., Pryor, Mont., June 19, 2013.

Hogan, Larry. Fort Smith, Mont., July 24, 2012.

Lawton, Jonathan. Crow Agency, Mont., August 12, 2012.

McCleary, Timothy. Email correspondence July 4, 2014, and phone conversation July 11, 2015.

Moen, Barry. Crow Agency, Mont., August 18, 2012.

Old Crow, Newton, Sr. Crow Agency, Mont., June 21, 2013.

Passes, Marlon. Garryowen, Mont., July 27, 2012.

Pretty On Top, Kenneth, Sr. Crow Agency, Mont., June 23, 2013.

Russell, Angela. Crow Agency, Mont., June 22, 2013.

Steward, Conrad "CJ." Crow Agency, Mont., June 17, 2013.

Stops At Pretty Places, Bobby Lee. Crow Agency, Mont., July 24, 2012.

Ward, Fannie Plain Feather. Pryor, Mont., July 23, 2012.

Whiteman, Geneva. Pryor, Mont., June 23, 2013.

Index

References to illustrations appear in italic type.

áassahke (clan aunts, clan uncles),
  16–17
adoption (Crow tribe), 48, 50, 111, 123,
  152, 155, 169, 184, 190, 211, 219,
  224
Akbaatashée, 90, 105, 106n7, 136n6
Akbaatatdía, 17, 20, 61, 134
alcohol: abuse of, 23, 101, 130, 135, 139,
  140–41; counseling, 140, 142
Allen, A. A., 129
All Tribes Baptist Church, 234
American Baptist (denomination), 4, 5,
  8, 35, 36, 139, 140, 141, 143, 147n1,
  150, 155, 196, 244
American Baptist Home Missionary
  Society, 7, 137, 147n1, 148
American Indian Religious Freedom
  Act, 22, 174n6
Ammerman, Nancy Tatom, 30, 44n35
ancestors, 8, 25–26, 104
angels, 61, 113, 164, 168, 176, 177, 217
Angelus Temple, *9*, 92, 129
animals: in Bible, 126n2; in medicine
  bundles, 18; Pentecostal suspicion
  of, 104; as spirit helpers, 90;
  traditional Crow respect for, 164,
  168, 217
Anko (Ankque), 168–70, 174n1, 174n4
anointing: of Crow hymns, 199; of the
  Holy Spirit, 9, 236; with oil, 64, 68,
  69, 90, 102, 105, 106n7, 134, 136n6
Antoine, Jim, 41n5, 72, 84
Apaches, 235
Apsáalooke (Crow): language, 180;
  tribe, 3, 6, 40

Apsáalooke Baptist Church, 36,
  222–23
arrow-throwing (game), 90, 99, 133,
  228
Assemblies of God, 9
Azusa Street: on Crow Reservation,
  96–97; in Los Angeles, 105n5

baaxpáa, 49–50, 169
baaxpée, 17–20, 42n17, 90, 108, 114n2,
  125, 165–66. *See also* medicine
ballgames (basketball), as religious
  controversy, 78–79, 125–26, 225
Bandini, Peter, 7
Bapticostals, 12
baptism: in the Holy Spirit, 12, 72, 92,
  93, 105n5; in water, 7, 37, 48, 155
Baptists, Crow Reservation, 6, 8, 11,
  12, 13, 20, 22, 26, 33, 96, 122,
  137–38, 152–53, 160, 162–63,
  177, 179, 186, 193, 202–3, 205,
  211, 214, 217, 221n5, 243, 244,
  248; and education, 7–8, 35, 148,
  150–51; history of, 7–8, 40n1,
  41n6, 41n8, 50, 149–51, 159,
  175–76. *See also* American Baptist
  (denomination); Independent
  Baptist (denomination); Southern
  Baptist (denomination)
Barcelo, Peter, 7
Bates, Tommy, 11
Battle of Little Bighorn, 136n4
Bear Cloud, Joe, Sr., 18, 36, 193, 195,
  221n5
bear root, 144, 173

253

drums, drumming: avoided during Crow hymns, 193; churches, 226; curses, 113–14; medicine, 18; peyote meetings, 21, 167, 184, 185, 188, 189, 190; powwows, 226, 235; Sun Dance, 20, 140, 145

eagle: bone whistle (Sun Dance), 20, 181; church mural, 73; feather fallen from, 147, 172–73; feather fan, 20; Pentecostal skepticism of, 104; on peyote banner, 22; on Sun Dance pole, 19
Eastern Montana College, 47, 52
Edgar public school, Billings, Mont., 49
El Shaddai Church, 95
end of the world (end times), 88, 100, 234, 235
Episcopal Church, 10, 217
eucharistic adoration, 14, 55, 60, 62, 65

Facebook, 135
Falls Down, Georgine Takes Gun, 18, 36, 194, 201–9, 221n5
Falls Down, Myron, 242
fasting: at Catholic mission, 55, 61, 62; in hills, 14, 17, 18, 19, 40, 45, 54–57, 90, 133, 176–78, 181, 195, 198, 229; indoors ("shut-ins"), 95; and medicine bundles, 17, 177; and Pentecostals, 9, 34, 38, 39, 91–97, 120, 134, 243; and sacred songs, 36, 149, 193, 198, 207, 221n5; and spirit helpers, 59, 90, 104, 164; during Sun Dance, 15, 19, 25, 120, 134, 153, 219, 246; during vision quest, 110
First Crow Indian Baptist Church, 8, 35, 139, 143, 148–50, 154n1
Fistler, Minnie Allen, 143
Flandreau Federal Indian School, 71
Fort Smith, 29, *54*, 55, 170

Francis of Assisi, Saint, 3, 68, 221n1; Society of, Third Order, 34, 64
Frey, Rodney, 17, 20, 42n16, 114n2, 174n1

Garryowen, Mont., 175
Gas Cap Hill, 60
giveaways, 16, 158, 185, 245
glossolalia, 49, 182n4. *See also* speaking in tongues
Goes Ahead, 8, 41n8
Goes Ahead, Carlson "Duke," 131, 241
Goes Ahead, Rhea, 34, 41n11, 87, 89–106
Goes Ahead, Ruby, 50, 92, 97
Good Luck, Alice, 96, 97
Good Luck, Tex, 96, 97
Gordon, Ray, 215
Graber, Dave, 193, 195, 199, 206
Graczyk, Randolph, 12, 20, 36, 44n37, 52, 61–62, 211–12, 213–21, 244

Hagin, Kenneth E., 234
hand games, 90, 99, 108, 109–11, 133, 169, 228
Hardin, Mont., 10, 41n11, 44n36, 51, 67, 98, 106n6, 122, 158, 171, 174n7
Hart, Betty, 143
Hart, Lawrence, 143
healers, healing: anointing oil, 68–69, 106n7, 136n6; Barry Moen's prayer and healing tent, 10, 233, 235; Catholic Church, 52, 64, 68, 72, 84, 86n2; Christianity, 12, 31, 37; Pentecostalism, 9–10, 11, 33, 38, 41n9, 89, 91, 92, 95, 98, 105n1, 129, 136n1, 236, 243; peyote, 21, 171, 182n1; sacred songs, 18, 36, 40, 193–94, 196, 202, 207–8; Sun Dance, 20, 108, 246; Traditionalism, 18, 38, 158, 173; women healers, 91–95, 201

plants, traditional Crow respect for, 125, 160, 164, 168

Plenty Coups, Chief, 7, 53n2, 103, 106n8

powwow, 10, 12, 36, 37, 72, 86n5, 90, 99, 103, *115,* 140, 145, 158, 172–73, 201, 212, 223, 225–26, 233–35, 237, 238, 239, 240, 245

Prando, Paul, 7

Presbyterian, 63–64, 65, 70n1

Pretty Eagle, Chief, 7, 229

Pretty Eagle Academy, 7, 86n3, 86n4

Pretty On Top, Hannah, 87, 117, 125, 232n1

Pretty On Top, John, 176, 181

Pretty On Top, Kenneth, Sr., 19, 26, 35, 43n30, 87, 115–26, 224, 231, 232n1, 245, 246

Pretty On Top, Kenny, Jr., 5

Pretty On Top family, 226

Pretty Shield, 4, 8, 40n1

prison ministry, 68, 137, 140, 146

prophecies, 9, 97, 128, 132, 235, 237, 243

prophet, 10, 11, 114, 132

Pryor, Mont., 7, 14, 19, 34, 36, 47, 49, 51, 61, 86n3, 91, 103, 107, 109, 114n1, 152, 208, 213–15

Pryor District, 8, 25, 33, 48, 71, 97, 98, 99, 106n8, 108, 131, 154n1, 170, 206

Pryor Gap, 95

Pryor Mountains, 105, 108

Pueblos, 62n1

push dance, 145

Real Bird, Edison, 174n4

Reno District, 9, 41n8, 109

revival, *6,* 10, 14, 36, 96–97, 98, 108, 122, 184, 186–87, 233–34, 237, 242

Rhema Bible Training College, 234, 235

roadman, peyote, 14, 21, 35, 155, 157, 161–62, 167, 170, 246

Roberts, Oral, 11, 108

Robinson, Charles (Father Charlie) 64, 65

Rock Above, Julia, 99

Rocky Boy Reservation (Chippewa-Cree), 237

rodeo, 35, 86n5, 139–42, 223

rosary, 51, 67, 220

Russell, Angela, 8, 20, 26, 35, 137, 148–54, 244, 246

sacred songs, 39, 41n9, 48, 138, 193–94, 202, 221. *See also* Crow hymns

sage, 43n32, 90, 144, 173, 229

Santa Fe, N.Mex., 179

Schambach, R. W., 129, 132

Second Vatican Council, 83, 211, 213, 214, 216, 221n3, 244

Sheridan, Wyo., 3, 10, 74, 76, 137, 148, 151, 203, 235

Shoshones, 19, 24, 59, 62n3, 154n1, 237, 247

Sinatra, Frank, 47–48, 53

Singer, Grace, 92

Singer, Victor, 92

Sioux, 61

"slain in the Spirit," 76, 78, 81, 84, 187

smudging, 45, 64, 90, 101–2, 103–4, 120–21, 140, 144, 162, 188

Society of Jesus (Jesuits), 6–7, 48, 51, 216

Southern Baptist (denomination), 19, 36, 212, 222, 223, 225, 244, 248n5

speaking in tongues, 12, 14, 48, 50, 72, 84, 85, 97–98, 108, 120, 182n4, 187, 243. *See also* glossolalia

spirit helper, 19, 56, 176, 177, 180, 214

Spirit of Life Lighthouse for the Nations Foursquare Church, 4, 8, 9, 26, 88, 115, 117, 126n1, 191, 232n1

spirits, 9, 55, 60, 61–62, 90, 101–3, 111, 112, 166, 217, 239

spiritual warfare, 91, 96, 105, 109, 234–35
Stands, Cecilia, 99
Star of David, 242
stars, 59, 61, 65, 164; star quilt, 218
Steubenville Franciscan University, 74
Stewart, Conrad "CJ," 35, 64, 88, 127–36, 241
Stewart, Joe, 129
Stewart, Nellie Pretty Eagle, *4, 9,* 92–93, 105n1, 127, 129, 199, *200*
St. Labre Indian School, 74, 86n3, 213
Stops At Pretty Places, Bobby (Robert), 34, 45, 63–70
Stray Calf, Austin, 171, 174n4
St. Vincent's Hospital (Billings, Mont.), 51, 219
St. Xavier, Mont., 92, 105n2, 111, 196
Sun Dance, 15, 18, 39, 42n15, 99, 133–34, 137, 140, 143, 145, 158, 186, 193, 198, 244, 246, 247; and Catholicism, 13, 14, 34, 36, 45, 54–62, 214, 216, 219–20; center pole, 14, 19–20, 55, 59, 61, 220, 246; Chief Pole, 59; Christian criticism of, 20, 23, 24–25, 79, 87, 90, 105, 120, 176, 181, 225, 227–28, 238; doll (effigy), 56–59; history among Crows, 19–20, 42n20, 62n2, 108, 152, 154n1; praying to Jesus in, 153; Shoshone-Crow way, 19–20, 42n21, 55, 59–60, 154n1, 214, 248n4
sweat lodge, 18–19, 27, 30, 36, 38, 42n19, 43n32, 52, 57, 116, 125, 133–34, 140, 146, 158, 165–68, 172, 175, 177, 180, 181, 186, 214, 217–18, 220, 225, 226–27, 245, 246, 247
syncretism, 35, 118

Takes Gun, Frank, 133
Tempe, Ariz., 142
Ten Bear, Joe, 158

Ten Bear, Tyrone, 158
Ten Bear family, 158, 174n4
Third Day Ministry, 233–35
"throwing away" a sick baby, Crow custom, 50, 53n1
Tinker, George, 13, 38, 41n12, 41n13, 44n38, 246–47, 248n7
tobacco (offering), 21, 50, 102–3, 161
Tobacco Dance Society, 13, 14, 34, 45, 48, 49–50, 99, 152
tongues. *See* speaking in tongues
Trehero, John, 19, 24, 60–61, 154n1
Trinity, 73
Trujillo, John. *See* Trehero, John
Two Leggings, 179, 182n2
Tyler, Leonard, 170, 174n3

United Graduate College and Seminary International, 91
United Nations, 131; Declaration on the Rights of Indigenous People, 136n2
University of Chicago, 36, 215–16
University of Montana, 47
Ursuline Sisters, 7
Utes, 62n3

vacation Bible schools, 10, 211
Vatican II. *See* Second Vatican Council
Venne, Carl, 64, 67
Veterans Park. *See* Warriors Park
visions, 3, 14, 17, 25, 34, 38, 39, 40, 45, 48, 51, 54–55, 56–58, 62, 62n3, 63, 65, 67–70, 73, 90, 98, 108, 120, 162, 164, 168, 193, 214, 234–35, 236, 237, 240, 243; quest, 9, 15, 30, 55, 110

Wagner, C. Peter, 91
Ward, Fannie Plain Feather, 34, 87, 107–14
Warriors Park, 4, *5,* 6, 130
Washington, D.C., 5, 128